DO-IT-YOURSELFER'S GUIDE TO FURNITURE REPAIR & REFINISHING

No. 894
$9.95

DO-IT-YOURSELFER'S GUIDE TO FURNITURE REPAIR & REFINISHING

BY PERCY W. BLANDFORD

TAB BOOKS
Blue Ridge Summit, Pa. 17214

FIRST EDITION

FIRST PRINTING— APRIL 1977

Copyright 1977 by TAB BOOKS

Printed in the United States
of America

Library of Congress Cataloging in Publication Data

Blandford, Percy W.
  Do-It-Yourselfer's guide to furniture repair & refinishing

  Includes index.
  1. Furniture - Repairing - Amateur's manuals.
2. Furniture finishing - Amateur's manuals.   I. Title.
TT199.B55   684.1'044   77-5552
ISBN 0-8306-7894-8
ISBN 0-8306-6894-2 pbk.

Preface

Every day more modern do-it-yourselfers are using the traditional furnituremaking skills that helped to create the world's finest furniture. The reason is simple pragmatism: Do-it-yourselfers would rather repair furniture than dump it; they'd rather refinish it than store it; they'd rather create than buy.

To the do-it-yourselfer, restoring furniture means creativity, fun—and savings. And that's what this book is all about.

There are enough step-by-step instructions here to help you perform just about any repair, any refinishing job on any piece of furniture. And you may be surprised how easy it is to use professional techniques. Carving, veneering, turning, antiquing, stainging, planing—they're all easy to learn, with a little practice, a little patience.

Fortunately, you don't need a lot of expensive equipment, just a few basic tools. And this book gives you plenty of instructions on how to handle those tools. You learn how to use them to make a piece of furniture as beautiful, as well-crafted as it ever was—or better!

Percy W. Blandford

Contents

SECTION 3 REFINISHING OLD FURNITURE

Index

Section 1
Finishing New Work

Selecting A Finish

Nearly all furniture has been made from wood during the thousands of years that man has had the skill to make things to add to his comfort. Metal, leather, fabrics, and plastics have their place, but wood has character, workability, and also durability.

Most modern furniture is wooden furniture. Wood is a natural product that comes from an enormous variety of trees. Different kinds of wood have different characteristics. The way a softwood is treated may be very different from what is done to a choice piece of hardwood.

The finishes of wood furniture can vary according to what the furniture is used for. A show piece can have a very different finish from something that will have to stand up to the hard knocks of a play room.

Different kinds of finishes can do different things. A finish can disguise the appearance of wood or can allow that grain to show through. Anyone who has an appreciation for wood will want the furniture to show its beauty as wood, but there are occasions when a more opaque finish would be better.

Why apply a finish at all? Wood is a porous material, and pores absorb dirt. It is this problem that makes the application of a finish almost essential. It is possible to leave some wood bare, but then it must be scrubbed periodically. Obviously, this would not do for a choice piece of cabinetwork.

Bare wood can be damaged. Comparatively slight abrasion or hitting can mark it. These marks can only be removed by working away the surface to below the depth of damage, and this is obviously undesirable. A finish on the surface provides a barrier to this sort of damage. Many finishes are harder or more resilient than wood.

Although the protective aspects of a finish are important, it is appearance that usually settles the choice of finish. Some woods are not attractive in themselves, but a comparatively plain wood with little grain showing can be beautified if the right finish is used.

The color of some woods may be uneven or unattractive. Fortunately, color can be altered by staining. Most staining, though, is a matter of intensifying color, not transforming it. Today very little antique furniture is in its natural color; its new color is usually a deeper shade of the original. Most traditional oak furniture has been stained a darker brown. Nearly all mahogany furniture has been made more red than it was originally.

Sometimes a piece of furniture with exposed parts made of fairly expensive wood may have unexposed parts made from cheap wood stained to match.

Staining lets wood grain show through; painting does not. This should be remembered. Plywood, which has its veneers cut around the circumference of a log, usually has a wide wavy grain that is unlike the grain of any other solid wood. And stained plywood looks just like what it is—stained plywood.

Bleaching has the opposite effect of staining. Instead of darkening the wood, it lightens it. Bleaching is sometimes used throughout a construction to get special effects. But more often bleaching is a way of lightening certain areas of wood to get them to match surrounding areas. Sometimes a part is bleached to match the whole construction. And in such cases, bleaching of a part may be followed by staining the whole thing.

A good staining enhances the wood grain. So it is usually preferable to keep staining light and aim for an even color that lets the character of the wood show through. Most stains soak in and do nothing except color the wood. But there are a few that have some body and partially cover or fill the grain. These have their uses for special effects, but in general they should be avoided. They can create a muddy appearance.

Wood is absorbent. Often if a finish is applied directly to bare wood, most of it will soak in. For some finishes a succession of coats applied in this way may be correct, but for many finishes the wood has to be sealed, or filled, first. Sealing is particularly important for woods with very open grain. Sometimes even after many applications of a finish to bare wood, the surface is filled with dents where the finishing material has settled into the hollows. Sealing is an easy method of preventing such unevenness.

Most opaque finishes are paint, but there are lacquers and other materials that are also opaque. In recent years the things used for opaque finishes have changed considerably, mainly due to the introduction of synthetic ingredients.

Some old furniture was painted, although the beauty of natural wood was always appreciated. There was a time when furniture made from good wood was covered with paint, embellished by gilding, and ornamented with artful carvings. At yet another time the whole surface of a piece of furniture was covered with carvings. But today most painted furniture requires no such trappings.

A painted finish has certain advantages and disadvantages. Wood furniture with a clear finish generally blends easily with other room furnishings. But a painted finish may clash if it is badly chosen. On new work a painted finish may be more appropriate in places where dust and dampness are expected. Paint is also the finish for furniture made from softwood or several different types of wood.

If protection is an important consideration, a gloss paint is usually tougher than a semigloss paint. It is also easier to clean. A glossy finish does not hold dirt the way duller finishes do.

In the past, stains, clear finishes, and paints were prepared by the user, and many craftsmen kept their own trade secrets. Today all these things can be bought readymade. They are compounded by experts and made up precisely according to formulas. However, there is a satisfaction in making your own finish, and some are quite simple to make. Making your own finish may even be cheaper in the long run.

Preparation of Wood

2

The success of any finish is dependent on what goes before. It is important that the final coat be applied properly, but if all the preparatory work has not been done thoroughly, the finish could be a disaster. If the finish is one that will show the grain, proper attention to the surface of the wood, before any treatment is applied, is most important. Even when paint is the final treatment, producing a good finish is much easier if the wood surface has been properly prepared.

BASIC CONSIDERATIONS

Wood is a fibrous material. In some woods the fibers of the grain are easily seen. When wood is worked, ragged fibers are produced. These ragged fibers cause surface roughness. The elimination of this roughness is what wood preparation is all about.

First cuts in wood leave coarse fibers. Sawing leaves a rough surface made up of these fibers. Planing smoothes down the roughness somewhat, but ragged fibers will still remain. Successive smoothing gradually reduces the raggedness until it virtually disappears.

Usually, particularly in repair work, the choice of wood is dictated by the need to match something already existing. But if the kind of wood used doesn't matter, it is usually best to avoid wood with very pronounced grain. Heavily grained wood is more difficult to bring to a smooth, even surface than wood with a less obvious grain. Lightly grained wood is easier to stain too: it soaks up stain more evenly.

A lot of woods contain resin or oil. Some softwoods have resin pockets, and any knots that break the surface may exude resin that can spoil finishes. Oils in some woods can work to the surface long after the wood has been made into furniture. Teak is one of these woods. Any finish applied to it has to take into account the oil. There are oil finishes that bring out the beauty of teak, but some finishes appropriate to other woods would not last on teak.

The first work done on wood is usually sawing. A coarse saw may be used to cut the wood from the log. Usually a finer power saw is used to bring the wood to the size needed for furniture. But using a power saw can be tricky. Pushing wood against a circular saw at too high a speed can cause tearing out of the fibers. The sawing should be slow and easy—especially if the wood is not going to be planed. Breakouts caused by hasty sawing can be too deep for even a planer to remove without taking the wood below size.

Wood that is machine planed often has very obvious ridges across the surface, due to forcing the wood over the cutters too quickly. But buying machine-planed wood, even if the planing is poor, is better than buying sawn wood: flaws not apparent in a sawn surface may show after planing.

Perfection in the cutters of a planer cannot be maintained. Using sharpened cutters just one time can dull them slightly. Usually this slight dullness doesn't matter, but blunt cutters are something else. They can cause problems. Blunt cutters pounding a wood surface will caseharden it: they will bend over fibers (instead of slicing them off) and press them into the surface. Later on, possibly not until the application of a liquid finish, those bent fibers can rise and cause roughness.

Sometimes it may be sufficient to follow careful machine planing with sanding. But if prolonged power sanding is needed to get a satisfactory surface, there is a risk of bending the fibers instead of cutting them. This is especially true if worn abrasive paper or cloth is used.

For the finest surface, machine planing should be followed by hand planing. If a power planer is unavailable, the surface may be planed with a jack plane, followed by a shooting plane for long edges. A smoothing plane is even better for producing a clean, even surface. The blades of hand planes should be sharpened straight across, but the blade corners should be rounded to prevent digging in. The shaving taken off a wood surface should have an even thickness right across. It shouldn't be thicker at the center. Set the mouth of the plane no wider than necessary. Have the cap iron reasonably close to the cutting edge. All these things contribute to smooth, fine cuts with a minimum risk of surface tearing.

On most woods the smoothing plane can be used *along* the grain. A first cut will show the way. If the result is not as smooth as expected, turn the wood around and try planing the other way.

Twisting grain (caused by a knot or burr on the tree) is sometimes a desirable feature on wood. If such a grain can be planed at all, it will be *across* the grain. If there is any doubt about the success of planing this sort of surface, it is better to sand.

For most woods, sanding after hand planing will produce a surface good enough to apply a finish to. But for some woods it is better to scrape after planing. A properly sharpened scraper has a finer cut than a plane in the best condition. A scraper does not remove much, but it leaves a smoother surface because it cuts off the finest wood fibers. A scraper is a piece of steel with a sharp edge. The oldtime cabinetmaker scraped with the edge of a piece of glass. On most woods, the scraper can be used in any direction in relation to the grain. When a planed surface is scraped, it should be gone over systematically. Even those areas that appear to have good surfaces should be scraped. The scraper can be safely used over irregular grain that would tear up under a plane.

If plywood is used with solid wood, it may be advisable to scrape the veneer. Generally, the appearance of the plywood can be improved and the finish made more nearly the same as the adjoining wood if it is scraped all over, even if sanding is to follow. Scraping removes many of the ends of fibers that are in plywood due to the way the wood is prepared. However, if the plywood has been veneered with choice wood, the surface may be too thin to withstand scraping, except on obvious irregularities or high spots.

SANDING

All these preceding steps get the wood to a good state so little sanding is needed. Sanding breaks off some minute fibers and bends others. The best finish results from doing no more sanding than is necessary to complete the preparatory processes. Much old furniture dates from the days before abrasive papers and cloths were made with any degree of precision. The usual grit was sand, which varied according to the rock from which it was produced. The marvelous finish on some antique furniture was produced by tools and had little or no treatment with abrasives.

The term *sanding* is a carryover from the distant past. Sand as a grit fell from use a long time ago; the term *sandpaper* as a name for all abrasives is really not accurate. It is only in comparatively recent times that there has been any standardization of abrasive grades. But even standardized grades are inconsistent. The best grading is probably by the number of grits per square inch. Fifty grits per square inch is very coarse, and 320 is very fine. Fineness may continue to 600 grits per square inch or more for very fine abrasives used on metal and fiberglass. Other grading systems use numbers and letters which have no specific meaning other than the traditional ones, and do not necessarily mean the same thing in different grits. Table 2-1 gives some approximate comparisons. There are also traditional categories: papers used on bare wood are *cabinet* papers; fine abrasives used to rub down finishes are *finishing* papers.

Table 2-1. Abrasive Grades—Approximate Equivalents

Use	Grits	Traditional	Glasspaper	Emery cloth
Finest (for finishes)	400	10/0 (ten nought)		
	320	9/0		
	280	8/0		
Very fine (for bare wood)	240	7/0		
	220	6/0		
Finest (commonly used on wood)	180	5/0	00 (flour)	0
	150	4/0	0	FF
Medium sanding	120	3/0	1	F
	100	2/0	1 1/2	1
Usual first sanding	80	0	F2 (fine 2)	1 1/2
	60	1/2	M2 (middle 2)	2
Rough sanding	50	1	S2 (strong 2)	3
	40	1 1/2	2 1/2	4
	36	2	3	

The next grit used after sand was powdered glass. It is still possible to get glasspaper, but it has been displaced by other grits. A common cheaper grit is flint, made from quartz or silica. Flint tends to wear quickly and clog with dust rapidly, so overall it may not be cheap. However, for surfaces that would clog in any case, such as removing an old finish, flint is worth using.

A good paper for general sanding of wood is one using garnet, a tawny mineral. This paper is fast cutting, with less tendency to clog, and each piece has a reasonable life. Another good paper is made from aluminum oxide, derived from bauxite. It is greyish, fast cutting, and long lasting. It can be used on bare wood but is particularly useful for rubbing down lacquer and other finishes.

Silicon carbide paper works better on metal and fiberglass, but it can be used on wood. Silicon carbide paper has crystals that are hard, sharp, and irregular, so they cut rapidly. The paper can be soaked in water or other solvent. Because of this the abrasive sheets are often called *wet and dry* paper. Using water allows dust to be flowed away, making for cleaner cutting. This is valuable when rubbing down hard finishes, but there are occasions when this paper may be used on bare wood.

Abrasives may come on paper or cloth backing and occasionally on other materials. In the cheaper papers the grit is held by a nonwaterproof glue. This means that damp atmosphere can weaken the glue, causing the grit to come loose after a few strokes. Warming the paper first will prevent this. Other grits are either fixed to the backing with waterproof adhesive or fused on by other means. Cloth backing is usually more durable than paper and is to be preferred for hand sanding of curves. Cloth-backed papers are essential for power sanding.

Abrasives are available in bands and disks to suit machines. But for hand sanding, standard size sheets are about 9 by 11 in. If used folded and freehand, the paper may not last long and the surface may not be as good as expected. For flat surfaces the paper should be wrapped around a block. It is best if the block has a surface slightly softer than the wood being sanded. The block can be cork, hard rubber, felt, or wood. But if it is wood, it should be faced with a sheet of one of the other materials. A facing about 3 by 5 in. will do. There are special sanding blocks with handles and chips to hold the paper, but most workers prefer to hold the paper on by hand (Fig. 2-1). Keep the face of the block clean. A piece of grit between the block and the paper can score the wood, particularly when finishing with a fine paper.

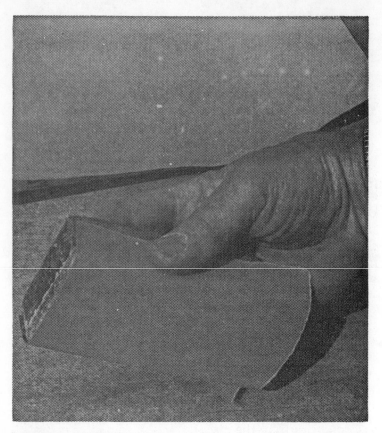

Fig. 2-1. Sandpaper wrapped around a wooden block can be used to sand flat surfaces.

Power sanders come in three forms: disk sanders, which sand in a circular motion; belt sanders, which use a band of abrasive cloth that moves over a pressure plate; and orbital (oscillating) sanders, in which a flat plate moves the abrasive sheet rapidly over a small area.

Disk sanders make curved scratches in the work, all of which have to be removed by later sanding. They can be used to reduce awkward shapes to size, but they are unsuitable for finishing. A belt sander has limitations too. It is excellent on narrow strips, but on broad surfaces there is a risk of the edge of the belt causing ridges. For finishing work, the orbital sander is a good choice.

The orbital sander has a vertical motor that operates a rectangular pad to which flat pieces of abrasive paper can be clipped (Fig. 2-2). Although the actual movement of the pad follows a curve, the sander does not leave visible cross-grain scratches.

Fig. 2-2. An orbital, or oscillating, sander.

Sanding of flat surfaces should normally be *with* the grain. The scratches from the abrasive will be less apparent this way. However, early sanding may be *diagonal* to the grain, particularly if there is unevenness from planing or other tool work. In any case, *final* strokes with fine abrasives have to be *with* the grain to remove any visible scratches.

When sanding flat surfaces near an edge, be careful not to let the abrasive dip and round the edge—unless a rounded edge is desired. Rounding edges unintentionally is very easy to do.

Do not be tempted to revert to planing once sanding has started. All blemishes that need planing should be dealt with *before* sanding begins. Grit from an abrasive can blunt a plane edge, and plane cuts after sanding are difficult to disguise.

Hand sanding can achieve the same results as power sanding, providing the abrasive used in hand sanding is of a finer grit. That means that hand sanding with 180 grit paper would produce the same surface as power sanding with 150 grit paper.

Where moldings or other shaped work has to be sanded, it's best to wrap the abrasive paper around a shaped piece of wood or around the finger. The problem with freehand sanding is the risk of rounding where an edge should be left square. Corners and angles in shaped work will have to be sanded carefully with the edge of a piece of abrasive paper. This job can be tedious, but there's no other way to sand such surfaces.

Abrasive papers are not the only method of sanding. Sanding used to be done with abrasive powder imbedded in cloth or a felt pad. Today such sanding can be used to rub down finishes between coats. It is also possible to sand with a fine powder, such as pumice or household scouring powder (dry), as a final smoothing after abrasive paper.

Steel wool is also used as an abrasive. But do not use the type sold for domestic scouring. Steel wool comes in grades: from 000 (finest) to 3 (coarsest). Grade 1 is the coarsest that need be used on furniture, and for finishing a wood surface 00 to 000 should be used. Steel wool can be used in places difficult to deal with using abrasive paper. Generally steel wool should be regarded as a final step after sanding. Some woods, particularly oak, can be discolored by the use of steel wool. It is important to remove particles of steel wool from the surface of any wood. A slightly dampened cloth will do this.

The best way to judge a sanded surface is with the fingertips. Do not try to judge smoothness with your eyesight.

Before a finish is applied, all dust must be removed from the wood surface. A cotton glove or a soft rag will do the job. Remember that the slightest trace of dust—visible or invisible—can mar a finish.

Usually sanding is quite successful if done with the wood dry. But sometimes a wet surface is best. On some woods, particularly some of the softer and more fibrous woods, fiber ends will bend, even with the sharpest tools and keenest abrasives. The fibers may straighten and spoil the surface when a liquid finish is applied. The best way to prevent at least some of this trouble is to wet the surface between sanding treatments. Moisture will make the bent fibers stand up. The wood should be left to dry, then sanded again.

Sometimes it's best to sand furniture parts *before* final assembly. They're more accessible then. But if all parts are accessible *after* assembly, it's common practice to wait until the whole thing is together. Sanded parts can take a lot of nicks and scratches while they are being transformed into a single piece of furniture.

There is also a case for sanding shaped parts before they are cut. If the end of a piece of molding butts against a flat surface, sanding it right up to the joint would be difficult in position. It would be better to sand *before* the joint is cut. If the joint is then made carefully, the finish will extend right into the angle. This applies to a miter, such as the corner of a frame. The strip of molding is sanded in the length before its miter joints are cut.

Round work is often sanded in the lathe. Any turned wood ought to be finished with progressively finer abrasives while in the lathe, but this is not enough. Such sanding is *across* the grain, so it is always advisable to further hand sand the broader surfaces *with* the grain.

BLEMISHES AND FLAWS

If the wood used is perfect and the workmanship is perfect, there is no need for any further treatment of the furniture before it is introduced to the finishing processes. However, wood is a natural material and it can have flaws. And faulty craftmanship can leave blemishes. But it is possible to deal with many defects so they are not visible in the finished work.

Some of this attention has to be given before sanding begins. Some of it may come intermediately. It may be advisable to do the first sanding and make repairs before further sanding. Some repairs are best delayed until after staining.

A dent doesn't mean that wood has been removed; it means that wood has been compressed. Sometimes sanding the area around a dent can bring the whole surface to the same level. Adding water to the dent will expend the squashed wood cells. And this expansion is sometimes enough to raise the wood to the correct level. Of course sanding may be necessary after expansion—but only after the dent has dried out.

Water alone may not always work, particularly with the less absorbent woods. In this case heat should be added. After dropping on a little water, dip a hot piece of steel in it until steam appears. The steam penetrates where water will not. The process may have to be repeated several times. A bad dent may have to be treated by filling, but it is more satisfactory to raise the wood if possible.

There are several compounds used to fill cracks, joints, knot holes, or sunken nails or screws. These compounds are called fillers or stoppings. Some older types have been superseded, and for most work in the home shop it is probably best to use a prepared stopping. If the work is to be given a painted finish, the appearance of the stopping is not important. If the surface will show through the finish, the stopping should be as inconspicuous as possible. If the wood is to be stained there is another problem. Some fillers will not take stain at all, so they have to be matched to the wood and used *after* staining. Other stoppings absorb stain differently from the surrounding wood, so the resulting shade may be slightly different.

Stick shellac or plastic fillers (sometimes called beaumontage) are good for covering sunken nails or small cracks. But they do not take stain and must be used after staining the wood. Oil putty (a mixture of whiting and linseed oil) is not recommended. It takes a long time to set and the oil absorbs into surrounding areas, discoloring the wood and making it take stain differently. This putty dries hard and brittle, which means it can easily come away from the wood.

Plastic water putty is effective. It comes in a powder and is mixed with water to form a thick paste. It is pressed into cracks or holes with a putty knife, screwdriver, or chisel. Any excess should be cleaned off quickly because it sets rapidly. It cannot be softened again with more water, so do not mix more than is needed. Sand the area thoroughly after it has dried. Stray bits of dried putty may show through the finish. If the wood is to be stained, test the stain on the filler—before the filler is used on the wood. The filler can be colored before mixing by adding colored powder.

Wood compound, a filler paste, is used in the same way as water putty and has similar effects and limitations. It takes about an hour to dry.

When it sets, Plastic Wood (wood plastic) is very much like natural wood. It is made of wood fibers with a plastic binder and comes in tubes as well as cans. For intermittent use, the tube is best because it excludes air and keeps the contents flexible. Like most fillers, plastic wood is pressed into the wood cavities. It does not contract as it dries, but is is usual to leave a little excess to be sanded off. Let the filler dry about 15 minutes before sanding.

Most fillers just fill gaps; they do not provide much strength. Most glues by themselves cannot fill gaps with any real holding power either. Most glues craze, or crack, too easily. The crazing takes away any strength. But if sawdust is mixed with glue, a strong bonding compound results. This mixture can be used to fill a crack or other exposed flaw, but it is particularly useful for joints that have not pulled close. If sawdust from the actual wood is used, it should make a close match. But the glue-sawdust mixture will not take stain.

For a painted finish, the color of any stopping or its ability to take stain does not matter. The important thing is a level surface. If softwoods are involved there is one more requirement. Resin can come through paint long after it has been applied. A barrier has to be provided, particularly over knots where the problem is worst. Fortunately a layer of shellac will hold back the resin.

Undesirable dark streaks in wood must be removed if a clear finish is to be applied. Sometimes streaks are less obvious after staining. It's even possible to stain dark areas less to get a more even color.

Bleaching is another way of getting rid of dark areas. Most bleaches will damage your skin, so always use rubber gloves when bleaching. Be sure to keep bleaches away from clothing too. Household laundry bleach is a good bleach to use on wood. Usually the correct mixture is 12 parts water and 1 part bleach. Apply the mixture with a cloth until the right wood color is reached. Then wash the surface with water to remove remaining bleach and allow to dry completely before taking any further step in finishing.

There are commercially produced bleaches for wood, but these are mostly intended for lightening the color all over for special effects. Check the label because some are very potent and may remove too much color.

Oxalic acid can also be used for bleaching. It can be bought from paint stores. Dissolve the crystals in hot water—how much water depends on the action required. Two ounces in a pint should be strong enough. Apply it hot and use several coats if necessary to get the right color. Then wash it off and allow the surface to dry before taking further steps in finishing.

Using bleaches requires more precautions than just wearing rubber gloves. Do not use metal containers for mixing bleaches; such containers may affect the action of the solution on wood, even to the point of staining instead of bleaching. To be safe, mix the solution in a glass container. Avoid metal-bound and bristle brushes. Old wood, even if cleaned off, will have its pores contaminated, and bleaching may become patchy or ineffective. If bleach gets on the skin, wash it off with plenty of water and use boric acid to neutralize it.

Paint Finishes

3

Since World War II there has been change after change in the constitution of paints, due mainly to the introduction of synthetic ingredients to replace traditional natural ones. The results have mostly been improvements in quality, but some of these alterations have affected the methods of application. Fortunately, paint manufacturers usually provide a considerable amount of information on their products. It's a good idea to read the instructions accompanying paints: old methods don't always work on new paints.

SOME BASICS

It is advisable to use a complete paint system produced by one manufacturer. This insures that the various coats and any sealers or fillers will be compatible with each other. Of course, sometimes it is possible to mix paint systems without any complications, but it's best to check the labels. The instructions in this chapter should be read in conjunction with the information provided by the paint manufacturer.

The word *paint* generally refers to an opaque finish. When paint is used on wood, the color of the wood and its grain are hidden. Traditionally, paint has been divided into two broad categories: enamel and lacquer. Most enamels dry slowly from the surface down, and they generally produce a relatively soft surface. Lacquer dries quickly to a hard, polishable surface. An enamel surface usually lasts longer than a lacquered one, which explains why most house paints are enamels. Both enamels and lacquers can produce glossy finishes, but a good lacquer can always outdo an enamel when it comes to creating a hard, high-shine surface.

Paints come in flat, semigloss, or full gloss finishes. They are generally used on walls, but they can also be applied to wood furniture. They cover well and a second coat can follow after overnight drying. Brushes or rollers can be used, and these can be cleaned with water. Water-base paint can be used if furniture has to match a wall, but the result will be less durable than if ordinary paints had been used.

Oil-base paint consists of pigment (usually a powder) mixed in an oil. The oil serves as the vehicle in which the color is dispersed. A third ingredient can be added—a drier, which speeds the drying of the paint. A thinner (traditionally turpentine) reduces the paint to a consistency that allows it to be brushed easily on the surface.

It is unusual today for someone to mix his own paint. Any paint shop can supply just about any color one would need. If a do-it-yourselfer insists on mixing his own paint, he should at least get the advice of someone experienced. Most people know that blue and yellow make green, but mixing paints that are already compounds can produce unexpected results. There is also the problem that dried paint may not be the same shade as it is when wet. The color may also be affected by the surface or undercoat below it.

However, if one wishes to produce his own colors (instead of mixing existing colors), he should start with white paint. Add color a little at a time and stir thoroughly by hand. All streakiness must be removed. At all stages add color slowly. You can always add more, but you cannot take it away after mixing. Remember to check the compatibility of all ingredients.

There are two-part paints. They are generally used on outdoor woodwork and boats. They produce a very hard, waterproof coat that resists salt water, solvents and heavy abrasion. These paints are seldom used on indoor furniture, but they are perfect for such things as lawn chairs and bar tops.

Two-part paints consist of resin and an accelerator, or hardener. When the two ingredients are brought together, a chemical reaction takes place and the paint hardens. Once the paint has hardened, nothing will reverse the process. Therefore, only sufficient paint is mixed for use in a specified time. Any that is mixed and unused will harden and be useless. This means that brushes must be cleaned before the hardening process begins.

Most painting jobs on furniture follow this sequence:

1. Preparation of the surface.
2. Sealing or filling of the surface, if necessary.
3. One or more priming coats of paint that provide a base for other coats.
4. One or more undercoats that provide the base for the last coat.
5. One (or two) top coats that provide the final visible surface.

Between some or all of these coats there will be rubbing down to remove irregularities.

Some paints do not require all these steps. Some painting jobs demand only one or two coats, but for the best finish on an important piece of furniture there must be several coats with adequate rubbing down between coats.

With smooth close-grained wood, it will often be possible to go straight into the use of priming paint. If the wood has a pronounced grain, something may have to be done before painting. Woods like oak have many large pores. These pores must be filled before painting.

Fillers are used to close the grain and leave a smooth surface on which to paint. Some paint manufacturers provide fillers or sealers for use under their paints. For open-grained wood the filler should be in paste form. If a filler is needed on close-grained wood, it can be liquid.

Fillers cannot be made at home; they must be bought readymade. Some woodworkers thin out paste fillers and brush them on as a first coat. The thinned paste penetrates better. Usually the thinning is done with turpentine or the manufacturer's solvent. Paste filler dries fairly quickly. It can be rubbed with a coarse cloth before it hardens. This forces filler into the grain and removes any excess. First rubs should be *across* the grain. Then change to a soft cloth and wipe gently *along* the grain until no excess filler is picked up.

A sealer is a coating applied to prevent subsequent coats of material (usually paint) from sinking into the wood. This material should not be confused with fillers, discussed above. A sealer is usually applied with a brush, like paint.

Shellac can be used as a sealer; it can prevent resin from oozing through a paint coat. Usually shellac is applied in two coats. The first may be thinned slightly with alcohol to give a better penetration. Then a stronger coat follows. It is applied evenly. Light sanding with a fine abrasive will provide a base for the paint. Chapter 6 gives details of shellac proportions.

Fir and other softwoods have very open grain. The open grain is even more pronounced in fir plywood, due to the way the veneers are cut. After these woods are sanded, a good sealer should be applied to them. The sealer creates a flat surface for paint so the grain will not show through. There are sealers especially made for fir. These sealers work very much like a first coat of paint.

Plywood made from hardwoods may be treated in the same way as solid woods of the same type. If the wood is close grained, sanding may be all that is needed before the first coat of paint.

Hardboard has a smooth, even surface. Sanding is inadvisable. If the surface is dirty, however, it may be washed with soap and water. Grease or oil can be removed with a degreasing solvent. But unless the hardboard is very soiled, there is probably no need for treatment before sealing.

Hardboard sealers should be used according to directions. The amount of sealer that hardboard will absorb varies. Some hardboards are very absorbent and may need several coats of sealer. The oil-tempered hardboards have a much greater resistance to absorption and may need little or no sealing. Sealers should be rubbed down lightly to produce a smooth surface.

Many modern paint systems do not call for the use of priming paint. To a certain extent the terms *undercoat* and *primer* are interchangeable. Primer is a fairly thin paint intended to penetrate the fibers of wood to provide a secure drip. An undercoat, in the most general terms, is a coat applied just before the final coat. But a primer is the first in the series of coats. If there has been no filling or sealing of a surface, a primer serves, to some extent, as a filler. Primers tend to be thin; they are usually grey or pink. If they are to be followed by several coats of other paint, their color does not matter.

It is possible to use water-base paint directly on wood as an undercoat. Synthetic or oil-base paint can be applied over it. An undercoat can be put directly over the wood or filler. However, undercoats cost more than primer and its alternatives, so this should be allowed for.

Undercoat paint is always flat to give the top coat a good mat surface to adhere to. The color of an undercoat may be the same or slightly different from that of the top coat. A slight difference in color makes it easier to see how well the final coat covers.

Usually, one top coat is all that is needed. And top coats do not necessarily have to have glossy surfaces. A glossy top coat must be sanded to remove the gloss (after drying) if subsequent top coats are to be applied. Putting gloss over untreated gloss may result in all kinds of troubles—uneven paint, runs, curtains, and blisters.

Sometimes a painted surface has to be rubbed down (sanded) between coats. A really hard surface may be rubbed down with fine abrasive paper, but if the surface powders easily, as it may with primer and undercoats, the abrasive paper has to be reasonably coarse to avoid clogging with paint dust. Garnet or other abrasive about 100 grit (2/0) should be about right. On early coats the sanding can be in all directions, but on later coats most of the sanding should be in the same direction as the brush strokes.

If rubbing down is to be done between top coats, it's best to do it with wet-and-dry finishing paper, used wet. Sanding by hand at this stage is important and should be thorough. Remove dust from this sanding with a damp cloth. If the final top coat has imperfections, such as roughness and blemishes, rub down the surface lightly with pumice powder on a damp cloth. As with sanding, this rubbing should be in the same direction as the final brush strokes.

BRUSHING

Applying paint by brush is a fairly simple process and most people have done it. But proper techniques always produce noticeably better results.

In the past, paint brushes were made with natural bristles, bound by metal in a wooden handle. These brushes are still a good choice, but today there are nylon bristles and other alternatives to natural bristle.

Brushes are made in a number of shapes and sizes. For normal painting there are flat brushes, which are graded according to their width. A flat brush is sometimes called a fitch brush, and its widths are designated X, XX, or XXX, according to the number of rows of bristle bundles (Fig. 3-1). The larger the brush, the more paint it will hold. Generally, a wide brush is less likely to leave brush marks than a narrower brush. However, the brush size should depend upon the kind of painting to be done. A 2 1/2 in. brush is a good general-purpose one; a 1 in. brush (or narrower) can be used for moldings or intricate work. Brushes come in different thicknesses too.

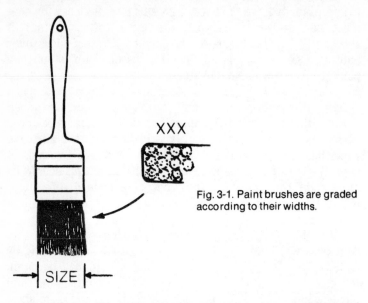

Fig. 3-1. Paint brushes are graded according to their widths.

Some manufacturers describe their best brushes as varnish brushes, the implication being that only the best is good enough for varnish. But a varnish brush is also the best paint brush. The quality of a brush can be determined by manipulating the bristles in the hand. They should be resilient, soft, and even, whether animal bristle or nylon. The ends of animal bristles may be split, which is a good thing. The ends of nylon bristles should be pointed and even. If the brush is described as chisel ended, the bristles are tapered from short to long like a chisel.

The life of a new brush can be extended if it is soaked in linseed oil for about a day. Never stand a brush on its bristles, but hang it so the bristles do not touch the bottom of the container. A simple way of doing this is shown in Fig. 3-2. If the chosen paint is a synthetic which is not compatible with linseed oil, use the solvent recommended by the makers. The object is to soak the bristles and permeate them with the protective oil.

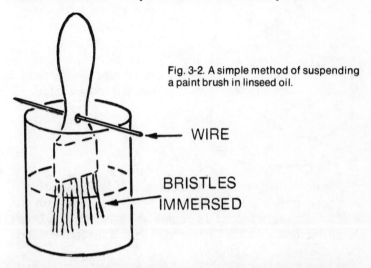

Fig. 3-2. A simple method of suspending a paint brush in linseed oil.

WIRE

BRISTLES
IMMERSED

To prepare the brush for use, squeeze out or shake out as much oil as possible and wash the bristles in turpentine or paint solvent. Repeat the process several times. Try to get rid of all surplus linseed oil before the brush is used in paint.

Traditionally paint has been stirred before use. With some paints this is still necessary and advisable, but read the instructions first. Some paints are better left unstirred. If there is a nearly clear film on top of the paint, it must be stirred. If there is a uniform color in the undisturbed paint, it is almost certainly a type that should not be stirred. If it is a paint that should be stirred and it has been standing for a long time, it may be helpful to turn the can over (with a secured lid, of course) for a few hours before opening and stirring. An electric stirrer is speedy, but if there is a considerable amount of very thick paste in the bottom of the can, it may be helpful to disturb this with a stick before using power.

At one time painters poured new paint into another can, or paint kettle. But today this is unnecessary. Modern paints can be used directly from the original can. However, wiping excess paint off onto the lip of a can may be messy. One way to avoid

37

the mess is to use a strike wire across the top of the can, as shown in Fig. 3-3.

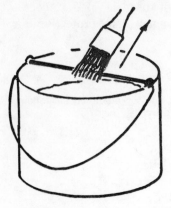

Fig. 3-3. A paint can with a strike wire.

Normally, only one-third to one-half of the bristle should be dipped in the paint. The brush should be held with the bristles slightly upwards to minimize dripping. The brush should be held with first finger and thumb a short distance above the tops of the bristles.

Again, read the instructions. Some synthetic paints cannot take too much brushing. Such paints demand a certain technique: Get the paint on the surface, spread it so it covers evenly, then finish with strokes all the same way. With paint that is not spoiled by excessive brushing, the brush strokes can be in several directions (Fig. 3-4). But the last strokes must be in the same direction.

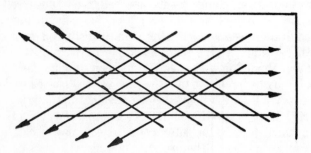

Fig. 3-4. Sometimes paint strokes can be in several directions.

Sometimes manufacturer's instruction say that the paint should be flowed on. This means that there must be enough

Fig. 3-5. Paint strokes should be toward an edge, not away from it.

brushing to spread it, but once the coat is reasonably even, the paint should be left to find its own level.

If the paint surface includes an edge, work towards it rather than away from it (Fig. 3-5). Brushing away from an edge (Fig. 3-6) can cause dripping.

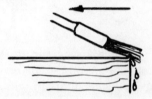

Fig. 3-6. Paint strokes away from an edge can cause dripping.

Painting on a horizontal surface is relatively easy. If the furniture can be moved about to bring the working surface horizontal, that is usually advisable. If paint must be put on a vertical surface, it is usually better to work up and down. Then painting can start at the top, and subsequent brushing can finish with a lifting stroke upwards (Fig. 3-7). If the vertical surface is wider than it is high, strokes will have to be horizontal so brush marks are lengthwise. Work is still best done from the top, going across the top edge first and working

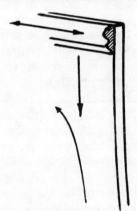

Fig. 3-7. Painting on vertical surfaces should be up and down.

39

down. But working on a vertical surface can produce runs or curtains. *Runs* are rivulets of excess paint that slide down the surface: *curtains* are layers of excess paint, shown in Fig. 3-8. Runs and curtains are less likely with up and down strokes, but even then it is important to make sure there is no excess paint left on the surface.

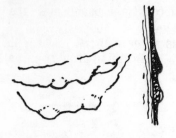

Fig. 3-8. Curtains are the result of excess paint on the surface.

When painting furniture indoors, it's important to keep plenty of light on the surface. A good lamp, as a supplement to regular room lighting, will reveal runs and areas where the paint is too thick.

Most furniture has angular or molded surfaces as well as flat surfaces. It should be standard procedure to paint the shaped parts *before* painting the flat parts. An excess of paint on nonflat surfaces can be brushed out onto an unpainted flat surface and covered later.

If necessary, excess paint can be absorbed with a nearly dry brush. The absorbed paint can be worked out on scrap wood.

If two different colors are to meet along a line, use masking tape. Paint one color up to the line (or across it) and put masking tape along the line on the painted side. The next color can be painted up to the edge of the tape, and it doesn't matter if an unsteady painting hand crosses over onto the tape. Make sure the adhesive of the masking tape will not lift the paint under it. Apply the tape only on dry paint. Take up the tape before the second color dries.

Painting should be done in as dustfree an atmosphere as possible. Fortunately, modern paints dry much quicker than traditional paints, but the first few hours after painting are important. Make sure no one can open a door and let in a draft. Consider your own clothes and those of anyone else present. Knitted clothing may harbor dust that can get on the paint. Smoking should be avoided. Some paints are flammable.

Do not be tempted to touch up half-dry paint. The new paint will not bond properly, and it will look bad when it dries. Wait until the paint dries, then sand down any imperfections and try again.

Most factory-made paints seldom need thinning. It is thick paint that causes curtains. If the paint is to be thinned, use only factory-recommended solutions. Turpentine is used in many paints, but some synthetic paints need special thinners. Be very sparing in the amount of thinner used. Add it in drops. Do not pour it. Quite a small amount will thin the paint appreciably. If it is thinned too much, new paint must be added. Do not thin in the middle of a paint job. The thinning may change the color.

BRUSH CLEANING

Neglecting a brush for even a short period can either make it useless for good work or cause a lot of work in restoring it to a workable condition. Brushes are often stood in water between jobs, but this is not satisfactory. Water keeps air from the bristles and prevents the paint in them from hardening, but this is its only advantage.

Brushes should be cleaned in turpentine, the recommended thinner, or certain special cleaning fluids. The brush may be suspended in the fluid overnight, after surplus paint has been squeezed out. The solvent should be squeezed out with a cloth, or it can be shaken out.

If water-base paint has been used, the brush should be washed out in water, preferably under a running faucet. If the bristles are manipulated by hand while the water is running, all the paint will come away easily. Cleaning the brush this way is better than leaving it in water overnight.

Brushes used in oil-base or synthetic paint should be cleaned in a solvent of some kind. Work the brush up and down in the solvent. Press the brush out on paper or cloth. Work the bristles between the fingers, but do not twist or bend the bristles. Do not beat the brush against anything to free it of solvent. This may damage the set of the bristles.

When all the paint has been removed, the brush should be dried and stored flat, wrapped in paper (Fig. 3-9). If a brush is stored unprotected, dirt will enter and the bristles will become distorted. However, brushes can be suspended in solvent or linseed oil. Linseed oil is a good preservative for brushes, but there are some paints affected by it.

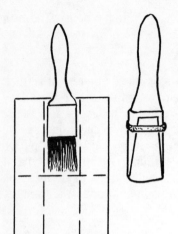

Fig. 3-9. One method of wrapping a paint brush for storage.

If paint has been left to harden in a brush, or if cleaning has not been as thorough as it should have been, there will have to be further steps in cleaning. Most of the hardened paint will be near the binding. The rest of the bristles may be clean.

Work the brush in solvent or cleaner. If a can is used, press the brush from all directions against the bottom. If necessary, use a blunt knife edge to scrape away lumps of paint (Fig. 3-10). A kitchen fork can even be used to dig out lumps (Fig.

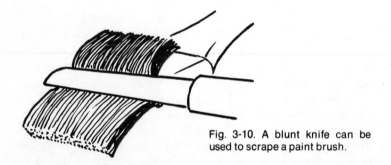

Fig. 3-10. A blunt knife can be used to scrape a paint brush.

3-11). Any scraping should be accompanied by soaking in solvent. Shake the brush to remove solvent.

If solvent alone does not complete the cleaning, use a strong solution of domestic detergent. Use the solution warm and work the bristles in it vigorously. Manipulate the bristles in the hand under a running faucet. Repeat the detergent

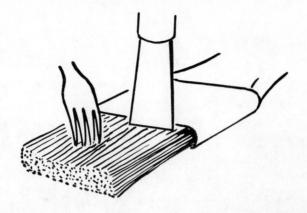

Fig. 3-11. A kitchen fork can be used to separate brush bristles.

treatment if necessary. Make sure all detergent is washed out with clean water. Then dry the brush.

Stains and Fillers

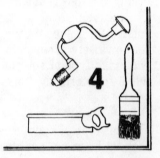

4

Stains and fillers make wood more attractive. Without them a lot of woods would be nothing more than fireplace fuel. But the proper use of stains and fillers implies a certain know-how, a certain practical knowledge of staining and filling techniques.

INTRODUCTION TO STAINS

Wood does not always have to be stained. Many woods are quite attractive with a clear finish over their natural color. However, there are several woods that are usually stained to what has been accepted as their normal furniture color. Mahogany usually has its redness emphasized. The brownness of oak and walnut may be intensified. To many people, the results are considered the natural color and are accepted as such. Some other woods are normally left in their original color.

Stain is also used when different woods have to be matched. The wood of a plywood panel may not be the same color as a surrounding framework, but both can be stained to a similar appearance. Stain can be used to give an inferior wood the appearance of quality. Woods that have an unattractive color can have their appearance enhanced by staining.

Stain should color wood without obscuring its appearance. The details of the grain should show through. Paints and other surface finishes obscure the grain and may be built up to completely hide the base material.

Stains should penetrate the wood. A stain should be applied evenly and smoothly so the finished wood will have an even color. A quick-drying stain may be difficult to get into the wood evenly, but too great a drying time would be inconvenient.

The vehicle of a stain's pigment is the solvent, which carries the color into the pores of the wood. Stains are made with a variety of solvents. A good range of colors is obtainable with each type of solvent, and it is the choice of solvent that mainly concerns the finisher.

OIL STAIN

This type of stain is very popular. Its solvent is a light oil, such as benzene, naphtha, or turpentine. Readymade stains are available in all quantities and in colors usually described by the name of wood they are intended to be used on. The actual colors include a variety of browns, reds, yellows, and oranges, as well as a deep black.

Oil stains penetrate well and quickly, but they have to be left at least a day to dry before anything else is applied on top of them. Stains may seep through a filler or some other finishes, but this can be prevented with a barrier of shellac.

Stains are usually brushed on. Spreading should be with a full brush and in the direction of the grain. Lift the brush over the previously applied stain when moving along a surface. Use plenty of stain. The aim is to get the whole surface covered quickly and evenly.

An oil stain will soak in rapidly and the intensity of color is partly dependent on the soaking time. When the color is right, use a cloth to wipe off surplus stain, stroking in the direction of the grain. Try to allow about the same amount of stain and the same length of soaking time for different sections. But *exact* timing is not critical. With reasonably even brushing and careful wiping, the result should be an even color.

With all stains it is a good policy to stain the least important parts first and do the important part (usually a top) last. It is helpful to work in a cross light and move the furniture about so the surface being worked on is horizontal, or nearly so, whenever possible.

There may be a problem of uneven absorption. Sapwood may soak up more than heartwood species. Extra stain can be brushed on the heartwood. In some things, end grain may be a problem. Exposed end grain may soak up stain rapidly so it is considerably darker than other surfaces. Quick wiping of the end grain will minimize this, but even then you may not be able to reduce the darkening much. The amount of end grain absorption can be reduced by partial sealing. A coat of thin shellac may be put on the end grain and allowed to soak in and dry before the stain is applied. Be careful that the shellac does not get on any adjoining side grain.

When the stain has dried to a mat surface, it will look slightly darker than it will after a clear gloss finish has been applied. If the result is not dark enough, more stain can be put over the first coat.

The solvents are flammable. This means taking the obvious precautions while working, but it is also advisable to destroy rags used for wiping. A fire could start by spontaneous combustion if oily cloths are allowed to accumulate.

WATER STAIN

Oil stains are readily available and convenient to use, but water stains can also penetrate the pores of wood.

Water stains come in powders. These are dissolved in hot water, in proportions indicated by the supplier, but the user can vary the intensity of a color by using different strengths. The water is stirred as the powder is poured in, then the mixture is left to cool before use. It can then be bottled and kept almost indefinitely.

A very large range of water stain powders are available. It is possible to buy certain basic colors and blend your own stain, or the powders can be bought already compounded to give particular wood colors. Concentrated mixtures can be mixed to get desired effects, with water added to lighten colors, or more stain added to darken.

A water stain leaves a transparent finish that does not affect the appearance of the wood. Drying time depends on temperature and humidity, but a few hours should be sufficient. One problem with the use of water stain is the raising of the grain, as mentioned in the section on preparing wood. Water stain has the same effect as treating the wood with water, but it would be unsatisfactory to rub down with abrasive paper after staining because this would affect the appearance of the stained wood. The wood should be wetted with clear water, allowed to dry, and then sanded. Sanding dust should be removed, then the stain applied.

Water stain is brushed on. There is some advantage in having a stiff brush. Use plenty of stain and brush *along* the grain. It is a help in getting even coverage to apply two coats of a lighter stain, rather than one coat of a dark stain. Excess water stain splashed on to plain wood is not as easy to disguise as oil stain. It is best to do the whole staining of a piece of furniture as quickly as possible. It is not usual to wipe with a cloth. Excess stain from corners or moldings may be lifted with a dry brush.

SPIRIT STAIN

Special colored powders may be dissolved in spirit (alcohol) to make stain. Spirit stains do not come in a large range of colors, but there are some that are not usually associated with wood shades, such as blue, green, and yellow, which are used for special effects. As with water stains, colors can be blended. The stains are obtained as powders, which dissolve easily. Concentrated mixtures can be made and thinned for use.

With alcohol as a solvent, penetration is quick, although not always deep. With near instantaneous drying, it is almost impossible to stain a large area and avoid brush marks. Consequently, spirit stain is not really a general-purpose one for large pieces of furniture. An exception is when spraying is possible—then an even effect is more easily obtained. Spirit stain is suitable for small things, where overlapped brushing (which causes streaking) does not occur. Moldings for picture frames and similar things may be spirit-stained. Spirit stain is also useful for touching up. It can be used where other stains have been and even over many finishes.

Brushing with spirit stains should be done rapidly. Keep the brush moving. Spread the stain with sweeps, but do not try to stretch the stain. Refill the brush as needed and try to always follow a wet edge, rather than on a dry one.

It is possible to continue with other finishing processes almost immediately after applying spirit stain, so there is an advantage when the work has to be completed quickly. But the difficulty of getting an even color on a large surface means that spirit stain is not the choice for a large area. And some of the colors fade easier than water and oil stains.

OTHER STAINS

It is possible to use other solvents for stains, but oil and water are the usual choices. Some staining is done with diluted paint. This may be described as pigmented oil stain. The coloring matter is a pigment which does not dissolve. Consequently, the result is not as transparent as other stains. It is brushed on and wiped off. Because its penetration is slight, its color can be lightened by wiping with a solvent, usually turpentine. In the treatment of new furniture, there is little use for pigmented oil stain. But it has uses in treating antique furniture or faking furniture to look old.

CHEMICAL COLORING

It is possible to alter the color of wood by using chemicals. What can be done depends on the particular wood. What has an effect on one wood may be ineffective on another. The resulting color is due to a chemical reaction. Some of the chemicals used are caustic, so rubber gloves and old clothing should be worn.

Oak and chestnut can be given a deep brown color with ammonia. The ammonia should be brushed on in a well ventilated area. Chestnut and oak are the only woods suitable for this treatment, but the quality of the warm brown color achieved is different from anything obtainable with liquid stains.

Another way of turning many woods a medium brown is to use permanganate of potash. This is bought as crystals to dissolve in water. The resulting mixture is safe to handle and use.

Acetic acid (cider vinegar) which has been left overnight to react with iron filings can be used on pine to give it a weathered grey appearance. Household lye and some domestic cleaning powders, dissolved in water, will turn some woods brown.

FILLERS

Filling is necessary on many woods to seal the tiny cells in the surface and the much larger visible hollows. Without filling, the finish would sink into the hollows and holes, revealing an unevenness on the surface. Some fillers applicable to painting have been described in Chapter 3. The color of a filler to be used under paint is unimportant, but when a clear finish is to follow, the color of the material used is vital. Fillers are broadly divided into paste fillers, for open-grained woods, and liquid fillers, for close-grained wood.

If the filler can absorb stain at the same rate as the wood fibers, the filler may be used *before* the wood is stained. In most cases it is better to do the staining first so the stain will achieve maximum penetration without any filler in the wood to restrict its progress. The filler's color, of course, must match that of the stain.

The filling material itself is a fine powder. The powder in most newer fillers is a finely ground crystal, called silex. The silex can be formed into a paste with linseed oil or other binder. A liquid sealer can be created by thinning this paste.

Not all woods can be classified as open or close grained. For intermediate types, a paste filler will have to be diluted slightly. Table 4-1 lists filler requirements of several woods.

Table 4-1. Requirements of Some Woods

Paste Filler	Medium Filler	Liquid Filler	No Filler
Ash	Butternut	Bass	Aspen
Chestnut	Korina	Beech	Cypress
Elm	Mahogany	Birch	Ebony
Hickory	Rosewood	Cedar	Gaboon
Lacewood	Sapele	Fir	Hemlock
Oak	Tigerwood	Gum	Holly
Padouk	Walnut	Maple	Magnolia
Teak		Poplar	Pine
		Sycamore	Redwood
			Spruce

PASTE FILLERS

Paste fillers come in many wood colors. In choosing a filler, let it be slightly darker, rather than lighter, than the stain because fillers tend to dry lighter. If paste fillers are mixed, prepare enough for the whole job in one mix and make sure there are no streaks or unmixed colors in the batch. It is difficult to get the exact color again if more has to be mixed.

If a filler needs thinning for brush application, use benzene. But thin it just enough to make brush spreading possible. Paste filler can be applied with a cloth, and some woodworkers favor an old hair brush or something similar.

If oil stain has been used, it is advisable to spread on a thin coat of shellac before filling. But with bare wood or other stains, the filler can be applied without other preparation. Try to spread the filler evenly. Leave it long enough to allow the surface to dull. Rub over this with a piece of coarse cloth, first across the grain to force the filler into the grain. Change to a soft cloth and wipe along the grain until all excess filler has been removed.

For shaped parts, coarse cloth may not go into the corners and hollows. A short-haired stiff brush will do the job though. Filler left on the surface will spoil the subsequent finish, so it is important to remove all filler that is not actually in the pores of the wood.

If the filler gets too hard to wipe off properly, dampen it with a cloth soaked in benzene. If you have doubts about all the pores being filled, a second application of filler is possible without affecting the first application. Although filler may dry in a short time, the filled surface should be left a day before moving on to the next treatment.

LIQUID FILLERS

Paste filler can be transformed into liquid filler by diluting it with benzene or turpentine. Liquid filler is brushed on and wiped after dulling. Shellac can be used as a liquid filler. It is brushed on, allowed to dry, then lightly sanded. This process is repeated at least once. There are white and orange shellacs. White suits light finishes, but orange can go over darker stains. Varnish should be used as a filler only when the finish is to be varnished.

Of course, a lot depends on the wood. Some woods do not require fillers—liquid or otherwise.

Varnishing

5

Varnish may be thought of as a paint without color. Varnishes have been used for thousands of years to give wood a clear glossy finish. And for all but the last half century, varnishes have consisted of natural resins and lacs, a natural oil vehicle, thinner, and a drier. In recent years some of these natural materials have been replaced with synthetic ones. Although some natural varnishes may still be obtainable, the newer types are superior in many ways.

Varnish can provide protection for outdoor woodwork and has been used on boats. It is not usually sprayed. Its finish is something like brushed shellac, but it is more durable and better able to resist attack by solvents and heavy objects.

The best synthetic varnishes produced today are intended mainly for use on the wooden parts of boats, but they are equally suitable for furniture. Almost all boat varnish now available is synthetic. Household synthetic varnish will probably be described as quick drying or four-hour varnish. A synthetic varnish consists of several types of manmade resins, special oil as a vehicle, and volatile thinners. Traditional varnish dries by evaporation, which can take a long time. There is some evaporation with a synthetic varnish, but a chemical reaction within the varnish provides most of the setting action.

Regular varnishes, whether synthetic or natural, are single solution. But there are two-part varnishes. After the two parts are mixed, there is a limited working time, during which the varnish must be applied. After that the varnish hardens fairly quickly but builds up a greater hardness over a few days. It is then *very* hard—even resisting some abrasives. It can even be polished with metal polish. It is fully waterproof and will resist several liquids that would attack other varnishes or paint.

APPLICATION

These notes apply to the use of synthetic varnish. Some additional notes applicable to natural resin varnish are at the end of this section.

Although modern varnish becomes dustproof in about two hours, the work area should be as dustfree as possible. Guard against drafts. Vacuum clean just before starting work. Some flow of air is necessary, but arrange this so there is no violent draft near the work.

Varnish is influenced by temperature. Although modern varnishes can be applied in a large range of temperatures, anything less than 65°F causes varnish to flow sluggishly. If the temperature is over about 85°F, varnish may get too liquid. If the work has to be done in cold conditions, it is helpful to warm the wood slightly and have the can of varnish standing in hot water (Fig. 5-1). If the room, varnish, and wood are maintained at about 70°F, conditions are ideal. Extreme temperatures should be avoided when storing varnish.

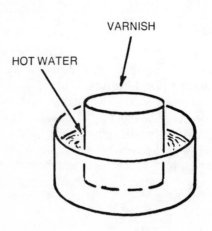

VARNISH

HOT WATER

Fig. 5-1. A method of softening cold varnish.

Preparation of the wood should be thorough. Grease and dirt interfere with the way the varnish behaves after it is applied, so see that the wood is kept clean.

When it comes to varnishing, brushes are very important. Brushes must be clean and should be used for varnishing only. Despite the greatest care in cleaning, some contamination from painting could be left in the brush and this would affect the varnishing. A new brush should have dust shaken or knocked out of it; then it should be washed in solvent and dried.

For storing, suspend varnish brushes in varnish. Since varnish will oxidize and form a skin on the surface if left in an open container, it is better to completely enclose the brushes in a container with a lid (Fig. 5-2). As with paint brushes, arrange varnish brushes so their bristles do not touch the bottom of the container. There can be some thinners in the varnish, but the bulk of the liquid should be varnish of the same type the brush has been used with. A varnish brush can be cleaned in the same way as a paint brush.

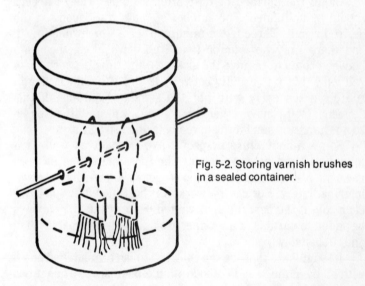

Fig. 5-2. Storing varnish brushes in a sealed container.

Most synthetic varnishes should not be stirred. Even a small amount of stirring can introduce bubbles which may not disappear until they break on the wood surface, leaving tiny blemishes. Handle the can carefully. Shaking it or dropping it before use may also cause annoying bubbles.

Some varnishes should be *flowed* on. This means using a minimum amount of brushing. Too much brushing also causes bubbles. Brush with the grain. Do not continue after the paint is exhausted from the brush. Do not be tempted to go back over the surface again for another smoothing with an exhausted brush. This may lift the varnish instead of smoothing it. With paint it is possible. With varnish it is inadvisable.

If bare wood is being varnished, thin the first coat with the thinners or solvent recommended by the manufacturers. This helps the first coat penetrate the wood and bond to it. The amount of thinning depends on the porosity of the wood, but quite a small amount of solvent should be sufficient. Never use shellac as a filler or primer under varnish.

A first coat may raise the grain, flipping up tiny wood fibers into the varnish. This may happen even though the wood was prepared carefully. Give this coat a thorough sanding to remove these fibers, but not so much as to go through to bare wood. The grade of abrasive paper will depend on circumstances, but 300-500 wet-or-dry should be satisfactory.

Clean the surface of dust after sanding. The next coat should be unthinned. The number of coats will depend on the desired result. Three is the minimum for a worthwhile finish, and there may be four or five. Rub down along the grain between coats to remove the gloss. Drying time between coats will vary, but it is usually between 12 and 24 hours. Trying to rub down too early will mar the semihard surface. If this happens, or if runs or other flaws occur, wait until the trouble spot is hard and sand it flush, ready to varnish again.

Some manufacturers specify a maximum as well as a minimum time between coats. The maximum time is when gloss may be put directly on top of gloss without rubbing down intermediately. For cabinetwork, it is best though to rub down each coat if the best finish is wanted. Extra coats may always be added to varnish at any time, providing the old coat is clean and rubbed down.

It is unlikely that the top coat will finish absolutely smooth with an even gloss and without minute blemishes. When it has hardened several days it can be rubbed down with pumice powder mixed in either water or light oil on a soft cloth. Rub hard enough to remove flaws and even the gloss, but work gently. Then wipe the surface clean.

No varnish will adhere to a damp surface or to an earlier coat that has not fully dried. Imperfections will show in the surface, and sanding will cause the varnish to pull and break up instead of smoothing out.

The general technique of varnishing is similar to painting. It is advisable to do parts of least importance first and work towards the more important surfaces. So far as possible, the surface being worked on should be horizontal, and it is helpful to have a light shining across the surface so progress can be gauged. Intricate parts are best varnished *before* adjoining level surfaces so excess varnish is more easily dispersed.

If a natural oil varnish is used, all of the above instructions apply, but there are some other points to note. It is possible to brush out a traditional varnish more, so work can be done in all directions, providing the final strokes are along the grain. Drying time is longer—at least 24 hours. So the period in which the surface can be affected by dust is longer—probably 12 hours. Traditional varnish is even more affected by heating fumes than synthetic varnish. Atmospheric conditions are also more important. If there is too much humidity, the varnish may dry with a cloudy effect, called *bloom*. The surface may not even dry completely. Temperature is important. Regard 65°F as the minimum. Applying traditional varnish below the minimum temperature may result in incomplete drying.

Shellac  6

Shellac has been used as a wood finish for a very long time. Much antique furniture was finished by French polishing, which is one method of applying shellac. For many centuries shellac has been used for finishing good quality furniture. It produced a mellow beauty and even sheen that could not be obtained by any of the other means available. Some modern materials have taken its place for some things, but shellac is still used for professional and amateur finishing of wood.

SOME PRELIMINARIES

Most shellac comes from India and adjoining regions, where the lac is exuded by an insect that lives on trees. The lac eventually surrounds the insect, killing it in the lac shell that forms. This lac shell is gathered, heated, and stretched into sheets, which are crushed into flakes. Shellac is imported in this flake form.

Shellac dissolves readily in denatured alcohol (methyl alcohol, methylated spirits). Shellac can be bought in this liquid form with varying concentrations. The merchant may describe the proportion of shellac to alcohol as a *cut*. The strongest concentration is usually a 5 lb cut, which means that 5 lb of shellac has been dissolved in one gallon of alcohol. There are weaker cuts, down to 2 lb or lower. Obviously, any concentration may be diluted, but it would be troublesome to add shellac to a weak concentration to make it stronger. So it is better to buy the stronger cut when varying needs are anticipated and dilute with alcohol when a weaker cut has to be used.

The normal type of shellac, whether in flakes or as a liquid, has a transparent orange color. Applying this shellac to wood affects the wood's color slightly. But this shellac works very well on darker woods and can be applied over just about any stain. For lighter colored woods, or those treated by bleaching, there is a white shellac, which is made by bleaching orange shellac. It is not absolutely colorless, but its tint is not obvious on the wood.

Unfortunately bleached shellac does not have a very long storage life and it is affected by dampness, which clouds its tint. Normal orange shellac keeps better and has a better resistance to moisture, but it does not stand up to heat, moisture, and most solvents as well as lacquer and other modern finishes. So orange shellac is not the finish for table and bar tops.

Shellac should be stored in bottles or jars. It is inadvisable to use metal containers. Do not leave shellac in uncovered containers because the alcohol will quickly evaporate. It is unsatisfactory to mix white and orange shellac, and nothing but alcohol should be used for thinning. Spirit stain can be mixed with shellac to produce something similar to varnish stain. This mixture can be used inside a box or other enclosed part, where one-coat stain and finish saves time, but this is not a treatment for an exposed part because the stain is in the shellac coat and not in the wood.

Shellac's value as a sealer and primer has already been mentioned. When shellac is applied to wood, plaster, or any porous material, it soaks in and prevents the entry of any other finishing material.

For sealing wood, shellac should be thin—a 2 lb or 3 lb cut will do. The alcohol in thin cuts takes the shellac into the pores, then evaporates to leave the shellac to a good depth. A thicker concentration might stay mostly on the surface, needing more rubbing down. If left too thick on the wood, shellac might craze and spoil the finish put over it.

BRUSHING

Shellac applied by brush gives an effect comparable to varnish. But shellac does not have as good a resistance to abrasion and many solvents. Many coats are needed, but because drying time is short, these can be applied at intervals of two hours or so. So three to six coats can be built up in a comparatively short time.

Generally, the best results are obtained with five or six coats of a tin-cut shellac, rather than just a few coats of a stronger shellac. Apply with a broad brush (3 in. for a large surface) and work *with* the grain. Work as quickly as possible. Do not brush excessively and go the whole length in one stroke if possible. Avoid working over a part several times: the quick-drying finish may drag on the brush and spoil the surface. If a sag or other blemish is not seen until it has partly dried, it is better to leave it to sand later. If the blemish is still liquid, work very lightly with just the tips of the bristles.

When brushing shellac on carvings, turnings, and other shaped parts, work quickly. Take care to get into the recesses. Lift away any excess shellac with a dry brush.

Shellac does not perform well in damp conditions, so work in a dry atmosphere. A shellac coat becomes dust proof in only a few minutes.

A first coat should be given a little more drying time than later coats. After each intermediate coat dries, sand lightly with a finishing paper. And after each sanding, go over the surface and remove dust with a cloth moistened with alcohol. Hard shellac sands as a white powder. If it does not, this is a sign that sanding has started too early.

Shellac will harden in the brush. So between coats put the brush in alcohol. Clean it with alcohol after use.

When the final coat has been applied, there will be a good casing of shellac over the wood, but the surface may not be as smooth as desired. The surface can be rubbed smooth with a fine steel wool. Rub with long strokes in the direction of the grain. Avoid circular or cross-grain rubbing and do not apply much pressure. Stop when the surface appears smooth. Follow with a wax polish.

FRENCH POLISHING

This method of polishing goes back a long way. Whether it has a special connection with the French is uncertain.

The glowing surface obtained by French polishing is considered superior to just about any other gloss finish. But there is a certain amount of labor involved. While skill improves with practice, it is patience as much as skill that gets good results. For many items of furniture, any other finish may be just as acceptable as French polishing. But if the finish is to go on antique furniture, French polish is the correct choice in nearly every case. A great many pieces of furniture now considered antiques were originally French polished.

Usually French polishing is done with thin shellac. There are mixtures on the market called "French polishes," but these are likely to be 2 1/2 lb cut shellacs. Some denatured alcohol contains resin. This makes a less satisfactory polish, so get shellac mixed with alcohol that is free from resin.

Some woodworkers favor additives that they claim improve the finish. Two are gum arabic and gum opal. These are added in very small amounts—not more than a teaspoon to a pint of French polish (or thin shellac). Stir in and leave at least half a day before using.

With nearly all woods, French polish is used without coloring. Normally any coloring comes from staining—before polishing. But if something different from the orange or white shellac color is wanted to match another part, small quantities of spirit stain can be mixed with the polish.

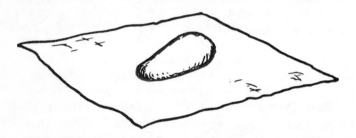

Fig. 6-1. A polishing pad's cloth should be about 9 in. square.

French polishing is done with a pad, usually cotton wrapped in a piece of old cotton cloth. The cloth must be free of lint. This pad should be a size that is convenient to handle. The inner cotton should about 2 or 3 in. across, so the outside cloth needs to be about 9 in. square (Fig. 6-1). To make the pad, the cloth is brought up around the cotton and twisted (Fig. 6-2). To prevent pads from hardening, store in an airtight jar.

There are three stages in French polishing: bodying in, building up, and spiriting out. Of course, the wood has to be brought to a good surface, as described earlier, then stained

Fig. 6-2. The cloth of a polishing pad should be twisted around the cotton.

and filled. If anything, French polishing emphasizes the quality of the wood surface. This is not a finish for disguising imperfections.

Bodying in is the process that puts a skin of shellac on the wood. Sprinkle shellac on the inner pad and cover it with the cloth. Twist the cloth up so the shellac oozes through. Rub across the grain and then with it (Fig. 6-3). Cover every part of

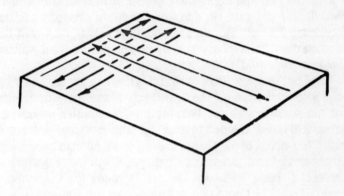

Fig. 6-3. The first rubbing strokes of the bodying in stage should be across the grain and then with it.

the surface, particularly the corners. Do not stop on the surface. Change to a circular motion or a figure-eight action (Fig. 6-4). Continue rubbing until all the polish in the pad is exhausted. Allow the surface to harden, then recharge the pad and repeat.

Try to cover the whole surface with an even film. It is the corners that suffer. Usually if you concentrate on the corners, the center of a panel will take care of itself. Recharging and rubbing may be repeated as many times as needed to give the

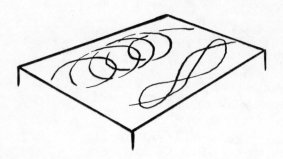

Fig. 6-4. After linear strokes, circular or figure-eight strokes should follow.

whole surface a good protective coating. Leave the work in a dust-free room for about a day.

Follow this by examining the surface in a light. There may be unevenness. Use fine steel wool lightly to remove this then charge the pad and apply more polish. If the pad sticks when moved over the surface, add a few drops of linseed oil to the outside of the pad. Get an even depth of polish, then wait for another day. If flaws are still there, the process and waiting should be repeated.

The building up stage is next. Lightly rub the surface with steel wool and wipe off the dust. Prepare the pad with polish, but not as much as for bodying in. The smaller amount of polish will cause the pad to drag, and this has to be prevented with a few drops of oil. Do not use any more oil than necessary. To check the pad, press it on paper. Oil will make a mark if present. If none is shown, the pad is ready for a few more drops of oil. The same test will show how wet the pad is with polish. If there is a definite wet trail when the pad is drawn lightly across the bodied-in surface, there is too much polish on the pad. If the pad marks are shiny, there is too much oil.

Work over the surface with circular or figure-eight movements in the same way as when bodying in. Stroke lightly. Do not rub hard. Make sure the whole area is covered. Do not put down or take up the pad from the center of the surface. Slide on or off at an edge. Do not stop on the surface. It is not swift rubbing that produces a good polish. There's no need to rush.

Recharge with polish as necessary and add spots of oil when needed. Continue until there is a good layer of polish over the surface of the wood. The layer need not have much of a shine or a very even gloss. Next, apply a coat of polish diluted with an equal quantity of alcohol. The result may look smeary, but it does not matter at this stage. Leave the work for at least five hours.

The next stage is spiriting out. Use a fresh pad with a double outer cloth. Dampen this with a little alcohol. Put the pad into an airtight jar for a short time so the alcohol permeates the pad. Wipe the surface with very light strokes. This should remove smears. Change to a dry clean pad and go over the whole surface, first with circular strokes and then with the grain. This burnishing action should bring up an even glow to the surface. Be careful not to use too much alcohol. This would dissolve too much of the surface that has been applied. The polished work should be left for two or three days to fully harden.

French polishing is a process for dealing with large areas. There are many fretted, carved, or molded parts that cannot be treated with a pad. Simple molding can be rubbed lengthwise, but shellac will have to be applied by brush to most other shaped parts, even if adjoining flat surfaces are polished with a pad.

Spray Finishes 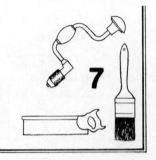 7

The spray gun offers an alternative way of applying a finish to furniture. Although some older finishing materials can be sprayed, lacquer is the most popular sprayed-on finish.

BASICS

Professional spraying equipment is comparatively bulky. The spray gun can be held in the hand, but the gun is connected by a hose to a compressor (usually electrically powered) that is big enough to serve the equipment. However, there are less bulky outfits that can be attached to a vacuum cleaner. Another type uses an electric vibrator in the spray unit. An aerosol can is a simple spray unit. But aerosol spraying should be regarded only as a means of touching up or dealing with small objects.

The simpler spray guns will only take very watery liquids, while the better spray units can cope with liquids with more body to them.

When spraying, space is an important factor. It is necessary to be able to get around the work. And spray painting in a small enclosed area is never a good idea.

There are two main types of spray guns. In a suction-feed gun, air blows over the outlet, picking up the liquid and atomizing it. In suction-feed guns, the air and fluid are mixed outside the unit (Fig. 7-1). This is described as an *external*

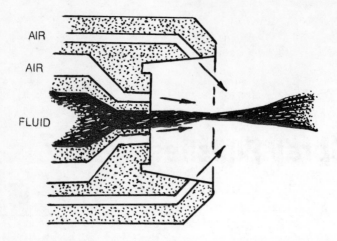

Fig. 7-1. Suction-feed spray guns mix air and fluid outside the nozzle.

mix. In a pressure-feed gun, the fluid is under pressure and there is an *internal mix* of air and fluid inside the nozzle (Fig. 7-2).

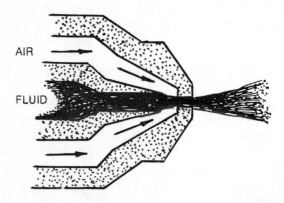

Fig. 7-2. Pressure-feed spray guns mix the fluid and air internally.

Only a pressure-feed gun can spray heavy liquids such as paint and enamel. But pressure-feed guns are less suitable for fast-drying liquids such as lacquer, which is better sprayed with a suction-feed gun. Many sunction-feed guns take glass jars which are quickly changed. The pressure-feed gun has a metal container.

The solvents used in some sprays can be uncomfortable—even dangerous—when breathed. Most sprays are flammable, so spraying should be done in a well ventilated place, preferably with a fan working. It is useful to have a turntable for the work. This is better than having to move oneself around a piece of furniture.

LACQUER

The main reason for the popularity of spray finishing is the fast-drying lacquer formulated to give a quick finish and a surface that is highly resilient. Modern lacquer is a complex chemical composition, which should be obtained already mixed. Lacquer is not a mixture to make yourself. Lacquers are formulated for a variety of purposes and care is needed to get the right type of lacquer intended for furniture. For most purposes there is a clear gloss furniture lacquer, but there is a water-white version for use on very light or bleached woods. If the gloss is not required there is a flat furniture lacquer. If the wood has not previously been sealed, there is a lacquer sealer to be used before the finishing lacquer.

There are colored lacquers too. These finishes are comparable to brush-painted finishes. But sprayed-on lacquers do not leave brush marks. Lacquers usually produce a tougher skin than most paints. Several special lacquers are also made, including a shading lacquer which is used to give shading around edges.

Lacquer will attack other finishes, usually by softening them, so lacquer should not be sprayed over any other finish.

Spraying lacquer usually demands a supply of lacquer thinners. And sometimes retarders are needed. These mixtures are slow drying and prevent the problem of blushing (becoming cloudy white), which may occur in humid conditions. These are lacquers intended for brushing, but the attraction of lacquer is its suitability for spraying.

Lacquer usually has to be thinned for spraying. How much thinning depends on the manufacturer's recommendations, but a pigmented lacquer will need more thinning than a clear one.

OTHER SPRAY FINISHES

Shellac should be thinned sufficiently to spray smoothly, to a 2 lb cut or thinner. Avoid spraying shellac in humid conditions.

Water-mixed paints can be used with a pressure-feed gun. Thin them with water to a consistency that will spray, but no thinner than the gun will handle.

Synthetic paints vary in their ingredients, and it may be necessary to experiment to discover if thinning is necessary. For the best finish, there will have to be pauses for drying between coats in the same way as when brushing. Some synthetics will work in a suction-feed gun, but all oil-mixed paints need a pressure gun.

Varnishes behave like synthetic paint and may require some thinning. Each coat will have to be given drying time.

Stains can be sprayed too, but the best penetration is obtained by brushing. However, with stains that are quick-drying and therefore likely to show brush marks, spraying should get a more even effect.

SPRAYING

Nothing must block the jet of a spray gun. This means that any pigment must be thoroughly mixed in the vehicle, and this mixture must be thoroughly mixed with the solvent or thinner for spraying. Thinning should be as recommended by the manufacturers, but insure that the result is a free-flowing mixture with the same consistency throughout. If there is any doubt, strain through a fine mesh screen or nylon stocking.

Test spray on a piece of cardboard or paper so any adjustments can be made before spraying the actual job. See that the mixture of air and fluid is atomizing correctly. Experiment with distance and note the pattern produced. Try vertical and horizontal spraying. Adjust the fluid flow to give a small pattern and try getting an even spread, then enlarge the pattern.

For most liquids, the distance from the gun to the surface should be betweeen 6 and 10 in. When the gun is close, more liquid is deposited on the surface. And the more liquid deposited, the faster the gun has to be moved to prevent build up. If the gun is too far from the work, the deposit of liquid will be too slow.

When spraying a flat surface, the gun should be used with a parallel action. Swinging in an arc is a common fault. It results in an uneven spread (Fig. 7-3). The gun should start moving *before* the trigger is pulled, and the trigger should be released *before* the gun has finished moving.

To cover an area, let the strokes overlap about half way to each band gets a double thickness (Fig. 7-4). Where a panel finishes at an edge, spray a band along the edge before doing the lengthwise bands. An outside corner is also treated in this

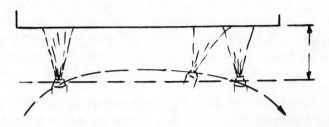

Fig. 7-3. Sweeping the spray gun in an arc can cause unevenness and runs.

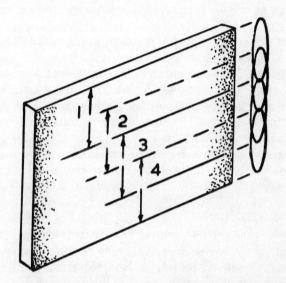

Fig. 7-4. Spray paint should be applied in overlapping bands.

way, with part of the band covering on each surface (Fig. 7-5). With a right-angled corner, it is difficult to avoid over-spraying some part, but try to spray each surface separately, with a minimum overlap around the corner. Spraying directly into a corner may cause an excess of fluid in the angle.

Fig. 7-5. One method of spraying a corner.

A vertical panel can be sprayed with either up and down motions or by horizontal bands. There are no problems like the risk of marks showing after brushing, so the direction of working is not important. What *is* important is an even coating.

On some items, spraying may be limited to a few parts. This means the part not to be sprayed has to be masked, but masking tape is not enough. Newspaper or cardboard has to be joined to the masking tape to catch any overspray.

There should be a spraying sequence thought out before spraying begins. In general, work from the least important to the most important. Spray the insides of cabinets before the outsides. Spray undersides and parts not normally visible. With legs, spray inside surfaces before the outsides. Spray edges before flat surfaces. Leave tops until last. When spraying a surface that adjoins one already sprayed, angle the gun so any spray that overshoots goes into the air over the edge and not around the corner.

Although lacquer dries very quickly, furniture should be left two hours before any rubbing down and the application of another coat.

SPRAYING FAULTS

Sags or runs are the result of an excess of fluid, usually on a vertical or sloping surface. This may be due to holding the gun still, not releasing the trigger before stopping, working too slowly, or getting too close.

Streaks are caused by uneven spraying. Unevenness can be caused by the gun being held at different distances or erratic overlapping.

Sometimes a sprayed surface can take on a texture like an orange peel. If the liquid has not been thinned enough or there is insufficient air pressure, this may happen. Overspraying on a previously sprayed surface can also cause the problem.

Blooming, or blushing, is caused by the absorption of moisture in the finish due to working in damp or humid conditions. It could also be caused by lacquer drying too quickly, which can be prevented by adding retarder.

Pin holes which may appear in the finish are probably caused by the lacquer not being thinned properly. Having the gun too close to the surface or the fluid pressure too high can also cause a pin-hole effect.

Defects in the pattern sprayed are likely to be due to particle blockages in the gun. Cleaning the gun will remove these, but the cause may be due to incorrectly mixed material or lack of filtering.

CLEANING A SPRAY GUN

It is important to clean a spray gun soon after use, particularly if a quick-drying finish has been used. Do not give the material a chance to harden in the gun. Have an extra container filled with solvent. This should be the thinner that goes with the material being sprayed.

With the air pressure off, let the fluid tube drip. Work the trigger to release trapped fluid. Wipe off any surplus. Operate the gun when it is filled with solvent. Give several brief squirts. Then seal the nozzle with a cloth and give the trigger a few quick pulls to agitate the solvent in the container and tube. Remove the gauge and squirt again. Remove the solvent container and operate the gun again to blow out any remaining solvent.

If a container needs cleaning, use solvent and a small brush, such as an old toothbrush. If other parts of the gun need cleaning, be careful not to damage air and fluid holes in the nozzle. Do not be tempted to poke through holes with a metal wire or pin. Poking around these areas is better done with a pointed piece of wood or a bristle taken from a broom. If water is used after water-base paint, follow cleaning with this by using turpentine or lacquer thinner to reduce the risk of rusting.

Many faults in a sprayed surface can be attributed to a blocked or dirty spray gun or to improperly prepared finishes. It is important that preparation and cleaning be done thoroughly. It is false economy to skimp on thinners or solvents used for cleaning.

Oil and Wax Polishes

8

It is remarkable that some furniture that has survived for hundreds of years still has a fine polish, a mellow patina. The ages seem to have enhanced the fine sheen. Such beauty is the result of expert craftsmanship—and either wax or oil polishes.

OIL POLISHING

Oil polishing takes a lot of time. And for this reason many people avoid it, preferring to use other methods. But oil polishing does produce beautiful finishes.

Many oils can be used, but the most common is linseed oil. It is possible to produce a finish on bare wood that is comparable to the finish on old furniture. The linseed oil is spread on, then polished off by vigorous rubbing with one or more cloths. Since most of the oil applied is rubbed off and only a thin film is left in the pores of the wood, the building up of a sheen takes many applications at intervals. Warming the oil by standing its container in hot water aids penetration of the oil. A good oil finish is unlikely to mark by heat or water.

Polishing may be started with coarse cloth. Rubbing has to be hard and kept up for some time—as much as 20 minutes. An alternative to the cloth is a stiff scrubbing brush. Cloth wrapped around a brick may be used on a flat surface. A power polisher may be used. It is the heat developed by friction that produces the polish.

All of this is tedious and time consuming. One way of speeding results is to add a little varnish and turpentine to the linseed oil. One or two early coats of this mixture may be brushed on, but later application should be friction polished with a cloth.

Instead of varnish, beeswax can be used. About 1 oz of beeswax should be dissolved in 1 pt of raw linseed oil. This mixture should be heated, but the linseed oil container should not be put on a hotplate or over a flame. Stand it in hot water and stir in the beeswax. Add about an equal amount of turpentine and allow the mixture to cool. Use it in the same way as the varnish-oil mixture.

There are several other mixtures, and it is possible to buy prepared oil polishes.

WAX POLISHING

Another finishing material with a long history is wax. Wax polish lasts longer than oil polish. Many modern polishes for reviving the appearance of furniture contain wax. Prepared wax polishes may be in paste or liquid form, and some of the liquid polishes come in spray containers. Liquid wax polishes may also include cleaning agents, which remove dirt as the polish is applied. Wax finishes may be marked by heat or water.

There are many kinds of waxes, but the most popular is beeswax, produced by the honey bee. Beeswax is usually white or yellowish brown. The hardest of natural waxes is carnauba, which comes from a Brazilian palm tree. It is a pale yellow. Although brittle when used alone, it can be mixed with other waxes, and is found in many prepared wax polishes.

Paraffin wax is well known. It comes from petroleum and is a translucent white. It is soft but can be used with other waxes. Ceresine is a hydrocarbon wax which may be mixed with carnauba wax.

Waxes may be bought in lump or block form for making your own polish. There are also several prepared versions that come ready to use. Mixing waxes involves the use of heat. But never heat a container of wax directly on a hotplate or flame. The wax may be damaged by too much heat and there could be risk of fire with most of them. Instead, stand the wax container in hot water, which may be kept hot by standing it over a hotplate or flame. To speed up melting, the wax should be shredded with a knife.

Turpentine is used with most waxes, either to make a liquid polish or to make a paste. A typical beeswax polish is made by melting 1 lb of shredded beeswax, then adding 1/2 pt of warmed turpentine. Stir well, then allow to cool. The shredded wax can be dissolved directly in cold turpentine, but this takes some time—probably a day.

Although carnauba can be dissolved in turpentine, the resulting polish is too hard and brittle, so another wax is introduced. This could be ceresine or paraffin wax. A suitable mixture is produced by melting together 1 lb of carnauba and the other wax, and adding 1 pt of turpentine. When cooled, this will be a paste. If it is too hard, it can be heated again and more turpentine can be added.

Normally wax polishes are used in their natural color. The creamy or yellowish tone does not affect the appearance of the natural or stained wood underneath. If coloring is wanted, oil stains can be mixed in while the wax is liquid, but only a small amount will be needed. Powdered stains can be used, particularly if a brown is needed for wax used on old furniture. But an excess of coloring matter may affect the polishing qualities of the wax.

Wax can be used on bare wood, but the building up of a good patina is a lengthy process. Unlike oil, wax does produce a film on the surface, where oil is mostly in the wood. Consequently, there is more of the base polishing material there to take a friction polish.

Since wax makes its own surface film and does not depend as much on penetrating the wood, it is standard procedure to seal the wood with something else before wax polishing. Wax can follow almost any of the other finishing materials, so new work can be given enough shellac, lacquer, or varnish to seal the pores before wax polishing.

If new work is prepared for wax polishing by sealing with another finish, level that finish and remove any shine before polishing. This can be done by sanding with finishing paper or by rubbing down with either cloth and water or oil and pumice powder. Remove all trace of abrasive before using wax.

Although it is necessary to apply wax all over the surface, care is needed to avoid getting thick patches of wax. One way of getting an even first coat is to use a pad very much like the one used to French polish. Put some paste wax on a cloth then wrap it in several layers of muslin.

Cover the surface with wax, then leave it for 10 minutes or so. Rub it briskly with another cloth, first polishing in all directions, then along the grain. For the first polish with a hard wax, considerable friction is needed and it may help to use a brush or cloth around a brick. Initial polishing is best done by hand, but later work can be done with power tools.

If a large area is to be covered, it may be better to concentrate on one part at a time. The final even sheen all over should not be difficult to obtain this way, especially if a final friction polish is done on the whole area.

Wax may be used to revive some other finish. Paste wax polish is the best treatment for a part that is well worn or is subject to much use. This will build up the best protective layer. However, some liquid and cream polishes will remove dirt, sticky finger marks, and similar things at the same time the polishing is done.

Many modern wax finishes have been formulated so little rubbing is needed and the considerable hard work of friction polishing is no longer necessary. Some of these polishes will also disguise marks left from hot or wet containers.

After the initial coat of wax polish has been put on, a softer cloth can be used for subsequent coats. But use a cloth without lint.

Some furniture polishes, intended for reviving a finish, are described as "no-rub." Their solvent evaporates and the deposit left may have a satisfactory gloss, but a light rub will usually improve it.

Wax polishes have a reasonable shelf life. But if polish becomes hard, it can be melted by placing the container in warm water and mixing in a very small amount of turpentine.

Any brushes used with wax can be cleaned with turpentine, which may have to be warmed to thoroughly penetrate and remove caked wax. Gasoline (not warmed, of course) will also dissolve wax from brushes or clean dirt from polishing cloths.

Special Wood Finishes

9

In modern furniture making there have been moves to introduce special effects that give wood a contemporary look. Whether these are acceptable or not depends on the eye of the beholder. But many of them, when used with discretion, can produce striking results.

LIMING

A novel effect can be obtained on oak, chestnut, and other open-grained wood by filling the crevices of the grain with something that contrasts with the color of the wood. This process is called liming. The name comes from the early use of lime to whiten parts of the grain in oak. Today, other substances are used instead, such as white filler and paints.

Usually liming is done on an unstained surface—one that has been properly prepared by a final sanding with fine abrasive paper. For the best results, any bent fibers are straightened by wetting the surface and allowing it to dry before sanding.

First seal the surface with a light coat of thinned bleached shellac (2 lb cut). There are several white fillers that can be used. Some are sold specially for the purpose. A wax filler can be used (zinc white in paraffin wax). Alternatively, use flat white or undercoat paint, thinned to a cream. But the paint should not be too fluid or the intensity of the white may not be good enough. Apply the paint with a brush, working in all directions so as to force the mixture into the grain. Wipe off with a cloth to remove paint from the surface without leaving smears. If you are not satisfied the first time, the process can be repeated.

Do not sand. Sanding would deposit particles of dust and grit in the filler or paint. Allow the "lime" ample time to dry. Pine will need at least a day to dry. Cover this with another coat of the thinned, bleached shellac. Lightly sand this and apply another coat. Sand again. The sanded shellac will seal the "lime" in the wood. Further treatment can be more shellac, possibly applied as French polish, or by sprayed lacquer, but whatever is used should be clear, without any orange or yellow tinge.

For variations on this process, the wood may be stained to give more contrast to the white "lime." Special effects can be obtained by using stains other than brown. A silver grey water stain can be used. A thinned black stain has a similar effect. Stains are used before any sealing. Color the wood after sanding and before applying thinned shellac sealer. After this, use the chosen "lime," as already described.

Although liming is particularly appropriate to oak, it can be used on other woods with grain sufficiently open to hold the liming material. Some mahoganies will take the finish. On pine a tinted filler can be used. Pine and other softer woods can be stained grey and a white wax filler used to give a driftwood effect.

SHADING

Wood does not have to be the same shade all over, although this may seem more natural and is usual for most furniture. In some cases there can be lighter and darker versions of the same color. On turned work, a bulbous part can be shaded lighter than the rest of the turning. In carved work, shading of the stain can increase emphasis where needed.

When shading, it is usually best to follow the color gradations of natural wear. That is, shade so that the color variations appear to be a result of aging and normal use. This is especially good advice for the restoring of antiques.

There are several ways of shading. A regular stain can be used, with more applied where a darker color is wanted. If a spray is used, there can be good control. Otherwise, use a cloth as well as a brush and let there be a gradual change from dark to light.

The stain can be applied heavily all over the surface and allowed to dry, then the parts which are to be lighter can be sanded until the desired effect is produced.

Oil stain may be applied, then the highlighted parts can be wiped with a cloth before the stain has dried.

It is also possible to apply shading after a finishing coat, particularly when spraying. There can be a first staining of the wood to what will be the lightest shading stain. After this has dried, more finish is sprayed over it.

Plan your shading. Examine professionally made shaded furniture. Although a haphazard shading is not wanted, do not go to the other extreme and shade with geometrical precision. Follow the lines of the furniture and make the color variations gradual. At a corner do not let the shading look like a mitered frame, but widen and round there (Fig. 9-1).

Fig. 9-1. The color gradations in shading should be gradual, especially around corners.

Shading has uses when woods are mixed in one piece of furniture. Maybe the only plywood available is not the same wood as the framing around it. Getting an exact color match by staining may be difficult. But shading, with its deliberate changing of hue, disguises the fact that the base woods are actually different.

BLOND FINISHES

Most furniture described as blond has been lightened by bleaching. Bleach is applied evenly and allowed to work. Even application is important to get a uniform result. No stains are used. The very light finish will show *any* defects in the wood, so flawless wood should be chosen and the workmanship should be good.

A bleached surface left too long untreated may attract dirt or begin to become discolored. So seal it quickly, either with bleached shellac or water-white lacquer. Do not use anything that will produce a yellow tinge. Sand this and follow with further finishing coats. Wax polish makes a good final treatment.

If the wood being given a blond finish is open grained, use a neutral-colored filler after bleaching and before sealing.

ACID TREATMENTS

Although stains have taken the place of many of the earlier more drastic treatments, their effect is only on the *color* of the wood. Some earlier treatments did things to the *character* of the wood as well.

Sulfuric and nitric acid, diluted with water, will eat away the soft parts of wood and leave the harder parts standing. One part acid to three parts water is about right.

WARNING

Never pour water into acid—always acid into water. Wear a heavy rubber apron or protective clothing and heavy rubber gloves.

In softwoods there are alternate light and dark grain lines. If acid eats away the light parts, the wood will look worn and aged. Use a wire scratch brush on the wood as the acid is applied. Wash off the acid with plenty of water and neutralize the wood with diluted ammonia before finishing. A grey stain can emphasize the apparent age and this can be followed with wax polish.

Special Opaque Finishes

When furniture is painted with a brush or sprayed with an opaque lacquer, the colors are normally uniformly applied, even if more than one color is used. But there are several other ways of using opaque substances, and some of the techniques can produce very attractive results.

GRAINING

For a long time, until sometime between World War I and II, many woodworkers tried to simulate the grain of wood by using paint. This technique is called graining. Graining is not an attempt to fool anyone; it is a novel way of giving wood a grainlike appearance.

Two colors are used: a base yellowish brown (a straw color) and a darker brown, something like the dark grain lines in spruce or fir. The flat base color is applied and allowed to dry. The second color, which is better if also flat, is then applied. It is allowed to partially dry. How long it is left to dry depends on the paint. Then a comb is drawn over the surface to scrape lines that expose the lighter color underneath. A painter's comb has broad flat teeth, but a coarse hair comb could be used. If the comb is drawn along the surface with a wavy motion, the result simulates a meandering wood grain. It is possible to simulate knots by leaving circles of dark paint. When the paint dries, it is sealed by one or more coats of varnish or clear lacquer.

TEXTURED AND MOTTLED FINISHES

Texturing paint is a technique comparable to graining, but the result is a paint surface almost like rough plaster. There are special prepared plasters to mix with water to give this effect, but paint can be adapted. The texture treatment suits some picture frames, but is not so appropriate for larger pieces of furniture.

Give the wood one or more coats of shellac or undercoat paint to provide a base. Use a flat paint and mix into it some plaster of Paris to make a thick stiff paste that can be applied with a brush, preferably one with stiffer bristles than the usual paint brush. Put on a thick coat. Go over this surface with a stiff brush or a hair comb, either in wavy lines along the wood or in a pattern of swirls or other shapes as desired. This will leave a pattern of ridges and hollows. Leave the work to harden.

There will usually be more roughness than is wanted, so go over the surface with medium abrasive paper to remove the high spots. Brush off any dust and give the surface a coat of paint in any shade. A gloss finish in a bright color will emphasize the texture of the surface.

A mottled effect can be obtained by applying one color on top of another. The lower color should be the lighter one. Apply this and let it dry. Put the second color on. While the top color is still wet, go over it with a wad of paper, picking up some of the top paint. This process will leave a random pattern where the lighter color shows through. Let this dry, then give it a coat of clear lacquer or varnish.

Another mottled finish, suitable for frames and other narrow things, also uses two colors or dark and light versions of the same color. The lighter coat is applied and allowed to dry. The second coat is applied with a brush or by dabbing with a cloth. Stipple with a clean cloth so some of the first coat shows through. The final effect is something like parchment. Cover with clear lacquer, varnish, or shellac.

UNEVEN EFFECTS

There are several finishes, most of which have been produced as a result of lacquer developments, in which the finished surface is uneven.

If a quick-drying lacquer is sprayed over a slow-drying elastic one, the top coat will crack. That is the principle. The first coat is sprayed on, using several coats if necessary. The special crackle lacquer is sprayed over this. In quite a short time it will crack and open up in an irregular pattern, showing the undercoat. The crackle coat should be allowed to dry, then covered with a clear lacquer. With the large variety of colors available, many interesting combinations are possible. Dark blue over light blue has a clean, bright effect.

A practice piece should be used first. There are no second chances with this technique.

There are special wrinkle lacquers which can be obtained in types that give different degrees of wrinkle. These may be brushed on in the usual thick consistency or thinned and sprayed. One type needs a special oven to finish it, but there is an air-dry type, although this really needs heat to form satisfactory wrinkles. Having an electric heater in the vicinity is enough. Follow the manufacturer's directions.

This is a one-coat finish, but the color can be changed by spraying with ordinary lacquer. An interesting effect can be obtained by spraying on another color with the gun angled so the new color is on only one side of the wrinkles.

Spattering is another interesting technique. Put on a base color and let it dry. Flick a second color onto the surface with a paint brush. One way to do this is to strike a charged paint brush with a piece of wood, forcing flecks of paint onto the surface. Obviously, some practice on scrap wood or paper is advisable to master the best technique and get the desired pattern of flecks.

The size and spacing of the flecks will depend on the distance, the amount of paint in the brush, and your handling of it. If the first spattering is too scattered for your liking, more can be spattered over the same area. Of course, there can be spots of different colors superimposed on each other, but each color should be allowed to dry before the next is applied.

MARBLING

Another skill of old-time painters was the production of a surface that looked like marble. The painter got this effect by using a brush or a feather. The method can still be used, of course, and can create an interesting finish on just about any flat wood surface.

Apply a light flat paint to the surface. Usually two colors are used for marbling, in addition to the initial flat coat. Blue and red are suitable, but marble has many hues, mostly in mild pastel shades. Dip the end of a feather in one color and pull the feather across the painted surface, moving it about in a wavy random pattern, varying the pressure so as to get different widths and intensities of line. Do the same thing with the second color. Where the wet colors join they will blend into each other as they do at some points in marble. Get a meandering mixed pattern of lines and curves that have some thin, hairlike parts and others that are quite thick.

The marbled surface should be allowed to dry. It can then be covered with a waterproof or heatproof lacquer.

Decorating  11

There are several ways of altering the appearance of wood surfaces without actually applying a finish. These techniques come under the heading of decorating.

DECALS

The history of slide-on transfer pictures goes back a long way, but many of the early techniques had faults so the results were not always as good as expected. It is now possible to get decals that work satisfactorily. And the number of different kinds of decals seems endless.

Application methods vary from decal to decal, so read the directions carefully. Most decals can be affixed to just about any flat wood surface, but any unevenness or raised grain may show through. So it is usually best to prepare a surface and apply at least one or two coats of finish before affixing decals. If the final finish is clear varnish or lacquer, the decal can go on before the last coat is applied. If the finish is paint, the decal can be applied over the top coat. But this leaves the decal vulnerable to abrasion. Most decals are quite tough, but it is better to give some more protection with a coat of clear varnish or lacquer. The solvents in some clear finishes may cause the decal to crack or loosen. Decals cannot be applied over wax or many other polishes, so clean with a solvent if an old surface is to be used.

PAPERING

Wall coverings can also be applied to furniture Papering produces special effects and can conceal irreparable flows. Some modern decorators paper furniture panels to match surrounding walls. Such a combination can be striking. Modern plastic-coated wall coverings provide quite a durable finish, which can be cleaned when necessary without damaging the paper. Usually a contact adhesive paper should be used on furniture. Conventional paste wallpaper comes away too easily.

The surface of the wood should be level. The paper can ease into cracks or holes, so the surface should be made good with filler. If the surface is dirty, clean with alcohol or other solvent.

Applying contact paper to furniture is a pretty straightforward process. Peel the backing off and place one edge of the contact paper on the surface being covered. Rub this edge down and lower the rest of the paper gradually, pressing it down little by little (Fig. 11-1). It is possible to lift and reposition to a limited extent, but too much of this may

Fig. 11-1. Applying contact paper.

weaken the final hold of the adhesive. A roller may be used, but wrinkles and air bubbles can be stroked out by hand. When you have the paper right, go over it with plenty of pressure.

Edges can be trimmed with a razor blade or a sharp knife. The paper will wrap over angles. To cover an edge (like a table edge), cut the paper as shown in Fig. 11-2. Fold one flap down and around the corner. Fold the other flap down and smooth it out (Fig. 11-3).

Fig. 11-2. Covering edges with contact paper.

Fig. 11-3. In covering an edge with contact paper, the flaps should be overlapped precisely.

MOLDINGS AND CARVINGS

Suppliers of materials for furniture making prepare shallow carvings and lengths of molding that can be applied to flat surfaces. The cheapest carvings are embossed. They have their patterns pressed on. There are also comparable plastic simulated carvings.

Moldings may be simple beads (Fig. 11-4) or carved patterns (Fig. 11-5). Carvings may be simple button motifs or elaborate floral clusters (Fig. 11-6).

Fig. 11-4. Some moldings are beads.

Moldings or strip carvings can be used to give interest to an otherwise plain flat surface (Fig. 11-7). Other carvings may be used to provide a center of interest, as on a pelmet over drapes (Fig. 11-8).

These applied decorations can be glued in place. But it's a good idea to reinforce the glue with a few tiny nails.

PYROGRAPHY

Pyrography is a modern name for what was once called pokerwork, from its original form in which a hot poker was

Fig. 11-5. Moldings can be carved patterns of all kinds.

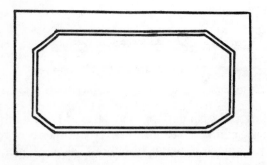

Fig. 11-6. Carvings for wood decoration, such as this floral design, can be very intricate.

Fig. 11-7. Strips of molding can be used to add interest to plain surfaces.

used to burn patterns into wood. The modern alternative to the poker is electrically heated and is something like a small electric soldering iron.

The tool is used like a pen and is used to draw patterns of burnt lines on the wood. The widths of lines can be varied with

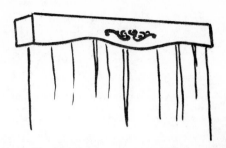

Fig. 11-8. Carvings can provide a focal point for furniture.

different points or by tilting a universal head. The speed of working also affects the intensity of line and its depth.

Pyrography should be used with restraint on most furniture. However, it can be used on children's furniture and a few kitchen items. It can be used in combination with color for decoration in places where a decal might otherwise be used. The pattern is outlined by burning and the spaces are colored. The result looks something like a stained glass window.

Pyrography is burning, so the wood is charred and some ash is produced. For a clean result, these particles should be lightly brushed or blown away, then the surface is given a coat or two of clear varnish or lacquer to prevent further spreading of any burnt dust.

FLOCK SPRAYING

There are methods which can give a wood surface a cloth-like appearance, not by putting on pieces of cloth, but by spraying particles of flock over an adhesive. Flock usually consists of short or pulverized fiber. Usually, the result of these techniques looks like felt. Flock usually is applied by spraying. Suede-Tex is one trade name. Many colors are available.

It is possible to spray almost anything. A complete piece of furniture can be covered. A drawer can be lined with flock for jewelry or cutlery.

The important tool is a hand-operated spray gun, which has a turbulation chamber to swirl the fibers as they are ejected. Usually, flock is sprayed onto a sticky undercoat which is the same color as the flock.

Section 2
Repairing Furniture

Furniture Woods

12

Most furniture repairs involve the incorporation of new pieces of wood. Ideally these will be the same sort of wood as was used originally. With old furniture that was stained and polished and has acquired the dirt of ages, it may not be easy to identify the original wood. If the old finish is to be stripped and the new and old wood given a new finish, clearing the old finish away may expose the bare wood sufficiently to identify it. In any case the grain markings may help in identification.

Fortunately it is often possible to stain a different wood to match the old. There are also ways of bleaching wood, but it is usually better to start with a light colored wood and stain it.

CABINET WOODS

At one time oak was plentiful all over Europe. English oak was reduced greatly by the needs of ship building, but much older substantial furniture was made of it. It is a dark brown, with a fairly open coarse grain. It is very durable, so old pieces of furniture may still be quite sound.

Austrian oak is milder, and Japanese oak is milder yet. The names designate the species and not necessarily where the wood comes from. These oaks plane more "sweetly" than English oak. A sharp plane can slide over them smoothly, removing a fine continuous shaving, leaving a very smooth surface. English oak may tear up and produce a more ragged

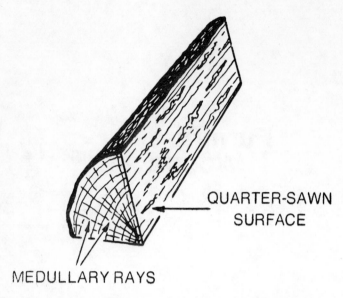

QUARTER-SAWN
SURFACE

MEDULLARY RAYS

Fig. 12-1. A quarter-sawn section of wood showing medullary rays.

shaving. American oaks can be found with similar grains, but there may have to be some staining to match color.

All woods have medullary rays (Fig. 12-1). But oak's medullary rays are very prominent. In the cross section of a tree there are annual rings (Fig. 12-2). The wood near the center is heartwood, which is strong and durable (Fig. 12-3). Farther out is sapwood, which is softer and may be more prone to rot.

If oak is cut radially (sometimes described as "quarter-sawn"), the medullary rays show as "figuring," or "feather grain," on the surface. Much old furniture made of oak has boards in prominent positions cut so the figuring shows. This figuring positively identifies the wood as oak. Even when the wood has not been cut radially, inspection of the end grain will show if there are medullary rays prominent enough to indicate oak.

European chestnut was sometimes used with oak or in place of it. It looks like oak except for the lack of medullary rays. So wood that appears to have the characteristics of oak but without the rays is probably chestnut. If chestnut cannot be obtained for a repair, it is probable that oak will match.

Beech grows prolifically in Europe. It has a close grain without prominent grain markings. It is not used much for

Fig. 12-2. The annual rings of a tree.

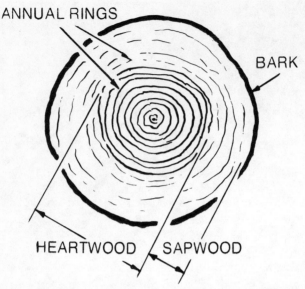

ANNUAL RINGS

BARK

HEARTWOOD / SAPWOOD

Fig. 12-3. The cross section of a tree showing the heartwood and the sapwood.

complete items of furniture, but because of its excellent turning qualities it is often used for the round parts of furniture. It is not a very durable wood, so beech that has been exposed to dampness may be rotten. Red or white beech should be obtainable for repairs.

Elm's color is very similar to oak's but its grain often winds in all directions. However, rock elm and some American elms have more uniform grains. European elm is likely to be found only in large plain furniture. European elm is hard and tough. Its grain may be difficult to match and a repair will probably have to be done with oak or other hardwood.

Mahogany is not native to Europe, but there was a long period when it was the favorite wood of European cabinetmakers. Much of this mahogany came from Spain, Cuba, or Honduras. All of these tend to be a rich brown with an attractive grain. The color can be emphasized. As several types of mahogany are still available, it should not be difficult to find what is needed for repairs. Sapele and gaboon are mahogany-like woods that might be used for repairs to mahogany.

There was a time when some English furniture was made of what was called satin walnut. In America this is better known as red or sweet gum and has a soft, even brown color with little sign of grain. It stains well, so it may be stained easily to match other woods.

Walnut was used in Europe and may be found in American furniture due to its fairly wide availability. Walnut should not be difficult to match.

Sycamore is almost white and may be radially cut like oak to show figuring. It was considered second to beech for turning and may be found as round parts in older furniture. Its clean look also makes it suitable for things associated with food.

Teak was used widely in furniture making at one time. It is brown but bleaches to near white in the sun. It is naturally oily and difficult to work. There is no other wood quite like it, so more teak will have to be found for a repair.

SOFTWOODS

Woods are usually classified as either hardwoods or softwoods. However, the names are not true guides to hardness because some softwoods are harder than some hardwoods. Softwoods are from coniferous trees. Hardwoods come from deciduous trees—trees that shed their leaves in the fall. All of the woods described so far are hardwoods. Softwoods were rarely used in furniture likely to have been imported by settlers, although some may have been brought from Scandinavia, where nearly all the local trees are softwood.

Softwoods are the many firs, pines, larches, and spruces. These are plentiful in the northern parts of the United States, so a lot of furniture has been made from them. Since the woods are still mostly available, there should be no difficulty in matching wood for repairs.

Most of the softwoods used for furniture are very soft, so older furniture may have suffered damage from knocks and normal wear. This could be regarded as a feature showing its age, but if repairs have to be made there are usually several softwoods that can be found with grain to make a reasonable match. Most softwoods contain resin, and it is the amount of resin and its disposition that gives the wood its appearance. Some of the pines that grow to great heights with few branches may have pronounced grain, with alternate dark and light brown lines. Some names are Columbian pine, Douglas fir or pine, and Oregon pine. These are not face woods for furniture, but they may be used constructionally. Pitch pine has an even more pronounced grain due to the heavy amount of resin. Pitch pine is difficult to bring to a good finish, but it may be found in such things as school desks.

Woods are being used from all parts of the world. World consumption of wood is such that some varieties are becoming rare and expensive, so substitutes have to be found. This means much furniture of recent years, particularly since the end of World War II, has been made of woods that we may never have heard of before. Some of them only have a brief popularity and may not be heard of again because they are no longer imported. This leads to difficulty in repair. If much repair work is expected it may be worthwhile retaining damaged furniture and discarded parts for the sake of the wood they may produce for repairing something else.

PLYWOOD

Plywood came into furniture making further back than might be expected, but some of the earlier plywood was of very poor quality and usually in the form of thin three-ply used for cabinet backs or drawer bottoms. Of course, in modern furniture there is considerable use made of plywood and various manufactured boards. While it would be incorrect to use these modern materials for repairing a genuine antique, their use would be sensible for any repair where they are appropriate and there is no need to retain all the original methods of construction.

Plywood is made from veneers, which are thin slices of wood. They are cut from a rotating log in long lengths. The method of cutting *around* the circumference of a rotating log results in a different grain marking from boards cut *across* a stationary log. This means that the appearance of a plywood panel may not match the grain of adjoining solid wood, even if it is all the same species. Not all wood is suitable for making plywood because veneers cannot always be rotary cut. Sometimes plywood comes with special veneer faces. These may be knife- or saw-cut veneers across a log, glued on. Oak is a wood that is difficult to rotary cut, but surface veneers that show figured grain may be glued on in sections.

Plywood usually has an uneven number of veneers. Their number is not necessarily an indication of total thickness. A larger number of veneers makes a stiffer panel than a smaller number. For instance, five 1/4 in. thick plies should be stiffer than three 1/4 in. thick plies (Fig. 12-4). If a thin decorative veneer is fixed to the front surface, another veneer of similar thickness but not necessarily decorative may be fixed for

Fig. 12-4. The more veneers in plywood, the stiffer it is.

compensation on the other side. This reduces any risk of distortion. Three veneers of equal thickness would provide a different strength in each direction, with a possible risk of twisting. This risk is reduced by making the center veneer thicker (Fig. 12-5).

Fig. 12-5. A thick center veneer in plywood can help prevent twisting.

Panels of plywood are made in many sizes. A common panel is 4 by 8 ft, which is as big as a man can comfortably carry. Thicknesses vary. Common sizes start at 3/16 in. and go up to about 3/4 in. Plywood also comes in metric thicknesses—from 4 to 18 mm.

There are several grades of most makes of plywood. If only one face is to be visible, an inferior face on the back may be acceptable for a lower price. Most plywood manufacturers divide their products into interior and exterior plywood, with the latter able to withstand outdoor conditions. However, a marine grade is available and is superior to the exterior grade. Interior plywood may have a glue which would be weakened in damp conditions. Exterior and marine grade will stand up to these conditions, and the best marine grades will stand immersion for a considerable time.

BLOCKBOARDS AND PARTICLE BOARDS

As an alternative to plywood, there are boards in which the core is made of solid strips. These boards are collectively called blockboard. Blockboard made with narrow strips is called laminboard (Fig. 12-6). With wider pieces it is called

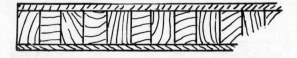

Fig. 12-6. Laminboard is made with narrow strips of wood.

battenboard (Fig. 12-7). The outer veneers resist any tendency to warp or twist.

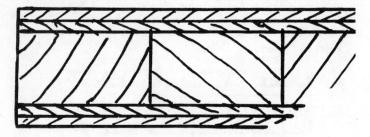

Fig. 12-7. Battenboard is made with wide pieces of wood.

Another thick board is made up of particles of wood embedded in a synthetic resin. This board is called particle board (Fig. 12-8). The board has constructional uses, but unfinished it has a rather unattractive appearance.

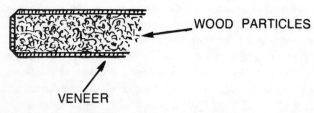

WOOD PARTICLES

VENEER

Fig. 12-8. Particle board consists of wood chips embedded in a synthetic resin.

Particle board may be veneered during manufacture, either with wood veneer or plastic with a wood grain appearance. Veneers may also be applied to the edges of stock size particle boards. It is also possible to get self-adhesive veneers to match those put on during manufacture, so cut and shaped edges can be made to match.

There may be less use for particle boards in repairs, but it has possibilities for replacement shelves and other interior work. If a new top is needed for a table or other working area, it may be possible to use a veneered piece or particle board.

FIBERBOARD

There are many boards manufactured from wood fiber. Some of the loosely bonded boards are used for insulation and temporary packing, but quite a hard material can be made when a suitable bonding agent is used and there is sufficient compression. Most forms of fiberboard have a smooth, tough face surface. The most common thickness is 1/8 in. Masonite is a well known make of fiberboard.

There are several grades of fiberboard. The softer and cheaper grades are not really suitable for furniture. Some of the better boards are given a treatment with oil during manufacturer that gives them a tough water-resistant quality. These boards are sometimes described as "oil tempered." These boards are the best choice for use in furniture.

If the original surface of fiberboard is not damaged, it can be extremely hard wearing. It can take most of the finishes used on other woods, and the smooth surface makes a good base for paint.

Although there may be some prejudice against fiberboard for use in good quality furniture, it is suitable for backs and other hidden parts. Fiberboard can be sprung to moderate curves. Some of it is available with fluted or other patterned surfaces. Sheets with a smooth surface on both sides are made, but they are less common than the type with one good side.

Tools

13

The amount of work involved in repairing furniture may vary from minor first aid to complete replacement of a larger part of the furniture. There may be a joint to be strengthened, some veneer to be patched, or a split to be glued. At the other extreme, repairs may be so massive that they amount to virtually a complete rebuilding job.

Except for extensive rebuilding, most furniture repair work is best done mainly with hand tools. If power tools are already owned, there will be occasions when they can be used, but initially it is better to have an assortment of hand tools. A large number of hand tools can be bought for the price of one power tool and offer considerably more versatility.

An exception might be an electric drill. Besides its use in making holes, it can be fitted with accessories that adapt it for sanding, sawing, and other functions. However, it is best to buy just a drill at first and add accessories later when the need for them is felt. Some accessories available may not be justified by the use they will be given.

In this chapter, some basic tools are discussed. There are obviously many other tools that can be used, particularly if advanced repairs are undertaken. There are other tools for such things as upholstery, carving, and turning, and these more specialized tools and processes are described elsewhere. The tools suggested here are suitable for a first tool kit. Many people already own most of these tools.

MEASURING AND MARKING TOOLS

Repairs cannot progress very far without measuring. However, much measuring with a rule can be avoided if parts can be compared directly. There is less chance of error if a new part is checked by being "offered up," or compared, to the old part it is to match than if a measurement is taken and transferred. Even when it is inconvenient to put the new piece against the old, dimensions can be transferred by use of a rod (Fig. 13-1). A rod can be any piece of wood which is marked in key positions. If several parts have to be made the same size, a rod can be used to mark each part to insure uniformity. If measurements are taken, there is always the risk of misreading the graduation of a rule or using a wrong dimension.

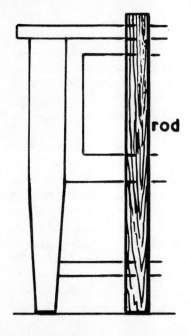

rod

Fig. 13.1. Using a rod is one way to insure uniform measurements.

A flexible rule that rolls into a case is probably the most convenient tool for most measuring. However, its lack of stiffness makes it unsuitable for drawing lines. A flat steel rule is better for things like setting gauges or the guides on power tools. Besides measuring, it can be used for drawing lines or testing for flatness.

Right angles have to be marked for joints, and wood that is planed may have to be tested for squareness. The usual tool for these jobs is a try square. A more handy square is called a combination square (Fig. 13-2). The head of the combination square slides on a rule and can be fixed in any position. It will mark or test 45° miters as well as right angles. Some sliding heads incorporate a spirit level, which can be used to test for surface flatness.

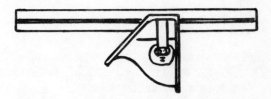

Fig. 13-2. A combination square.

The combination square can also be used with a pencil as a marking gauge. Set to the right distance, it can be draw along to make a line parallel with an edge (Fig. 13-3). For most purposes this is all that is needed, although a marking gauge that can be adjusted to scratch a line any distance from an edge is useful too.

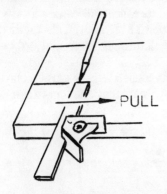

PULL

Fig. 13-3. Use the combination square and a pencil as a marking gauge.

Most marking of wood is with a pencil. But if an accurate cut has to be made across the grain, it is better to use a knife. This severs the fibers of the grain so they are less likely to break out under the saw or other tool. If a cut is to be made on an end piece, the knife line should be "squared" around all four sides (Fig. 3-4). It may be a help in accurate sawing to chisel a bevel on the waste side of the line (Fig. 13-5). Any

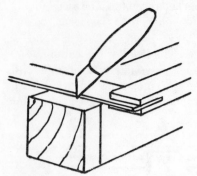

Fig. 13-4. Squaring the end of a piece of wood with a knife.

sharp knife can be used, but a utility knife with replaceable blades is probably more convenient to use.

When furniture joints loosen, it is likely that the whole structure will be distorted. So when regluing or bracing, it is important to keep parts aligned properly. Symmetry can be checked by standing back as far as possible and viewing the piece from several directions.

With most furniture, symmetry can also be checked by measuring diagonals. With a chair or stool, distances measured diagonally from leg to leg should be equal. If these distances are checked with a rod, differences can be noted immediately and the final correct distance will come midway between the marks of the first test (Fig. 13-6). This method can be used anywhere the structure is supposed to be symmetrical.

Curved parts, such as bulbous turned legs or carved claw feet, cannot be measured across with a rule. The tool to use is

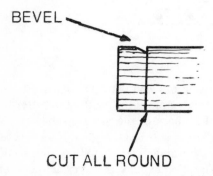

BEVEL

CUT ALL ROUND

Fig. 13-5. Chiseling a bevel on the waste side of a cut can help to insure accurate sawing.

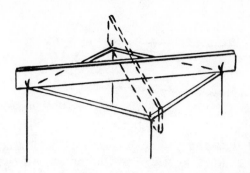

Fig. 13-6. Checking diagonals with a rod.

a pair of calipers. Simple friction-joint calipers are satisfactory (Fig. 13-7).

A pair of dividers is useful for transferring measurements and scratching circles. Heavy, sturdy dividers are best for woodworking.

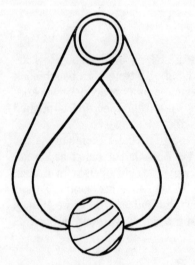

Fig. 13-7. Friction-joint calipers.

SAWS

There is no one saw that will satisfactorily make all cuts needed in woodwork. For most precision cutting and joint making, the first choice should be a backsaw (Fig. 13-8). Recommended size is 10 or 12 in. long with about 14 to 16 teeth per inch. This is the saw for accurate cutting close to a line. It

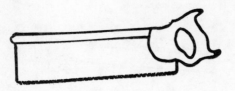

Fig. 13-8. A backsaw.

does not leave much raggedness. It is not the tool for reducing a large piece of wood to size. The tool for general coarser cutting is an 18 in. panel saw with about 8 teeth per inch (Fig. 13-9).

Fig. 13-9. A panel saw.

A lot of sawing is done on the bench. And a good tool for holding wood in place while sawing on a bench is a bench hook (Fig. 13-10). One end of the bench hook is braced, or hooked, against the edge of the bench while the other end is pushed against with the wood to be sawn.

Control of a saw is best if the first finger points along the side of the handle (Fig. 13-11). Although a panel saw may sometimes be used when the wood is held upright in a vise, most cutting has to be done with the wood horizontal. This is best arranged at knee height so the wood is held by kneeling on it. A trestle can be used, but a chair without a back is

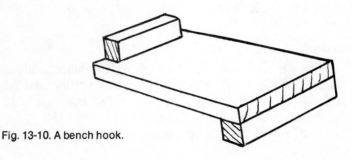

Fig. 13-10. A bench hook.

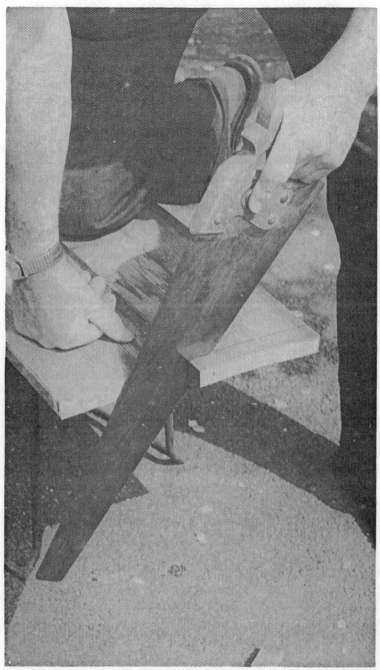

Fig. 13-11. The correct way to hold a saw.

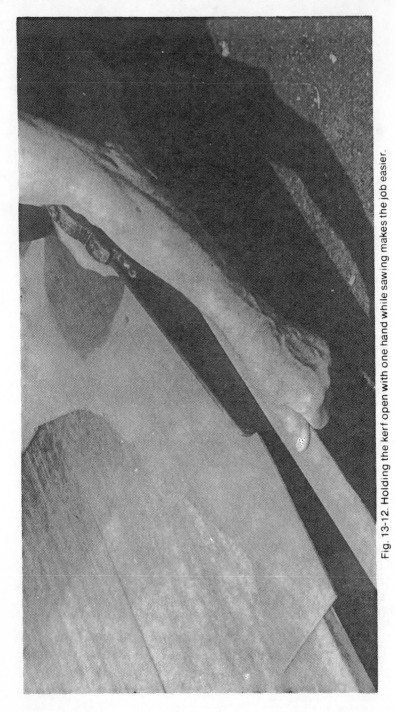

Fig. 13-12. Holding the kerf open with one hand while sawing makes the job easier.

satisfactory. For wood of moderate thickness, a saw cuts best if its edge is at about 45° to the surface. But for thin wood, there will be a cleaner cut if the saw is more horizontal. For cutting plywood or hardboard it is better to use a backsaw in one hand while the cut is held slightly open with the other hand (Fig. 13-12).

Backsaws and panel saws have teeth designed for cutting *across* the grain, but they will also cut along the grain. For considerable hand cutting along the grain, there is a ripsaw. However, a ripsaw is unlikely to be used very often because most wood comes from the supplier already near the right size. If much conversion of larger stock is expected, it will be better to use a power saw, probably a circular table saw.

A saw relies on the sharpness and set of its teeth for accurate and easy work. The set is the way alternate teeth are bent in opposite directions so the cut, or kerf, is wider than the thickness of the metal in the blade. Without a good set, the saw would bind in a deep cut. Professional sharpening and setting is advisable. So that as much use as possible is gotten from the saw between these treatments, be careful that there are no screws or nails in the wood being cut. Store the saw where other tools cannot fall against the teeth.

Curves are sawn with a narrow-bladed saw. A power jigsaw is good for curves. But there are hand saws for sawing curves too. It is possible to get a saw handle with three or more blades. Usually, one blade is a panel saw blade, but at least one blade is for cutting curves (a compass saw or keyhole saw). These saws tend to be coarse and are suitable for roughing out larger pieces of wood. For finer curves, there is a scroll, or coping, saw which has a throwaway blade tensioned in a frame (Fig. 13-13). The blade can be turned in the frame to allow the back of the frame to give clearance to the wood in different directions. A similar and even finer saw is the fretsaw. The fretsaw usually has a deeper frame to allow cutting farther from an edge (Fig. 13-14). Coping saw blades are usually about 1/8 in. wide. But most fretsaw blades are less than 1/16 in. wide, so they are delicate and do not last long. However, for intricate cuts, they are the only tool.

A coping saw may be set with the teeth pointing away from the handle and used while the wood is upright in a vise. But it is usual to have fretsaw teeth pointing towards the handle; then the fretsaw can be used while sitting in front of a notched piece

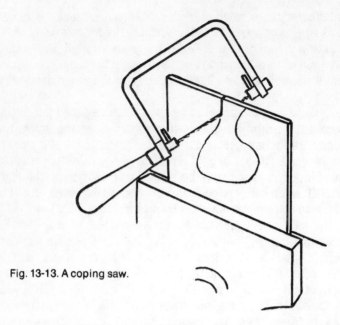

Fig. 13-13. A coping saw.

of wood that forms a cutting table (Fig. 13-14). A coping saw can be used the same way. The advantage of working like this is that the face side of the wood is upwards and the cut is easily seen because any raggedness due to sawing is on the underside. When using any saw intended for curves, it is important to keep it moving up and down, even when not going forward. Otherwise it may bind in the cut.

Besides the power jigsaw, there is also the bandsaw for cutting curves. A bandsaw consists of a continuous cutting band that runs over two or more guide wheels. In a

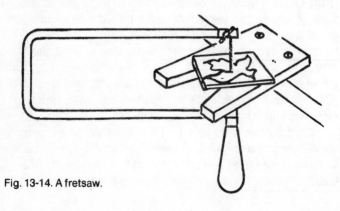

Fig. 13-14. A fretsaw.

comprehensively equipped shop, a bandsaw will often be used for work that would otherwise be done by a backsaw.

A less common power saw for curves is the saber saw (Fig. 13-15). The saber saw is a handheld saw that has a vertical reciprocating blade. The advantage of the saber saw is that the cut is downwards and the kerf is clean on the top surface so lines are easier to follow. A jigsaw also has a vertical reciprocating blade, but the cut is upwards and tends to leave a ragged edge on the face side of the wood.

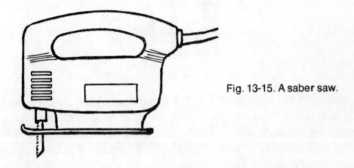

Fig. 13-15. A saber saw.

CLAMPS

In furniture repairing there is more need to press and hold things than in most other types of woodwork. Quite often regular clamps and other holding devices are inappropriate and the worker has to exercise his ingenuity with improvisations. Although standard clamps and other manufactured holding equipment are valuable, cord, rope, and wedges may be better in some circumstances.

Ordinary C-clamps (Fig. 13-16) in several sizes should be in the tool kit. Usually, two C-clamps of the same size are needed, so they should be bought in pairs. Large clamps will

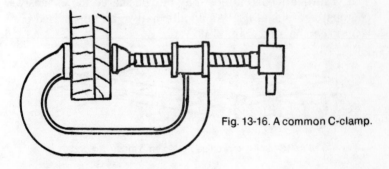

Fig. 13-16. A common C-clamp.

115

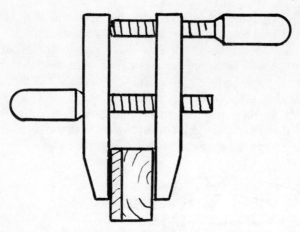

Fig. 13-17. A typical wooden clamp.

usually close sufficiently to do the same work as small clamps. If not, wood packing blocks may be used. However, very large clamps may be too clumsy for delicate work. There are various types of sliding clamps, and wooden clamps can be useful too (Fig. 13-17).

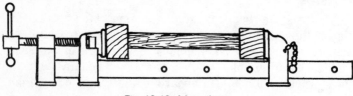

Fig. 13-18. A bar clamp.

The best tools for pulling the joints of frameworks tight are bar clamps (Fig. 13-18). They are usually used in pairs. The usual type has a sliding head which can be locked in place on a bar. However, bar clamps may be considered too expensive for just occasional use. As an alternative, an improvised bar clamp can be used (Fig. 13-19).

Fig. 13-19. An improvised bar clamp made of wood.

Fig. 13-20. Wedges driven against blocks of wood to hold glued parts in place.

A wedge can exert considerable pressure. Suppose a curved hair back has to be laminated with several thin strips of wood. Wedges driven against temporary blocks of wood can pull the parts together (Fig. 13-20). If this idea is used for normal clamping, there is a risk of movement due to the sideways hammering (Fig. 13-21). It is sometimes better to use two "folding" wedges working against each other to give a parallel pressure (Fig. 13-22).

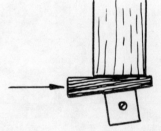

Fig. 13-21. Hammering against a wedge can knock parts out of place.

Cord or rope can be tied around parts that are to be pulled together, but usually there has to be some means of increasing pressure. One way is to drive a wedge under the rope (Fig.

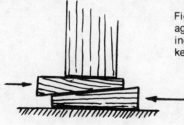

Fig. 13-22. Folding wedges work against each other, so hammering each wedge alternately can keep parts in position.

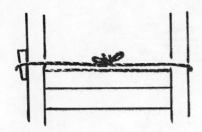

Fig. 13-23. A simple wedge and a rope can operate as a vise.

13-23). Rope under pressure may pull enough to mark wood, so pad with cloth or shaped pieces of wood.

A Spanish windlass uses cord or rope to apply pressure (Fig. 13-24). Remember that sometimes cord or rope under pressure can mark wood, so protective coverings may be in order.

A simple, little known clamping device is shown in Fig. 13-25. It's called a dog. If two boards are to be glued edge to edge, a dog is driven temporarily into each end. The dog's legs

Fig. 13-24. A Spanish windlass.

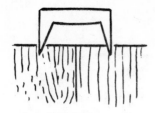

Fig. 13-25. Clamping can be done with a dog.

are edge shaped with the taper on the inside, so the act of driving presses the surfaces together.

PLANES AND CHISELS

Many joints can be made by skillful sawing, but there are many places where wood has to be shaped with a chisel. The standard chisel is called a firmer chisel (Fig. 13-26). A bevel-edged chisel (Fig. 13-27) will do all that a firmer chisel can and also get into corners. A 1/2 in. bevel-edged chisel is

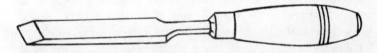

Fig. 13-26. A firmer chisel.

probably a good first choice. Other widths may follow. These chisels will stand up to hitting with a hammer or mallet, but there are longer more slender paring chisels that are not intended to be hit. They are useful for more delicate hand work. They can be used on shaped work and are good for removing surplus glue from a long dado joint.

A chisel curved in its cross section is called a gouge. If it is sharpened inside the curve, it is described as "in-cannelled" and is used for paring the inside of curves (Fig. 13-28). If sharpened outside, it is "out-cannelled" and is used for

Fig. 13-27. A bevel-edged chisel.

Fig. 13-28. The blade of an in-cannelled gouge.

hollowing (Fig. 13-29). For normal repairs there is likely to be little use for gouges. Most carving is done with gouges, but these are special types that come in a very large range of sizes and curves (Fig. 13-30). Gouges are also used for turning on a lathe. These are sharpened outside but are longer and stronger than gouges used for other woodwork.

Surfaces can be smoothed with a plane. At first it is probably sufficient to have a steel smoothing plane, such as the Stanley No. 4 or 4 1/2, which can be used on machine-planed wood (Fig. 13-31A). If larger pieces are to be planed or rough-sawn, wood has to be converted with the slightly longer jack plane (Fig. 13-31B). For very long straight pieces, there is the even longer trying plane (Fig. 13-31C). These are all similar except for the longer soles, which span unevenness in the wood to get surfaces level by taking off the high spots.

For work across the grain there are block planes that can be held in one hand (Fig. 13-31D). These have their cutting "iron" at a lower angle. Block planes are useful for final fitting of joints on hardwoods.

There are also special rabbet planes for cutting rabbets such as those in a picture frame.

A plow plane is used for making grooves. It is also possible to make grooves with adaptions of a table saw or a spindle molder, so anyone planning an extensively equipped shop will have to weigh up the relative advantages of hand tools and their equivalent power tools.

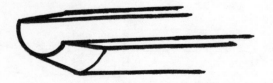

Fig. 13-29. The blade of an out-cannelled gouge.

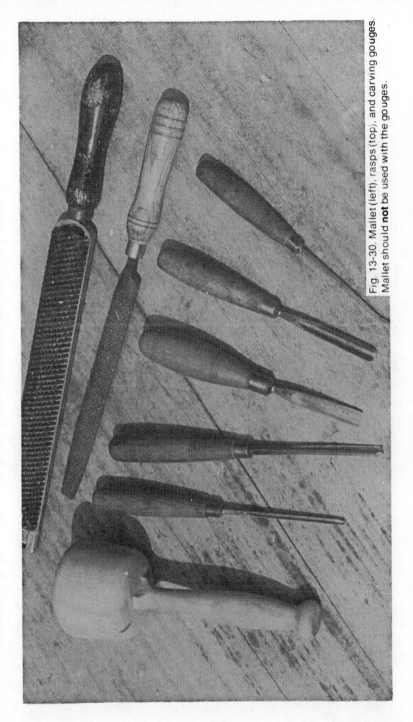

Fig. 13-30. Mallet (left), rasps (top), and carving gouges. Mallet should **not** be used with the gouges.

121

Fig. 13-31. Common woodworking planes.

An alternative to a plane or chisel is a Surform tool (Fig. 13-32). This tool has many small cutting edges in a throwaway blade, and its frame is shaped so that it can be used like a plane or file. There are flat and curved versions.

Fig. 13-32. Surform tools are used for cutting and forming a variety of materials—everything from wood to plastics. (Courtesy Stanley Tools)

Ordinary planes have a cap iron over the cutting iron (Fig. 13-33). This breaks off the shavings and prevents tearing of the surface. Some special planes have single irons. The use of the word *iron* as applied to cutting blades dates from the days when most of the blade was iron and only the cutting edge was steel. But modern blades are all steel.

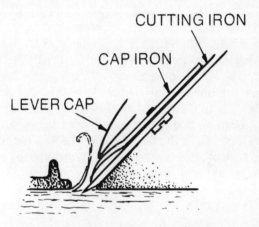

CUTTING IRON

CAP IRON

LEVER CAP

Fig. 13-33. The cutting section of a plane.

Plane irons and chisels have to be kept sharp. Excess metal can be removed by grinding, but be careful of over heating, which will take the temper out of the steel. Have a can of water alongside the grinder and dip the tool into it frequently. Modern plane irons are thin and may not need grinding, but chisels usually have one grinding bevel and another "sharpening" bevel (Fig. 13-34). A thin plane iron only has the sharpening bevel. Sharpening should be done fre-

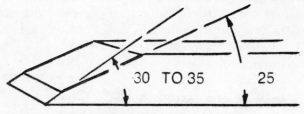

Fig. 13-34. The two bevels of a chisel.

quently to get best results, but grinding of chisels need only come when the sharpening bevel has become very long. Anyone without a grinder can have the tools ground professionally.

Sharpening is done on an oilstone. Some types have a coarse and a fine side. The coarse side removes metal quickly, but the fine side is needed to provide a good cutting edge. For sharpening, it is best to set the stone into a box or a block of wood. Use a thin oil (kerosene or sewing machine oil, not car lubricant) on the stone. Hold the tool bevel downwards with one hand controlling and the other pressing (Fig. 13-35). Slide the tool along the full length of the stone, over the whole stone surface keeping the angle the same all the time. When the edge is sharp, wipe off the oil and rub a finger gently towards the edge down the flat side. A roughness at the edge indicates a "wire edge," a tiny sliver of steel clinging to the sharp edge. The wire edge shows that the two sides have been rubbed enough to meet. Give the blade a few rubs with the flat side to the stone, then slice across a piece of scrap wood to remove the wire edge.

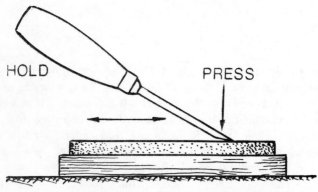

Fig. 13-35. Sharpening a chisel on an oilstone.

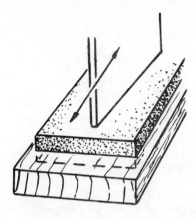

Fig. 13-36. A cabinet scraper's edge is filed flat.

With some hardwoods the grain is often difficult to work. The twisted grain that provides much of the beauty of the wood when polished is not the sort that can be planed properly in any direction. Such a surface has to be scraped. The basic cabinet scraper is a rectangular piece of steel. Its edge is filed straight, rubbed on an oilstone (Fig. 13-36), then rubbed with a piece of hard steel. There are tools for this rubbing, but a gouge or chisel will do. The effect is to turn over the edge (shown exaggerated in Fig. 13-37). The scraper is pushed over the wood at an angle which makes this edge cut (Fig. 13-38). It is usual to hold the scraper with both thumbs pushing while the fingers at each side pull the scraper to a slight curve. There are curved scrapers for shaped work.

There are tools, some made like planes, which hold a scraper blade correctly, and there are others which use special throwaway scraper blades for the same purpose. It is also possible to scrape with the edge of a piece of glass.

Fig. 13-37. A cross section of the edge of a scraper.

Fig. 13-38. The scraper must be used at an angle in order to cut.

Sanding, whether hand or power, is not a substitute for planing or scraping. Scraping is a finishing process and should not be used for shaping or levelling roughness.

DRILLS AND AWLS

In almost every repair there are holes to be made. At one time the basic drill was a carpenter's bit brace with an assortment of bits. This still has its uses, and one is worth having (Fig. 13-39). The square ends of bits give a much more positive drive than the round ends of bits used in a self-centering chuck. Bits used in a brace have more control of depth because of the slow speed, but most drilling today is done with an electric drill.

Fig. 13-39. A carpenter's bit brace.

Fig. 13-40. A drill bit.

For small holes, such as are needed for screws, the bits have the same shape as those used for metal (Fig. 13-40). But for holes bigger than about 1/4 in. diameter, it is better to use special bits. For deep holes these may look like metalworking bits, but the ends are sharpened to cut wood (Fig. 13-41) with spurs to make a clean circle. For shallower and larger holes there are spade bits (Fig. 13-42).

Fig. 13-41. The end of a woodworking bit.

For countersinking screw heads there are countersink bits to fit electric drills, but it's usually better to countersink with a countersink bit in a brace. The usual type has a "rose" end

Fig. 13-42. The cutting end of a spade bit.

127

(Fig. 13-43). A similar bit or a flat one can be used for countersinking holes in hinges and other fittings.

For extremely large holes, there are expansive bits, hole saws, and other devices.

Fig. 13-43. The rose end of a countersink bit.

If a hole must be a certain depth, some sort of stop can be used. This may be a piece of wood with a hole that stops the bit (Fig. 13-44), or you can buy clip-on depth stops that serve the same purpose.

Fig. 13-44. A piece of wood on a bit can act as a depth gauge.

Sometimes it is best to use an electric drill in a stand, particularly when dowelling or making holes that have to be perpendicular to the surface. Usually there is an adjustable stop on the pillar, which can be used to control the depth of a hole.

If a hole is to go right through, something should be done to prevent breakout at the opposite side. A second piece of wood may be held against the first, either in a vise or a clamp. If the second piece of wood has a smooth surface and is harder than the wood being drilled, the hole will go through cleanly.

An alternative method of preventing breakout involves drilling from two directions. If the drill bit has a long point, the bit can be withdrawn when the point comes through the far side. Then the hole can be finished up by drilling from the far side. This makes the cleanest hole.

The center of any drill bit does not cut. In hardwoods it is helpful to first make a small "pilot" hole, no bigger than the diameter of the base of the point. This makes drilling easier and guides the drill. A pilot hole is particularly helpful when dealing with heavy graining or knots, which might deflect the drill.

Although most drilling is done with bits, a plain awl is worth having for starting the smallest screws. A bradawl is also useful for small screws. It is an awl with the end filed to a chisel edge. The chisel edge is entered *across* the line of grain and worked to and fro as it is pushed in.

HAMMERS AND SCREWDRIVERS

The best hammer for driving nails in quality furniture is a cross peen (Fig. 13-45). The flat face does most of the hammering, but the cross peen will get into corners and may be used for small nails held between finger and thumb. A size about 12 oz. is a good general hammer, but for small nails and

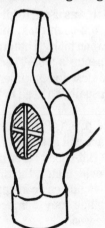

Fig. 13-45. A cross peen hammer is used on quality furniture.

tacks it may be as light as 4 oz. If nails have to be sunk below the surface, a punch is used (Fig. 13-46). Then the hole is filled with stopping.

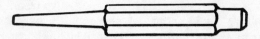

Fig. 13-46. A punch is used for countersinking nails.

A hammer should *not* be used directly on furniture wood. If it has to be hit during assembly, a piece of scrap should be used as a cushion. It is probably better to use a hammer with a softer face, even over the scrap wood. This can be a wooden mallet, or it can be a plastic-faced hammer or mallet (Fig. 13-47).

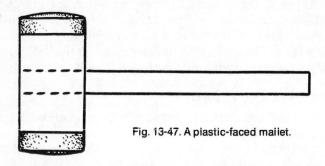

Fig. 13-47. A plastic-faced mallet.

When all chisel handles were wood, it was usual to hit them with a mallet. This is still advisable, although most modern plastic chisel handles are undamaged when hit by a hammer.

A claw hammer is more of a carpenter's tool. There are special hammers for upholstery. But almost any hammer may be used for funiture repairs. There is usually no need to buy a new one.

If a nail has to be withdrawn, use pliers. Put a piece of scrap wood under the pliers so the surface will not be marked.

The ordinary slotted screw takes a flat-ended screwdriver (Fig. 13-48). And the screwdriver should match the slot as closely as possible. Otherwise an overhanging end can damage the surrounding wood, or a narrow blade may damage the screw head or come out and damage the wood.

Fig. 13-48. An ordinary flat-ended screwdriver.

The Phillips head screw was evolved to minimize the risk of power screwdrivers jumping off the screw. But there are hand screwdrivers for these screws too (Fig. 13-49).

There are ratchet and pump-action screwdrivers that speed production when large numbers of screws have to be driven. The bits can be changed to suit different sizes of screws, but many times a variety of plain screwdrivers may be a better investment.

A long screwdriver is easier to use than a short one, but there are sometimes places where only a short screwdriver can be used, so a few short screwdrivers are needed. Sometimes a large screw needs more leverage than can be given by an ordinary screwdriver. This can be provided by a screwdriver bit in a brace. Automatic screwdrivers that fit electric drills are production tools and should be avoided for repair work.

METALWORKING TOOLS

The metalwork in most furniture repairs usually consists of cutting off nails or screws, altering fittings, and adapting stock metal items to suit the job. So metalworking is auxiliary to woodworking and comparatively few tools are needed.

Fig. 13-49. The Phillips head screw.

A full-size hacksaw frame that takes about 12 in. blades is advisable. A variety of blades should be kept to suit the cutting of brass and steel in thick and thin section. Use finer teeth for thinner metals and tubes; coarse teeth span the thickness and do not cut properly. There are small hacksaw frames that take 6 in. blades. These are useful for the light cuts often needed on fittings, where the full-size frame would be clumsy.

Files come in many shapes and cuts. An 8 in. half-round double-cut file is a good general-purpose file, but there will be uses for round and triangular files, as well as small files for getting inside keyholes and other fittings.

Some small-hole drill bits for wood can be used on metal, but the better quality high-speed steel types are advised. Cheaper drills may be good enough for wood but will not remain sharp for long on metal. Holes in metal should be started with a center-punched dent. The center punch should have a point ground at about 60°.

Nail ends and thin wire can be cut with a pair of side or end cutters, which are like sharp pincers. Some pliers also have cutting edges. Thin sheet metal may be cut with snips, which have a scissors action.

Much metalworking can only be done with the aid of a vise. Most repair metalworking can be done with a vise that clamps to the edge of a table or bench. For holding polished work, the vise jaws should be covered with pieces of aluminum or other soft sheet metal. Thin sheet metal may be bent in the vise, either by bending over with a piece of wood or hitting with a hammer. If you use a hammer, place a piece of flat stout metal against the sheet metal to cushion the blow and spread the pressure.

Although the small amount of metalworking involved in furniture repairs may be marked out with a pencil, it is more accurate to scratch lines with a scriber, a sharply pointed piece of steel. An awl can be used too.

If the furniture metalwork involves nuts and bolts, use wrenches of the proper size. Using pliers to tighten nuts will damage them and spoil appearance. It would be better to use parallel-action grips or an adjustable wrench.

Construction Methods

14

You don't have to be a skilled cabinetmaker to repair furniture, but it is helpful to understand how the piece of furniture was made so the repair can be compatible. If the work is on antique furniture, it is obvious that any new work should match the old. With more recent furniture, the repair may be by any convenient method.

There are sometimes subtle points to watch when dealing with antiques, and it may be wise to consult a dealer or other specialist before undertaking a repair to a valuable piece of furniture. A lot of care should be taken when trying to match new fixtures to the old. Old fixtures, such as hinges and catches, are most likely to have been cast brass. But many new fixtures may be made from sheet brass. Flaps of an old hinge may be solid; modern hinges are likely to be hollow sheet brass. Similarly, modern decorative handles and catches may be pressed from sheet brass instead of being cast. They may not even be brass but a metal or plastic with a brassed surface. Not many older fixtures were plated in any way, so plated handles and other parts would be inappropriate on some antique furniture.

All of this means that for antique furniture you may have to search for a specialist supplier of appropriate fixtures. The only way, in some cases, may be to get what you want from some other piece of furniture which has been abandoned or damaged. Those who do much antique restoring collect fixtures and screws and nails from old furniture. Even sound wood from furniture that is beyond repair is kept. Antique restoration is often something of a jigsaw puzzle, using material obtained from one or more cannibalized pieces of furniture to complete another.

GLUE

For many centuries the usual glue for wood was made from animal parts. This rather foul smelling mixture was made into flat slabs that looked something like dark brown resin. In the cold state it was fairly brittle. This was prepared for use by first breaking it into small pieces. The pieces were put into water and heated to form a thick solution.

This type of glue was followed by a similar glue derived from fish. This glue does not smell as unpleasant as animal glue, and some types are obtainable in the form of beads or flakes, which make preparation for use easier. Glue of this type is acceptable for antique furniture repairs. In all gluing it is advisable to remove traces of earlier adhesives, but if this cannot be done completely, fish glue should bond satisfactorily with animal glue.

Nearly all modern glues are synthetics and usually stronger than animal or fish glues. Most are also unaffected by heat once set, and any are either completely waterproof for all practical purposes or have a very high dampness resistance.

In general, a glue in one part is usually not as strong as one supplied in two parts, but many one-part glues have adequate strength for furniture in the home. The two-part glues are more water resistant, so they can be used where dampness is anticipated. An expert might see the difference between a traditional animal glue and a modern synthetic glue by examining the glue line, so modern glues should not be used in the repair of antique furniture if the final effect is to be authentic.

One-part liquid glues that are supplied in plastic containers with an applicator are convenient, but be sure they really are wood glues. If an adhesive is called an "all-purpose" glue, it is probably not of sufficient strength for furniture joints.

There are several two-part synthetic glues on the market. Usually, one part is the glue, and the other part is a setting agent, or hardener. The glue will not set until the setting agent is added. The agent is added just before using the glue, or by putting one part on each surface. The setting time depends on temperature. With some glues the hardener can be obtained in different strengths to give different setting times.

The strongest and most waterproof of the two-part glues is epoxy. Besides joining wood to wood, this is one of the few glues that can be used successfully on metals and plastics.

With all of the synthetic glues, there is no way of reversing the process once they have set. Some of them set extremely hard. The excess glue is best removed with a chisel or scraper after the glue hardens slightly. For veneers there is some advantage in using traditional glue because heat over the veneer (possibly with a domestic iron) can be used to soften the glue and allow adjustment, which would not be possible with a synthetic glue.

Traditional glues require the meeting surfaces to be tightly clamped together until the glue has set. Most synthetic glues do not require tight clamping. In fact, excessive squeezing may "starve" the joint by pushing out too much glue. Close contact is necessary until the glue has set, but use no more pressure than is needed to hold the parts together. If there is too much glue between surfaces, strength will be severely compromised. If the type of repair is such that a uniform close contact is impossible, sawdust should be mixed with the glue. This gives the glue something to bond to and avoids the crazing and weakening that would otherwise occur in the more open parts.

Wood glues are ineffective with many other materials. It may be possible to use them with leather or paper on wood, but for bonding plastic to wood there are adhesives, often called "impact adhesives," that will bond such things as laminated plastic (Formica) table tops. The name indicates that they bond on impact, so it is necessary to get the parts positioned correctly first time. It can usually be arranged by using temporary guide pieces.

SCREWS AND NAILS

Wood screws are designated by gauge number (outside diameter of the threads) and length. Although common screws are steel, it is more usual to see brass or other alloy screws in good-quality furniture. Steel screws in some woods will rust because of chemicals in the wood, even in dry conditions.

Fig. 14-1. A typical flat-head slotted screw.

There are several gauge thicknesses available for each length screw. Thin brass screws may be brittle and shear off while being driven, so do not use a screw thinner than necessary. Some common sizes are: 4 gauge by 1/2 in., 6 gauge by 3/4 in., 8 gauge by 1 in., 10 gauge by 1 1/2 in.

The most common screw in woodworking is the flat-head, slotted screw (Fig. 14-1). A Phillips screw (Fig. 14-2) is comparatively recent and would not be found in antique furniture. But otherwise the Phillips screw can be very useful. Screws can have round heads too (Fig. 14-3); the round head, of course, will be visible on the surface. Even when a fitting has countersunk screw holes, a flat-head screw may not have a satisfactory appearance, so the combined countersunk and round head may be preferred (Fig. 14-4).

Fig. 14-2. The Phillips screw head.

Fig. 14-3. A round-headed screw.

The differences between a bolt and a machine screw is in the amount of screw thread. A bolt has threads only on part of the shank (Fig. 14-5), while a screw has threads on the entire shank (Fig. 14-6). Diameters may be designated by gauge numbers, but they are more likely to be distinguished by

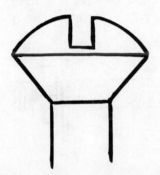

Fig. 14-4. A countersunk-round screw head.

length. As with wood screws, length is a measurement of the part of the screw that goes into the wood. Heads may be similar to those on wood screws, although larger bolts and screws may have square or hexagonal heads to take wrenches (Fig. 14-5). A carriage bolt is convenient for *moving* parts of furniture: The shank is square under the head to prevent the bolt's turning in the wood (Fig. 14-7). Although a machine screw may have a nut, it is more likely to screw into a tapped

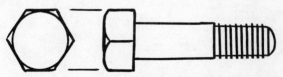

Fig. 14-5. The shank of a bolt is only partly threaded.

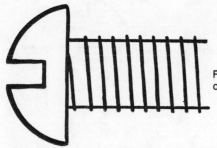

Fig. 14-6. The shank of a screw is completely threaded.

hole (Fig. 14-8). Bolts or screws used in wood may have a washer or nut under the head.

There are several forms of self-tapping sheet metal screws. They are not used much in furniture, but they will cut their own thread in sheet metal because they're made from hardened steel. Several heads and points are available. A

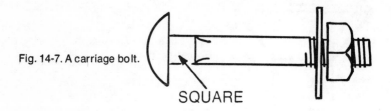

Fig. 14-7. A carriage bolt.

SQUARE

common type has a shallow head and a gimlet point (Fig. 14-9). It should not be confused with a wood screw; it would not hold very well if driven into wood.

In good-quality cabinetwork there are few nails. They are more often used in general carpentry, particularly on exterior construction. However, there are places where nails are

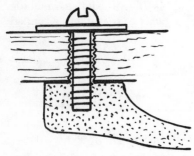

Fig. 14-8. A machine screw in a tapped hole.

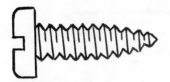

Fig. 14-9. You can buy sheet metal screws with shallow heads and gimlet points.

appropriate, as when fixing a back to a cabinet. A nail does not have the property of pulling a joint together as a screw does, and there is the risk that when a nail is driven into one place, the shock of the blow may loosen another nail or a joint elsewhere. A heavy hammer or iron block should be held against the place being hit, whenever possible, to cushion the blow.

Nails are categorized by their length. Common nails and some special nails are described in penny sizes, from 2d (1 in. long) through 10d (3 in. long) to 60d (6 in. long). It is probably wiser to specify actual length when ordering nails. Common and box nails have large flat heads (Fig. 14-10). These are carpentry and joinery nails and are probably best avoided in repairing furniture.

Fig. 14-10. Common and box nails have flat heads and shouldn't be used in repairing furniture.

Casing nails have deep tapered countersunk heads (Fig. 14-11); and finishing nails have a brad head (Fig. 14-12). Both are less conspicuous and can be punched below the surface and covered with stopping. There are several other nails with small heads intended for fiberboard and wallboard; they also have value in holding moldings and other light constructional parts during repair.

Most nails are steel, but the risk of corrosion is reduced with aluminum or brass nails. Both aluminum and brass nails should not be too thin or they will buckle as they are driven.

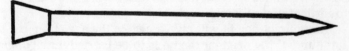

Fig. 14-11. A casing nail.

Fig. 14-12. A finishing nail.

Undersize holes may be drilled first to reduce the risk of buckling, but the hole should not go the full depth and be no bigger than necessary or the grip of the nail will be reduced. The majority of nails are smooth, but their grip can be improved if they are given grooves (ring-shanked).

Screws and nails may be given decorative heads and may be plated or given an antique or other finish to match fittings. It is also possible to get screws that can have shaped covers fitted over them after driving.

Nails in very old furniture may be the "cut" type (Fig. 14-13). They are individually stamped from sheet iron. It would be inappropriate to replace them with modern nails in a repair. Fortunately, there are specialist suppliers of cut nails.

Fig. 14-13. A cut nail.

JOINTS

There are an enormous number of joints used in furniture. They provide strength and offer side grain surfaces for glue, which does not hold very well on end grain. At one time they were all handmade. There were accepted joints for particular purposes, with little variation in good-quality cabinetwork. With the coming of machinery, variations on the traditional joints were developed, variations that took advantage of machine convenience and precision. New joints were evolved that were aimed at complete machine cutting without regard to earlier handcut joints.

Examining joints will give a clue to the age of a piece of furniture. If the original theme is to be carried through, any joints in repair work should match those used before. In old

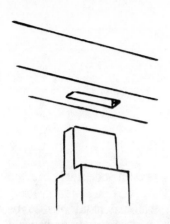

Fig. 14-14. A simple mortise and tenon joint.

furniture the most common joint is the mortise and tenon. In its simplest form, with both parts the same thickness, the tenon (the projecting part) and the mortise (the hole) are one-third the thickness of the wood (Fig. 14-14). A blind, or stub, mortise and tenon joint does not go right through (Fig. 14-15). At a corner the joint is haunched (Fig. 14-16).

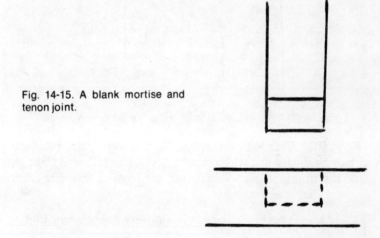

Fig. 14-15. A blank mortise and tenon joint.

It is not impossible to make mortise and tenon joints by machinery, but this is really a hand tool joint. It is less trouble, and often equally effective, to use dowels, with two or more in each joint (Fig. 14-17). There are templates and gauges for use with electric drills to insure matching parts. It would be inappropriate to use a dowelled joint when all other joints are

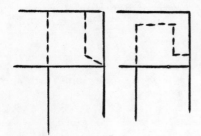

Fig. 14-16. A haunched mortise and tenon joint.

mortise and tenon, but otherwise this is an acceptable method of jointing.

For type of construction in which a shelf has to be supported by an upright, the usual joint is a dado or housing

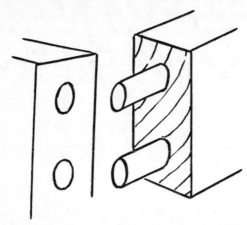

Fig. 14-17. A mortise and tenon joint can be made with dowels.

(Fig. 14-18). This joint was originally a handcut joint, but since it can be easily cut with power tools, it has followed through into the machine age. To prevent the front of the joint from

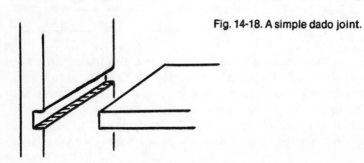

Fig. 14-18. A simple dado joint.

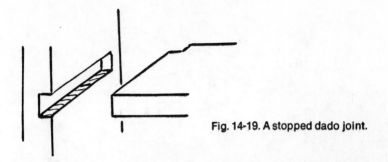

Fig. 14-19. A stopped dado joint.

showing, a stopped dado can be used (Fig. 14-19). An ordinary dado joint has adequate strength when the main load is downwards on the shelf. If there is also an end pull, the end of the shelf may be dovetailed (Fig. 14-20). Doing this on one side is usually enough, but it could be done on both sides.

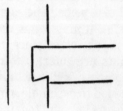

Fig. 14-20. A dado joint can be dovetailed for added strength.

If an edge is notched, it is a rabbet joint (Fig. 14-21). A dado and rabbet joint will make a corner (fig. 14-22). There can be rabbets in both pieces (Fig. 14-23), and a joint that

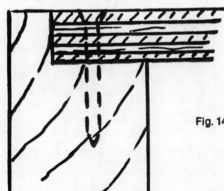

Fig. 14-21. A typical rabbet joint.

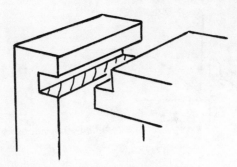

Fig. 14-22. Rabbet and dado joints can be used together to join corners.

shows the minimum of end grain is a dado, tongue, and rabbet (Fig. 14-24).

A joint in which pieces cross and one or both surfaces are flush is called a cross lap joint (Fig. 14-25). If the pieces are different thicknesses, not more than half is cut from the thinner piece. The joint may be an end lap on a corner (Fig. 14-26). It may come where the end of one piece comes partway along the other piece as a middle lap. In both these cases, lap joints are inferior to mortise and tenon joints. However, in repair work it is not always possible to get the end movement needed to assemble a mortise and tenon joint, but it is possible to get a lap joint together from the side.

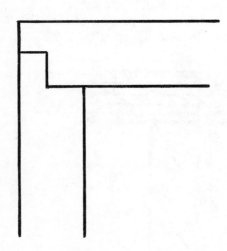

Fig. 14-23. Rabbets can be cut in both connecting pieces.

144

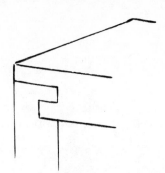

Fig. 14-24. The basic joints can be used in combination, as in this dado-tongue-rabbet joint.

The joint that is truly the cabinetmaker's is the dovetail. The basic version is the through dovetail (Fig. 14-27). The dovetails shown in the figure are separated by pins in the

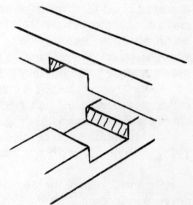

Fig. 14-25. A cross lap joint.

opposing piece. The dovetail is the wedge-shaped part; the parts to the side of it, the pins. In traditional handcut dovetails, the pins were narrower than the dovetails. Some cabinet-

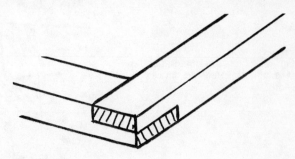

Fig. 14-26. An end lap joint.

145

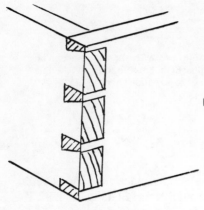

Fig. 14-27. A typical dovetail joint.

makers prided themselves on making the pins exceptionally narrow. This may have been an exhibition of their skill, but it could not have been as strong as pins of more reasonable width. However, if a repair calls for dovetails to match narrow pins in antique furniture, they will have to be attempted.

A more recent method of cutting dovetails, using a conical cutter and template in an electric drill, produces pins and dovetails of the same width (Fig. 14-28).

The dovetail joint can be combined with a dado (Fig. 14-29), or with a lap when it has to resist an end strain (Fig. 14-30).

A common use of the dovetail is the stopped, or half blind, dovetail in fixing a drawer side to the front (Fig. 14-31). There

Fig. 14-28. It is possible to cut the pins and dovetails to the same width.

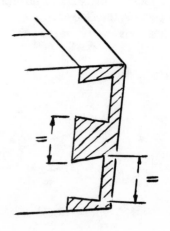

Fig. 11-29. Dovetail and dado
joints can be combined

can be considerable strain when a heavily loaded drawer is
pulled, and this dovetail has all the qualities needed.

There are occasions in repair work when only part of a
piece of wood needs replacing, possibly because it would be
difficult to remove one end without damaging the other parts,
or because only one end is damaged enough to justify
replacing. Glue would not hold if the new and old parts merely
butted together. A joint has to be devised to allow the glue to
grip side grain. One way is to half lap the parts together (Fig.
14-32). The meeting ends can be bevelled. Although bevelled
ends do not make the meeting surfaces exactly parallel with
the lines of grain, a slope of at least 1 in 7 gives a good glued
joint (Fig. 14-33).

There are a number of metal and plastic brackets and
reinforcing plates that can be used to strengthen weakened

Fig. 14-30. A lap joint can be
strengthened by combining it
with a dovetail.

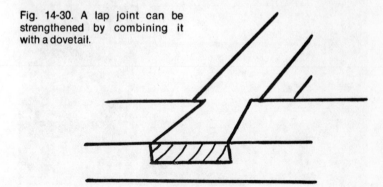

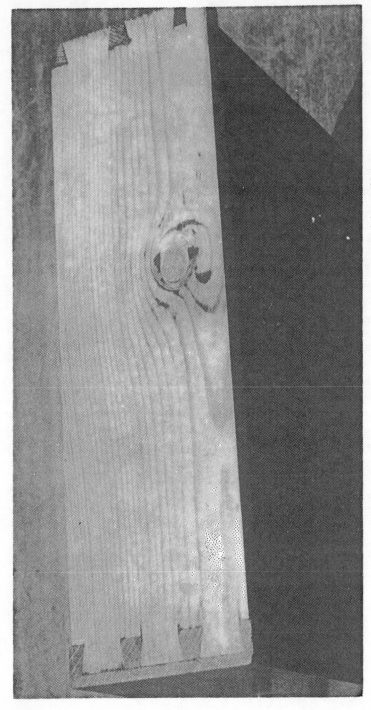

Fig. 14-31. The front side of a drawer can be secured by a stopped dovetail joint.

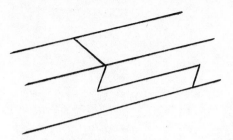

Fig. 14-32. A half lap joint.

joints, and there are ways of building by reinforcements inconspicuously so existing joints which have weakened can be held. Details of these repair joints are given in Chapter 15.

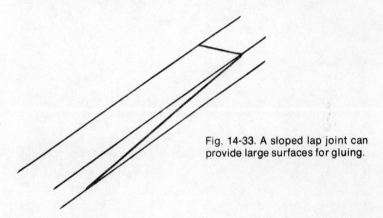

Fig. 14-33. A sloped lap joint can provide large surfaces for gluing.

Dealing With Minor Damage

15

A piece of furniture may suffer damage which affects it structurally. The finish may also be damaged, but ways of dealing with this sort of damage are covered in Section 3. Of course, structural damage may warrant the replacement of a part or the splicing on of a major new section, but there are many ways that existing weakened or broken parts can be made good. Usually this means less work than replacing parts. And in many cases, preserving the original material can be extremely important.

REGLUING

A common fault is the breaking down of a glued joint without the wood becoming fractured. There are two versions of this problem: joints that are loose but cannot be pulled apart because other parts of the structure are holding them, and those joints that can be taken apart.

The repaired joint will be stronger if most of the old glue can be removed because some glues are not compatible with others. If the old glue cannot be scraped away because of inaccessibility, the joint should be supplemented with screws, nails, or dowels.

If a joint can be separated, use a scraper or a chisel to remove chunks of glue. Then scratch the joint surfaces with an awl or a saw to break through to expose new surfaces (Fig.

15-1). Inside a mortise, or hole, use the awl to scratch through the old glue. The important thing is to tear into the surfaces so fibers untainted by the old glue are exposed without reducing the surface as a whole.

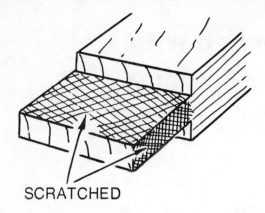

SCRATCHED

Fig. 15-1. A glue/sawdust mixture can be pressed into a joint with a knife.

If the parts of the joint have become very open due to rocking, it is inadvisable to depend solely on glue to fill the spaces. It may be possible to insert a wood shaving alongside a tenon to build up the surface (with glue all round it of course). A shaving, or even a piece of paper, could be wrapped around a loose dowel. If all else fails, mix sawdust with the glue so it becomes a putty-like paste. Use the mixture in the joint. If this is done, be careful not to starve the joint of glue in some places. It may be better to use the more fluid, ordinary glue deeper in the hole and put the sawdust/glue only where needed.

If a joint cannot be fully separated, it will almost certainly wobble enough to expose part of the inside. All surfaces that can be reached should be freed of old glue as far as possible and scratched to penetrate the fibers. Much can be done with a slim knife blade and fine awl. A razor blade will sometimes be useful. If there is an open part within a joint which cannot be reached, liquid glue may be squirted in with a syringe. The throwaway hypodermic syringes used in hospitals may be given a second life for this work.

It may also be possible to use the glue/sawdust mixture a little at a time and press it progressively into the hidden part of the joint with a knife (Fig. 15-2).

Fig. 15-2. A glue/sawdust mixture can be pressed into a joint with a knife.

Such a joint may finish with adequate strength due to the glue only, but it is unlikely that new glue will penetrate as far as could be wished, particularly if it is a joint that does not open very far. Consequently, further strengthening may be advisable. This should usually be done before the glue has hardened and before any clamps are removed. Clamps should be used with blocks to spread the pressure and reduce the risk of marking surfaces. Cloth or paper may be put between a block and a surface for further protection. Round the edges of blocks used as pads to avoid an abrupt change which could mark a finished surface (Fig. 15-3). Watch a joint as pressure is applied. See that it is going together straight. Don't squeeze excessively. Stop when the joint is obviously closed. Putting on

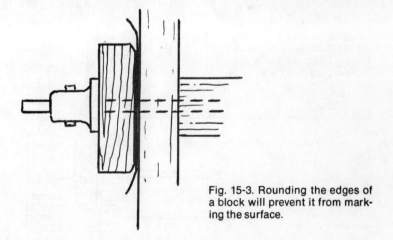

Fig. 15-3. Rounding the edges of a block will prevent it from marking the surface.

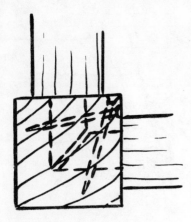

Fig. 15-4. A joint can be reinforced with nails.

more pressure after that will only distort fibers, either at the joint, or worse, on the surfaces under the pressure pads. Leave clamps in position until you are certain the glue has set.

REINFORCING JOINTS

A simple reinforcement is to use nails, preferably driven from a less obvious surface, like the inside of a table leg (Fig. 15-4). As with clamping, take the precaution of supporting the opposite surface on a padded solid support to minimize any risk of damage to the finish.

However, if there is a choice, use screws for joint reinforcement. It is more craftsmanlike. If there is a clearance hole for the neck of the screw and a hole to aid penetration through the dowel or tenon (Fig. 15-5), some expansion will

Fig. 15-5. When it comes to reinforcing joints, screws are usually more secure than nails.

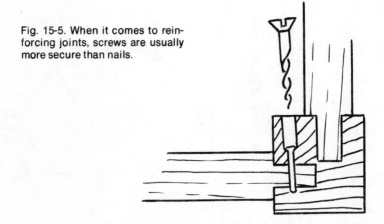

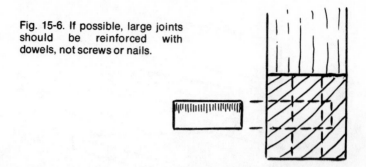

Fig. 15-6. If possible, large joints should be reinforced with dowels, not screws or nails.

take place as the screw is driven. The expansion will strengthen the joint by pushing the glued surfaces closer together. But remember that the glue still must be soft.

For larger joints, better reinforcement comes from the use of dowels instead of nails or screws. Dowels should not be so large as to weaken the inner wood by drilling away too much, but a diameter of dowel about the same as the thickness of a tenon or not more than half the thickness of the constructional dowel, would be satisfactory. Drill into the clamped joint enough to allow the dowel to go through the mating parts without breaking out the opposite side (Fig. 15-6). If it is a joint that can be taken apart, an even more secure dowel-reinforced joint can be arranged. The center for the hole in the inner part is drilled independently, slightly nearer where the parts butt together, so when the joint is assembled the holes do not quite match (Fig. 15-7). The end of the dowel is bevelled, so it will enter the offset hole as it is driven and pull the parts closer together as it forces its way through.

If tenon has broken off or is so damaged that there would be insufficient strength if it was reglued, a new tenon can be

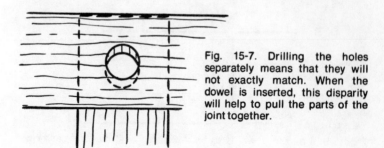

Fig. 15-7. Drilling the holes separately means that they will not exactly match. When the dowel is inserted, this disparity will help to pull the parts of the joint together.

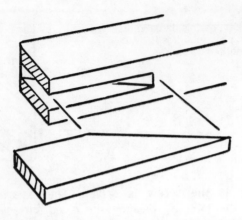

Fig. 15-8. Some reinforcements call for tenons to be scarfed into long grooves.

made by scarfing it into a long groove (Fig. 15-8). Making the groove twice as long as it is deep should give adequate gluing surface.

When dowels break off, it is usually possible to drill into the broken piece to remove it so a new dowel can be glued in. To reduce the risk of the drill straying or starting offcenter, level the broken end and mark the center with a deep dot from a center punch or awl (Fig. 15-9). If the mating hole is worn out of shape, it may be better to use a slightly larger diameter new dowel and open out the worn hole to the new size with a suitable drill. However, be careful not to weaken either of the parts by drilling away too much wood. If the larger size would shave surrounding wood dangerously thin, it may be better to keep to the same size and rely on filling spaces with glue and sawdust or shavings. If there is sufficient wood to allow dowels

Fig. 15-9. If an old dowel is to be drilled out, first mark its center with a punch.

Fig. 15-10. Before inserting a new dowel, bevel its edges and groove the side.

to penetrate further, there can be some gain in strength by drilling deeper.

A dowel entering a hole acts something like a piston in a cylinder, compressing the air inside, with the risk of bursting the hole, often pushing glue aside or into the bottom of the hole so the more important surfaces around the circumference of the dowel are left with little or no glue. When fitting a new dowel, it is helpful to bevel the ends and make a groove in the length (Fig. 15-10) with a saw or any tool that will scratch a slight hollow. This dowel will drive in without catching, and any excess glue and the compressed air will find its way out via the groove, resulting in a tight joint with a good spread of glue.

If the joint is so weakened that repairs within the structure may not be adequate, further reinforcement can be used. In most such structures the inside is not normally viewed, so strengthening can be done there. If there is room, wood blocks may be glued in or fastened with thin nails driven diagonally (Fig. 15-11). If there has been any surface treatment, scrape this away and roughen the exposed wood before gluing. Even if there has not been any surface treatment, it may be advisable to give the surfaces a light scraping to remove dirt and present a new surface to the joint. It may be possible to

Fig. 15-11. A corner of a structure can sometimes be reinforced with a block.

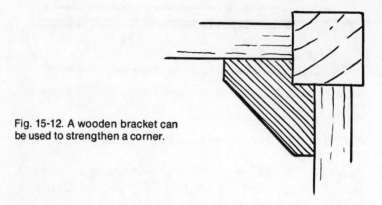

Fig. 15-12. A wooden bracket can be used to strengthen a corner.

merely rub the blocks in the glue and leave them without clamping, if the design is such that there is no way of using clamps.

In a corner where two rails join a leg, it may be better to make a wooden bracket fitted around the parts (Fig. 15-12). This could be fixed with glue, but the end grain, due to the diagonal cut, may not give the best gripping surface for glue. The joint can be strengthened and pulled tight by screws driven at an angle (Fig. 15-13). If the bracket is cut with slightly too wide an angle, its points will meet the rails first; further tightening closes the entire joint.

Similar wood blocks can be used in other joints. A table top can have blocks or a continuous strip fastened to the supporting rail (Fig. 15-14). There are plastic and metal strips intended for use in angles of ready-to-assemble furniture or

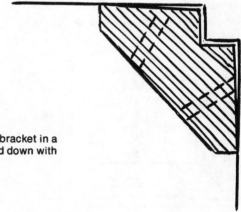

Fig. 15-13. A wooden bracket in a corner can be fastened down with screws.

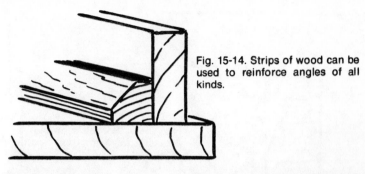

Fig. 15-14. Strips of wood can be used to reinforce angles of all kinds.

adjustable shelves. Some are blocks to be screwed in both directions, like the wood blocks, or they may be in two parts with a machine screw to pull them together (Fig. 15-15). The two-part type is useful in a repair where one structure tends to pull away from another because of warping, twisting, or other cause.

Another way of dealing with a loose top on surrounding rails is to use pocket screwing. A hole is drilled diagonally from inside, and a notch is cut out to let the screw head pull in (Fig. 15-16). For the greatest strength, the point of the screw needs to go as far as possible into the top, so care is needed to drill adequately without actually breaking through the top.

Metal repair plates can be bought in flat, straight, and angle patterns of various sizes. In furniture where they can be hidden, they can provide rigidity in a repair, often greater than is possible by any wood reinforcing. An angle plate can be fastened into the underside of a weak miter joint or behind the corner of a picture or mirror frame (Fig. 15-17).

Fig. 15-15. Parts can be pulled together with blocks and screws.

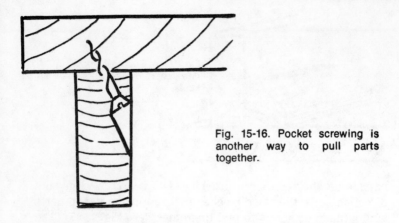

Fig. 15-16. Pocket screwing is another way to pull parts together.

A straight repair plate can be used where two adjoining parts have to be held together. The angle type of bracket can be used inside corners, as in an old chest where the sides no longer hold together. There is not much that can be done to make a bracket draw a joint tight, as can be done with diagonal screwing through a wood block, but there are a couple of tricks that may help. If an angled bracket is sprung so it is slightly less than right angle, it will have a slight tightening effect as it is screwed down. It is also helpful to drill for screws towards the corner (Fig. 15-18). As the screw head pulls down into the countersink of the bracket it will pull the corner tighter.

Another device with some repair applications is the corrugated fastener. The corrugations are at a slight angle on each side of the center, so as it is driven, a joint across its center is pulled closer. The device may be considered crude

Fig. 15-17. Miter joints can be secured with angle plates.

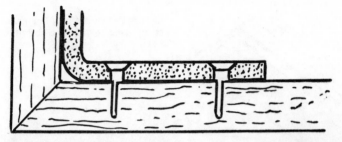

Fig. 15-18. Angle plates should be fastened down with screws near the corner.

and mostly only suitable for rough carpentry, but in a place like the underside of a plinth, this is a good reinforcement (Fig. 15-19). Another method for corner joining is to cut the head off a nail and file a second point, then bend the ends and drive them in hard enough to bury the whole nail flush with the surface (Fig. 15-20).

REESTABLISHING SCREWS

Sometimes screws no longer hold in the wood. This may happen at the hinges of a heavy door or at some much used fitting. The simple answer is a larger screw, but this may not be practicable, particularly when the hole in a metal fitting is involved. There may be no room for a larger screw head, particularly in a hinge, and the result might look clumsy on

Fig. 15-19. Corrugated fasteners can be used to pull a miter joint together.

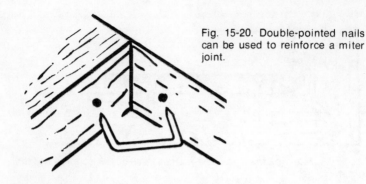

Fig. 15-20. Double-pointed nails can be used to reinforce a miter joint.

some fittings. A longer screw of the same diameter may gain extra hold at the point, but point hold may last for only a short time.

Most stoppings and wood plastics do not have much strength, so it would not be satisfactory to plug a hole with them and drive the screw again. It may be possible to push a sliver of wood into the hole and drive the screw again, but this tends to push the screw out of line. Most glues crystalize and break away after setting around a screw, so they would not provide strength. The only adhesive that would secure a slackened screw would be epoxy glue. This will bond to both the metal and the wood. It will adhere so strongly that it may be impossible to withdraw the screw later.

An alternative, particularly where large screws are involved, is to drill out the hole and insert a plug. The plug can

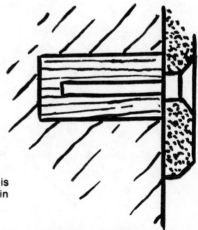

Fig. 15-21. Sometimes a plug is the best way to hold a screw in place.

be a piece of dowel rod (Fig. 15-21). Take it slightly deeper than the screw is to penetrate, glue it in place, and drill again as if starting a new screw. Make a clearance hole for the screw neck, and an undersize hole for the threaded part.

Instead of a piece of dowel rod, one of the plugs intended for fixing to masonry can be used, either a fibrous or a plastic type. Plastic plugs are especially useful in particle board (Fig. 15-22).

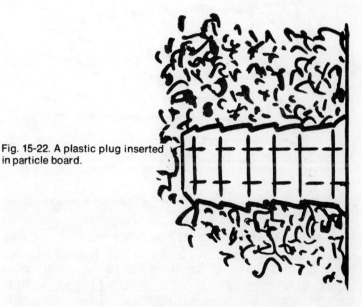

Fig. 15-22. A plastic plug inserted in particle board.

Screws do not hold well in end grain. Even if a repair is made by plugging the hole, there may be a risk of the joint coming away. Another way of using a dowel to reinforce a screw driven with the grain is to arrange it across the wood at a position where the screw can go into it (Fig. 15-23). The dowel need not go right through. The hole may be drilled from a hidden surface without breaking through any exposed surface. Position the dowel so the screw can have as many threads as possible in the cross grain of the dowel.

ADDING NEW WOOD

When new wood must be added to furniture in order to make repairs, one of the first considerations is matching the grain. Ideally, the repair will be made with wood of the same

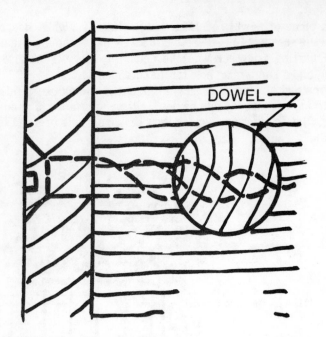

Fig. 15-23. A screw inserted in a dowel will hold better than a screw forced into regular wood.

kind. Although a careful craftsman might make the new part exactly to size and achieve a perfect match, it would be much easier for him (and certainly for a less confident worker) to join on an oversize piece of wood and bring the new wood to size after it has become an extension of the old part. Even with

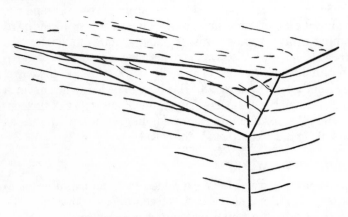

Fig. 15-24. A damaged corner cut away.

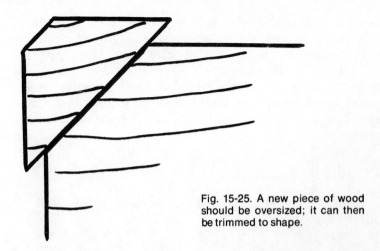

Fig. 15-25. A new piece of wood should be oversized; it can then be trimmed to shape.

the greatest care, it is possible to find a slight error of alignment or of matching shape after joining on, so leaving a little surplus wood permits adjustment.

An example is a fractured edge. Say the damage is cut away at an angle, both in the length and across the edge (Fig. 15-24). A new piece can be cut approximately to shape and glued on (Fig. 15-25), then the surplus wood can be planed off. This is a simple example, but this same technique can be used with a part that has to be worked to a curve or carved after fixing. Match the grain, leave enough spare wood to work on, then treat the part as a whole when the glue has set. In this way the new work will blend into the old.

If it is necessary to join on a complete new piece, there can be a lapped joint or a splice. The new part can usually be identical to the old, but if the old part is curved, the new piece should have extra wood for working into shape (Fig. 15-26).

If the edge of a long piece (like a square table leg) has to be cut away for repairs, the ends of the replacement part should be cut at angles (Fig. 15-27). This cut makes for a much

Fig. 15-26. New wood added to a curved piece can be cut down to shape.

better fit. If the cuts are made carefully, a very inconspicuous joint can be formed. The action of clamping the open end will force the other end tightly into the acute angle. If the repair is easily gotten at after gluing, it is helpful to leave considerable excess wood to be cleaned off later. This means that tool marks can be cut away during finishing to size. In a less accessible place, it may be better to cut the repair piece close to size.

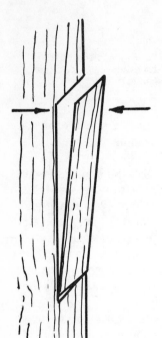

Fig. 15-27. A replacement piece for an edge should be cut at an angle.

Sometimes new wood must be inset into a damaged surface. First look at the piece from several angles before cutting out. A simple rectangle puts two cuts *across* the grain. Even with careful fitting, these cuts are likely to remain apparent (Fig. 15-28). An ellipse with its long axis in the direction of the grain will be less obvious (Fig. 15-29). But having a curve brings problems in cutting and fitting. Another alternative is to use a long diamond shape (Fig. 15-30). This shape avoids cuts directly across the grain so it is easier to disguise.

If the damage is within reasonable distance from an end, it may be better to make the replacement part continue out to

Fig. 15-28. Inlaid wood is sometimes quite conspicuous.

the end. This procedure will reduce the number of cuts not directly along the grain (Fig. 15-31). A further step, if the surface is not too big, is to extend the replacement part out to both ends. Then the only joints will be *with* the grain and might pass as normal joints between boards making up the top.

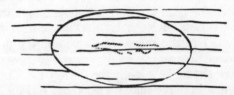

Fig. 15-29. An ellipse-shaped piece usually makes a less conspicuous inlay.

For a surface repair there is no need to cut more deeply than necessary to remove the damage. The wood may be chopped out or removed with a router. A power router insures an even depth cleanly cut, but the unevenness from cutting out with a chisel will not matter. No matter how deep the damage is, it is advisable with most woods to go at least 1/4 in. deep. A thin replacement piece may warp eventually. Trim the edges of the routed area vertically, but make the repair piece with slightly bevelled edges (Fig. 15-32).

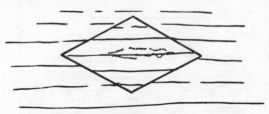

Fig. 15-30. A long diamond-shaped inlay.

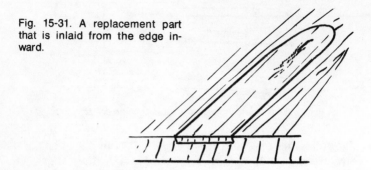

Fig. 15-31. A replacement part that is inlaid from the edge inward.

It is best to proceed slowly. Cut the recess approximately to shape and make the replacement patch slightly larger than the first recess cuts. Trim the patch to its final shape and use it with the underside downwards as a template to mark the final shape of the recess, preferably marking with a sharp thin-bladed knife. Trim the recess to shape and try the patch in place, but do not press it in.

The patch should be slightly too thick. Glue it in place and press it down with paper under a wood block (Fig. 15-33). Use clamps if possible. Failing that, hand pressure may get the patch in, then weights can be left on top until the glue has set. Finally, plane and sand the patch level.

Before the days of plywood, blockboard, and particle board, the only way to make a broad panel like a table top was to joint boards edge to edge (Fig. 15-34). Such a builtup panel can easily warp, shrink, expand, or otherwise distort. But much old furniture was built with builtup panels. It is not sufficient to repair such panels by fixing stout battens

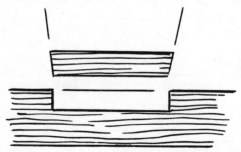

Fig. 15-32. A repair inlay should have beveled edges.

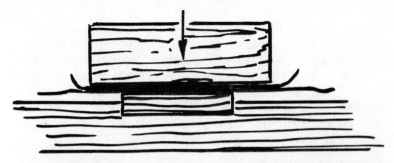

Fig. 15-33. Press the inlay down with a wooden block. Use paper between the block and the inlay.

underneath because the wood needs to expand and contract. Even with properly seasoned wood, a table top 2 ft wide may

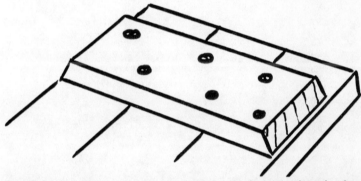

Fig. 15-34. At one time, all large panels were made by joining boards edge to edge.

expand and shrink as much as 1/4 in. in the width because of changes in temperature and humidity.

Of course, if the piece of furniture is not an antique, or there is no reason for keeping the old top, it may be better to

Fig. 15-35. Screw slots allow for movement.

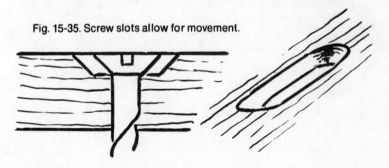

replace it with a new top made from manufactured board. If the old top is to be retained, any battens put across it should be screwed on, without glue, and each screw should have a slot (except perhaps the center one). A round hole for the center screw keeps the batten central, but the slots will allow some movement (Fig. 15-35). How much movement to expect depends on many factors, but allowing too much is better than not enough, so 1/2 in. slots are reasonable.

Veneering  16

The process of veneering consists of laying down and gluing together sheets of thin wood upon a solid base. The art goes back at least as far as the days of the Roman Empire, and there is evidence of a form of veneering in ancient Egypt. There are several reasons for veneering. A rather plain base wood may be covered by a decorative veneer. Expensive solid wood may be avoided by using a cheap base wood veneered with a layer of the expensive wood to achieve a similar appearance to the solid wood. Some woods, particularly those with attractive grains, may not be suitable for use in solid form, or they may not be obtainable in pieces large enough for furniture.

Early veneers were cut by hand sawing. This means they were comparatively thick by modern standards. Old furniture may be found with these thick veneers, and it is unlikely that new veneer of comparable thickness will be available. For patching, it may be possible to build up the thickness with several layers of modern veneer. Sometimes, working on antique furniture means cutting your own veneers, but fortunately with a power saw instead of by hand.

Modern veneers may be cut by saw or knife, depending on the wood and its grain or the effect desired. Most modern veneers are cut from logs by a stationary knife. The log rotates as the knife slices off a thin layer of wood. Of course, plywood is made up of veneers laid across each other, but these ply veneers are usually thicker than those intended to be laid on a solid backing.

Allied with wood veneers are the plastic laminates used to provide tough working surfaces that are immune to many of the liquids that attack wood and mark many of the finishes applied to wood. Some of these plastic laminates may be given a wood grain appearance. Some even have genuine wood veneer embedded in clear plastic. However, there is no attempt to make the plastic deceive anyone into thinking it is genuine wood, although some of the plastic laminates have an appearance remarkably close to the genuine article. Such plastic laminates are comparatively recent and have many uses on modern furniture. But they should not be used on old furniture if the piece is to retain its authenticity. If this is unimportant, plastic laminate (such as Formica) can be used to give a new life and appearance to something like a battered table top that is beyond refurbishing in any other way.

There are plastic veneers available. These are not really veneers in the cabinetmaking sense, but are more like paper and may have uses in covering plain furniture to give a decorative effect. These materials may be supplied as unbacked sheets to be stuck down with the adhesive. Another version has the veneer on a paper backing which has to be soaked or peeled off. These paperlike materials may be wrapped over edges and trimmed with a razor blade or sharp knife after fixing. Some of these materials have grain effects, which simulate the appearance of real wood. However, too much should not be expected of these thin pieces of plastic, but they do have a reasonable life span as temporary covering for utility furniture. Light-patterned plastic veneer, or even wall paper, can be used to brighten the inside of a drawer. This is particularly suitable where age has given the wood an unattractive appearance.

A further variation on this is genuine veneer in strip form with paper backing. The strips are designed to cover edges. They can be bought to match the veneers used on manufactured boards, or they may be supplied with veneered boards which have bare edges. The veneer strips may be applied by hand pressure after the backing has been stripped.

If veneer is used on a base wood, consideration should be given to stresses. If the base wood is fairly substantial and firmly fixed, there should be no problem. But if the base wood is light, there is a risk of distortion if veneer is applied to one side only. The distortion happens over a period of maybe a year; the veneered surface may pull hollow. This can be counteracted by veneering *both* sides. If the second side is unimportant, the veneer used there can be a cheap plain one.

MATERIALS

Veneers are available in panels and natural pieces. It is unlikely that a large piece will be needed in a repair, but it should be remembered that a sawn veneer cannot be any wider than the tree trunk from which it was cut, so widths may have to be made up by joining edges. Knife-cut veneers produced on a rotary machine can be almost any width. At one time, knife-cut veneers were supplied in several thicknesses. But stock veneers in the quality decorative woods are nearly all in standard thicknesses. Most veneers produced in America are 1/28 in. thick. This is slightly under 1 mm. English veneers (some of which are imported) may be 1/40 in. thick.

A lot of very old furniture has inlaid bands or borders made up of pieces of veneer arranged in patterns. These veneers range from 1/8 to 1 in. thickness. These were laid in or around veneered panels or sometimes inset into solid wood. Although it would be possible to make up a section of banding in a repair, it would be very tedious and it might be difficult to get a sufficient variety of veneers to match the existing work. Fortunately, these bands can still be bought ready made, and it is likely that one of the stock patterns will match the old work, as the designs continue traditional patterns.

In some of these borders there are other materials besides wood. Celluloid was used, being one of the earliest uses of synthetic plastics in furniture. Brass was also included, and imitation tortoiseshell was used to glisten. Musical instruments often had these special bands.

TOOLS

Most minor repairs to veneer can be done without special tools. If the tools and techniques for fixing larger pieces of veneer are understood, more ambitious repairs or complete replacements are possible.

Veneers are quite fragile and are susceptible to splitting and breaking, so they should be handled carefully and preferably kept between boards to protect them and reduce warping and twisting. which can be very marked in some woods.

Cutting may be done on a piece of stout plywood or a piece of hardboard over a solid support. Most cutting can be done with a sharp thin-bladed knife, used against a straight edge or template. Cut so that any tendency for the knife to catch in the grain will be towards the waste part (Fig. 16-1), if the cut is not directly across or along the grain. If there is a risk of breaking out at the end of a cut toward an edge, cut both ways, from the ends towards the center.

Fig. 16-1. Lay the straightedge along the cutting line. Shield the pattern side with the straightedge so that a mistake will damage only the waste wood side.

All ordinary saws are too coarse for cutting veneers, but there are saws with very fine teeth that can be used along a straight edge or around a template. The handle is offset to allow for this (Fig. 16-2). A knife, by the nature of its action, leaves a slight bevel on an edge, but a saw can produce a vertical cut. So if no finishing work is to be done on an edge, a saw should produce a closer joint than a knife. However, edges often have to be trimmed for a final fit, and this may be done with a chisel or finely set small block plane. These tools can correct the bevel from a knife.

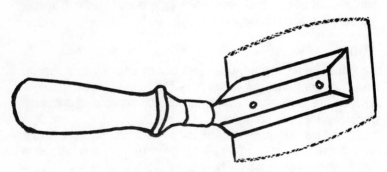

Fig. 16-2. A saw for cutting veneers.

There are several special tools for trimming edges after veneer has been laid. One has a knife in a handle like a plane. Another is like a chisel with a hollow end. For normal repair work, a chisel, knife, or plane will do all the trimming needed. The special tools should be purchased only if a large amount of veneering is to be done.

Laying a veneer usually means roughing up the base surface so the glue can get a better grip. This can be done by pulling saw teeth sideways.

Veneers are laid on glue and have to be pressed down and maintained in contact until the glue has set. Most of the glues already described can be used, but there are advantages to using a water-soluble heat-sensitive glue, particularly when repairing old veneering fixed originally with animal or fish glue. If this sort of glue cannot be obtained, one of the white glues in squeeze bottles should be satisfactory. There is some advantage in using a quick-setting glue: the veneer becomes secure in a short time and pressure need only be brief. Another problem may be staining. Veneers are so thin that glue may soak right through. This may not spoil adhesion, but there may be a stain showing on the surface after the glue has dried. This usually cannot be sanded out because the wood is permeated. The only treatment may be bleaching. It is better to use a glue known not to penetrate. Constantine of New York and other veneer specialist supplies offer specially formulated veneer glue.

Veneers can be pressed down with a roller, which may be a handled type (Fig. 16-3) or even a discard domestic pastry roller. But pressure can also be applied with a veneer hammer. This is not a percussion tool, as the name suggests, but more of a squeegee (Fig. 16-4). This tool is used with both hands or with one hand over the hammer's head. It is drawn with plenty of pressure in a zig-zag manner across the veneer

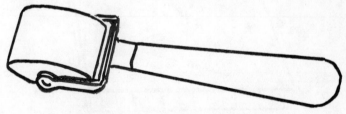

Fig. 16-3. A roller for pressing down veneers.

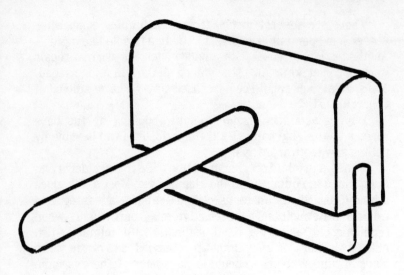

Fig. 16-4. A veneer hammer.

(Fig. 16-4). The object is to bring the veneer and the base surface into the closest contact and to work any surplus glue or air bubbles to the edges. For small repairs, a hammer with a cross peen can be drawn across the newly glued part in the same way.

Fig. 16-5. The veneer hammer should be used in a zigzag motion.

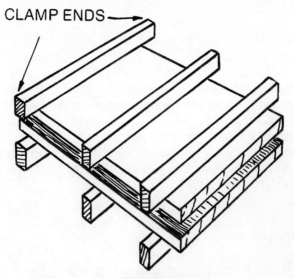

Fig. 16-6. A simple caul.

If a quick-setting glue is used, prolonged pressure is unnecessary, but in traditional gluing of veneers, large areas were clamped in a caul. The caul was merely an arrangement of boards (blockboard today) with strips across the clamps at the ends (Fig. 16-6). The cross strips were curved along the bottom so pressure could be maintained at the center and along the full width (Fig. 16-7). The caul is still a good tool to use today.

REPAIRS

A common fault in old veneer is a blister. The glue underneath has ceased to hold and a bubblelike projection has appeared. This may have been caused by moisture soaking

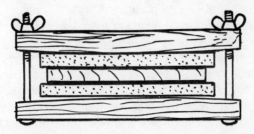

Fig. 16-7. The bottom edges of a caul's cross strips are curved so pressure can be maintained uniformly.

through or by excessive heat. Blisters can be detected early by tapping over the surface with the knuckle. A different note will indicate failure of the glue.

Use a razor blade or very fine knife to cut in the direction of the grain along what is judged to be the center of the blister. Do not go any further than necessary. Use the point of a knife to insert glue into the bubble (Fig. 16-8). Do this to both sides, but be careful not to break or slit the fibers of the veneer. If it is a large blister it may be possible to get more glue in with the fingers. By surface pressure and stroking, try to spread the glue to the furthermost parts.

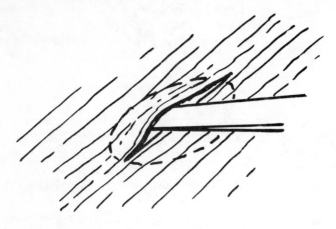

Fig. 16-8. Once a wood blister is slit, a knife can be used to insert glue.

Press down, moderately at first, working from the edges of the blister to the cut. Any surplus glue which comes out should be wiped with a damp cloth. Use a roller, veneer hammer, or a cross peen hammer to finally press down. If it is necessary to apply more prolonged pressure, put paper over the blister and a block of wood over that. Use a clamp if possible or put weights on the block.

If a small area has been damaged, it is sometimes possible to disguise it with some sort of stopping, as described in Section 3, but except for the most minor damage it is better to cut it away and insert a new piece. It is usually possible to cut through the veneer and pry it away. To avoid marking the surrounding undamaged veneer, it is advisable to work in two stages. With a pencil, outline the area to be replaced and cut *inside* the outline to get the waste out from that area (Fig. 16-9). Then trim to the limits of the outline. Try to scrape old glue away down to the wood, without going too deeply.

Fig. 16-9. Cutting inside the outlined damaged area.

Repairing damaged veneers near an edge is usually pretty simple. Cut out a long V enclosing the damage and make a patch to go in. Let the piece stick out a bit along the edge and trim it after the glue has set (Fig. 16-10).

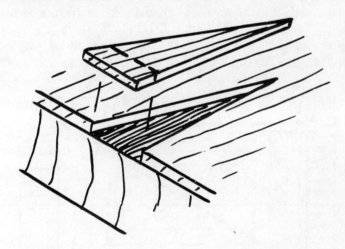

Fig. 16-10. Repairing veneer damage near an edge.

Any sort of cut will show when the repair has been finished. Usually the main problem is making the patch fit the opening. A bad fit is more obvious with irregular cuts; straight cuts usually create better fits. However, irregular cuts can be made with better precision with special punches. Each punch has a cutting end which works like a leather punch, but the cutting end has an irregular shape (Fig. 16-11). The punch cuts around the defect. Then it is used on the new veneer to cut a perfectly matching patch that should glue in to be practically unnoticeable.

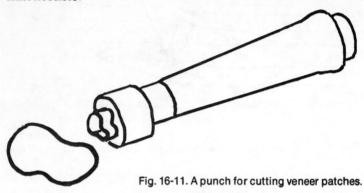

Fig. 16-11. A punch for cutting veneer patches.

A lot of veneering looks like solid wood, with a very normal looking grain. But veneers also lend themselves to patterns. Four panels may be arranged around a center, with a border of veneer cut across the grain (Fig. 16-12). There are many elaborations on this and other builtup patterns of varying complexity. The making of pictures in marquetry is an example. But without going that far, some cabinetmakers use

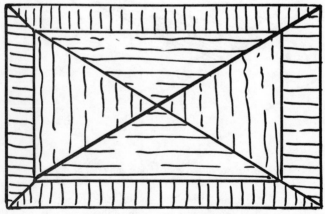

Fig. 16-12. Veneers can be laid in patterns.

veneers in different woods and shapes to make patterns. A chess board is an example.

When a repair involves the replacement of parts of several adjoining veneers in one of these patterned panels, it is usually best to prefabricate the builtup patch and fit it in as a unit. If two pieces of veneer have to be cut to match each other, it is usually possible to cut both at once. Allow a little surplus at the meeting edges. Let these overlap and slice or saw through both (Fig. 16-13). For accuracy and security against movement, the two pieces can be clamped down before cutting.

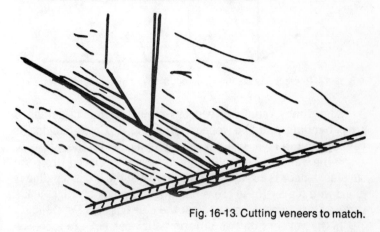

Fig. 16-13. Cutting veneers to match.

If a patch made of more than one piece is builtup, masking tape or a special veneer tape can be used on the surface over the joint to hold it until glued and set. It is a good idea to do this over all new joints. These tapes should peel without leaving marks, but if not, sand the tape away. But remember the extreme thinness of the veneers and sand cautiously, or you may find you have to repair your repair!

It is sometimes difficult to keep veneer in position during repairs. There are veneer pins, which are extremely thin nails, that can be driven just far enough to hold the veneer until the glue has set. Ordinary domestic dressmaking pins are just as good. When a pin is driven, it pushes fibers aside. It does not remove any wood. Consequently, it is possible to make a pin hole close again by swelling the fibers with water. Do not soak the whole thing, particularly if a water-soluble glue has been used, but put just a spot of water over each hole and leave it for a few minutes.

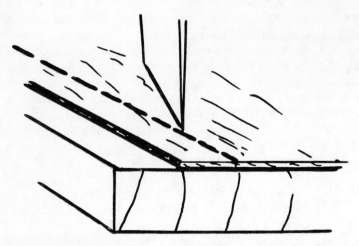

Fig. 16-14. Replace the adjoining veneer first; cut off any surplus veneer.

Sometimes repairing veneers means replacing damaged cross-banding and the veneer adjoining it. Cross-banding is veneer that has a grain running opposite to the grain of adjoining veneer. The adjoining veneer is replaced first; the surplus veneer is cut off (Fig. 16-14). Then the cross-banding is glued into place. If the cross-banding lies along an edge, leave some excess to be cut away after the glue has set (Fig. 16-15).

If the veneers on two different surfaces have to meet, be careful not to undercut when trimming the first veneer. See that it is level with the other surface and does not fall away (Fig. 16-16). Then glue on the other veneer. Leave some surplus and trim that carefully (Fig. 16-17). Finally, very lightly bevel the edge or slightly round it with just one stroke

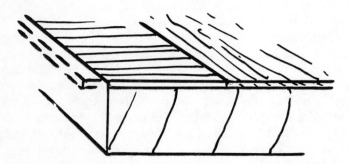

Fig. 16-15. Cross-banding laid along an edge should be oversized; surplus can be cut off.

Fig. 16-16. Veneers laid on two different surfaces, say around a corner, have to be carefully matched. The first veneer laid should be flush with the second surface.

with abrasive paper. There is very little veneer overlapping on the angle, but if it is left sharp, it may catch and break away.

If veneer has to follow a curve, it may be possible to spring it into shape. But even then it may crack if it has the grain crosswise. Breaking is less likely if the veneer is first dampened. Allow the moisture to penetrate for about 10 minutes before bending the veneer. It may be bent and left curved until dry, then glued in place. Alternatively, apply glue and bend the dampened (not wet) veneer in place. Use an iron on it to dry out the moisture.

LAMINATED PLASTIC

Formica and other laminated plastics have much in common with veneer. But laminated plastics are much more durable. There is little risk of damage after Formica has been glued down, and the surface usually lasts a long time.

There are tools which cut the material to shape. But it can be sawn and filed or even planed—although the plane will need frequent sharpening.

Fig. 16-17. Let the second veneer cover the edge of the first.

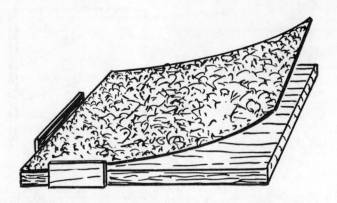

Fig. 16-18. Use blocks as guides for laying laminated plastic.

Although there are adhesives that allow movement after the plastic contacts the wood surface, the usual contact adhesive requires correct location the *first time*. It is also important to exclude air *as* the material is laid; working out bubbles of air *after* laying is difficult or impossible. This means that it is necessary to provide guides to position and lower the material into place.

In the usual table top, with the laminated plastic going to the edge, there should be temporary blocks projecting above the surface as guides (Fig. 16-18). Then the plastic can be pressed against them and lowered in a curved sweep with one hand while the other strokes the surface down, thus avoiding pockets of air.

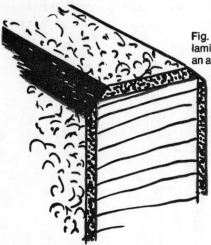

Fig. 16-19. Bevelling the edges of laminated plastic usually leaves an attractive black surface.

Patching laminated plastic is possible, but since there is no way of softening the impact adhesive, any part cut away may also pull out wood fibers or leave uneven patches of glue. This means that before putting in a patch, the wood surface will have to be levelled so the new piece will become flush with the old surface.

An alternative is to put a new piece of the same material over the old. The same adhesive will work, but the old surface should be thoroughly sanded so it will take the adhesive.

Putting laminated plastic around edges is very much like veneer edging. However, with the plastic, the bevel has to be more pronounced: laminated plastic is thicker than most veneers. Usually such bevelling leaves a black line between the two decorative surfaces, but this can be quite attractive (Fig. 16-19).

Wood Defects  17

Wood is a natural product and is subject to defects. Manmade products may be produced with a uniformity of appearance and with durability. However, there is something lacking in these synthetic materials. In general, they do not have the beauty and mystique that wood has. So if one loves wood, he must be willing to deal with its defects.

ROT

Attacks by fungi cause decay and rot. The effect cannot be reversed and there is no cure. Fungi are parasitic growths; some of them live on the organic matter in wood. Fungus seeds, or spores, float about in the air and may settle on wood at any time, but moist conditions are needed for them to attack the wood. If the moisture content of the wood is less than 20%, there should be no attack. Fairly temperate conditions favor attack. It is unlikely below freezing or in very hot conditions.

Fortunately, most furniture kept in normal room conditions will have less than 20% moisture content, but sometimes conditions are set up that invite attack. A liquid spilt on the top of a cabinet may leak to the inside, where lack of ventilation causes the moist conditions that enable fungus to become established. Nondurable woods (many of the softwoods and some of the hardwoods) are most likely to be attacked. A piece of wood which has both sapwood and heartwood in it may be attacked only in the vulnerable sapwood.

If a spore settles on receptive wood, it sends out roots, or hypae, which spread through the natural cavities in the wood (Fig. 17-1). These roots take away cellulose from the wood, and this causes a complete breakdown of the character of the wood. As the fungus feeds on the wood, it produces more spores, which are spread elsewhere in the same wood or may be carried by air, hands, or tools to other wood.

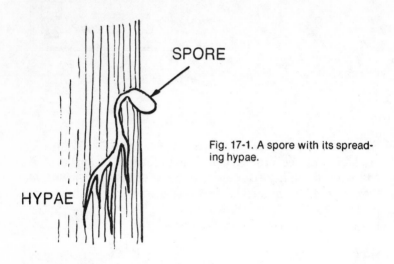

Fig. 17-1. A spore with its spreading hypae.

Rot and decay may be divided broadly into dry and wet rot. The differences are not important to a furniture repairer. They both need drastic treatment. Dry rot is not aptly named because it can only occur in the presence of moisture and air. It flourishes in stagnant air. The wood changes color. Almost any color is possible, but the general effect is usually lighter in color than the overall tint of the particular wood. The wood will soften and lose weight. There is a musty smell. In an extreme case the wood will disintegrate to a powder. If it has not gone as far, tapping the wood will produce much deader sound at the rotted part than on the sound wood. The fungus looks like a soft white spongy cushion.

The only treatment is removal of the rotted wood, which should be burned to destroy spores that can escape to attack other wood. Unfortunately, wood adjoining the infected area can carry live spores and hypae, so some good wood will have to be cut away too. The recommended cutting area is illustrated in Fig. 17-2. In some furniture of modest size these distances are enough to enclose the entire woodwork and make the destruction of the whole piece advisable. Allowing active spores to remain in wood which is still receptive can only mean a spread of rot, with a risk to other nearby wood.

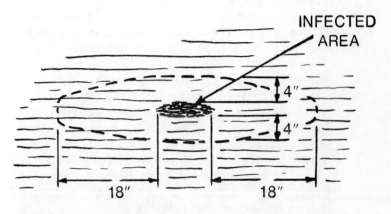

Fig. 17-2. The recommended cutting area for eliminating wood that can carry spores and hypae.

Since both air and moisture are needed for rot to develop, good ventilation should be provided for remaining wood. Any replacement parts should be of durable wood, preferably heartwood. Sound wood in the vicinity should be treated with a preservative, particularly if it is of the nondurable type. The spores can live on nearby objects of all kinds, so precautions have to be taken. A blowtorch flame played over masonry can kill spores. A solution of 4% sodium fluoride in water will sterilize masonry or metal.

Buying old furniture infected by rot is risky. Even if treated, it could bring spores into contact with other furniture and cause trouble there.

Avoiding rot is much easier than attempting to treat it after it has become established. Precautions to take are:

1. Use wood with a moisture content below 20%. Most properly seasoned furniture wood is likely to have a moisture content of no more than 15%. Forced drying by heat is inadvisable because having wood too dry affects its workability and makes it brittle. Because

dried furniture takes moisture again from the air to bring its moisture content up to normal (12% to 15% in room conditions), it can expand and distort.

2. Insure adequate ventilation. In most pieces of furniture that are normally dry, there is little risk. Problems come if liquid gets inside or something is stored inside that gives off moisture.

3. Treat new and surrounding wood with preservative. This should be done while the wood is dry and before any surface treatment. Anything put on the surface, such as paint or varnish, will act as a barrier to the entry of moisture and may be adequate alone.

4. Choose woods with a good resistance to rot. In a repair this may not be possible because woods have to match. Some woods resist attack by rot because of their chemical constituents. Teak and red cedar are examples. The manufactured woods have a resistance to rot. Particle board is more synthetic resin than wood and should not be affected by dampness. Plywood has glue barriers that resist rot.

There are some fungi that attack wood while it is curing. Their effect on the wood at the furniture stage may be some discoloring or staining, but otherwise the qualities of the wood are unaffected. Discoloring in itself is not necessarily a sign of rot, and some of the other signs should also be looked for if rot is suspected.

Modern synthetic resins have made it possible to preserve rotten wood. By permeating the rotten wood with a resin which eventually bonds what is left into a solid mass, it is possible to retain church timbers and parts of ships that would otherwise have disintegrated. The technique may yet become possible for important parts of furniture, but normally the only treatment for rot is to remove and destroy.

BORERS

Rot is not a very great menace to furniture used in normal household conditions. A greater problem may come from insects. The damage is done by their larvae, which bore through the wood. There may be small holes on the surface where entry was made, but under the surface there may be a maze of tunnels. (Fig. 17-3).

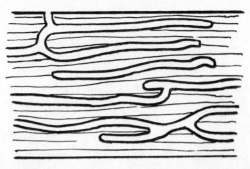

Fig. 17-3. Borers can weaken the structure of wood by tunneling.

All of this may only be apparent after the wood is cut through. If the pupae are still active, cuts may be seen below the boreholes in certain seasons—early summer in the Northern Hemisphere. It is unlikely that furniture can survive a century or more without being attacked in this way. This means that there are likely to be worm holes in old furniture, although the piece may have been treated to kill the borers. It is not unknown for furniture fakers to drill imitation worm holes as some evidence of antiquity!

The cycle commences with a beetle laying its eggs in a tiny crevice in wood. When the larvae appear from the eggs, they start eating the wood, boring farther into it for more food. This goes on for a long time, maybe a year or more. Eventually the larvae get near the surface and turn into pupae and eventually into beetles, which break out and the whole cycle starts again (Fig. 17-4).

The beetles that cause the trouble may be no more than 1/8 in. long. Most of those that attack furniture in the home are about this size.

If there has been an attack by borers, there must be a thorough application of an insecticide. Some common fluids, such as kerosene, benzene, and turpentine may be used, but it is probably better to use a specially compounded commercial insecticide. Although there may be some benefit in painting on insecticide, sure results only come from injecting into individual holes. There are ways of insuring good penetration by fumigation. This must be done professionally, but a badly affected piece may be worth the expense of having this done.

Although particle board is as immune to borer attack as it is to rot, plywood of some types can be vulnerable to borers.

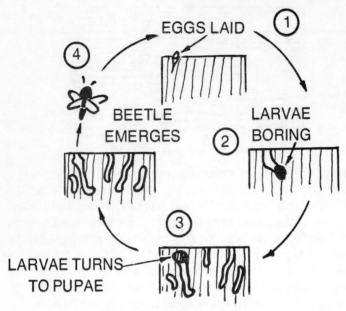

EGGS LAID

BEETLE EMERGES

LARVAE BORING

LARVAE TURNS TO PUPAE

Fig. 17-4. The life cycle of a borer.

The larvae may not like the glue, but that does not stop them from burrowing through individual plies between glue lines. Older plywood, with nonwaterproof glue, is particularly vulnerable. Drawer bottoms and cabinet backs made from old plywood may be the home of borers. If these panels can be removed and burned, it is better to replace them than to treat them. Use plenty of preservative on the new plywood and the adjoining wood.

PRESERVATIVES

Fortunately, most of the furniture woods, particularly heartwoods, are unlikely to be affected by rot unless they are used in moisture-laden areas (like bathrooms or laundries). Though good home conditions provide some protection against borers, there is a risk of their attack almost anywhere.

Fortunately there are preservatives that can be applied to wood to give protection against both rot and borers. Some of these are more appropriate to outdoor use and are used on fence posts and the exteriors of wooden buildings. These are unsuitable for furniture because of their appearance or smell. Tar oil products are in this group. There are some organic solvent types, such as chloronapthalenes, copper and zinc napthenates, and pentachlorophenol. There are also waterborne preservatives, such as copper or chrome arsenate, fluoride dinitrophenol, and sodium fluoride.

Wood preservatives are available under trade names, and the small amounts needed in furniture repair are most simply obtained this way. In professional treatment the preservative is forced into the wood. Alternatively the wood is soaked in the hot or cold preservative and then left for the liquid to diffuse through the grain.

These methods of application are not usually available or appropriate in furniture making and repair. Sufficient protection may be given by painting preservative on with a brush or spraying. Of course, the preservative is only effective if it can soak in. So the wood must be clean and bare. Some preservatives affect the grip of glues. Because of this it may be better to delay treating with preservative until after construction and before any finish has been applied. In many cases some of the surrounding finish will have been removed as well, so this is an opportunity to treat old as well as new wood in the piece of furniture. Surface treatments with polish or paint offer some protection against attack by borers, although obviously they only hide any action already taking place inside the wood. Quite often the hidden parts of the wood are without this protection, and their hidden parts may attract the beetle and her eggs, so these parts should be treated particularly well with preservative.

Be sure that the selected preservative is suitable for use on wood that will be painted, polished, or otherwise finished. The organic solvent types will take most finishes. Waterborne preservatives should be allowed to dry; they will leave salt deposits on the surface. The deposits should be wiped off cleanly. Then the surface can take paint, polish, varnish, or stain.

Most preservatives, other than the waterborne ones, are combustible during application. Some give off vapors which may be unpleasant, if not actually dangerous, when breathed, so application should be outdoors or in a well ventilated place.

CRACKS AND KNOTS

As wood dries out, minute cracks in the grain may open. This often occurs after the wood has been worked and before the final finish. But sometimes a crack does not appear until some time after the furniture has been in use. These natural cracks do not affect strength, so they only need to be treated for the sake of appearance. Normally some form of stopping is used. But just as the crack has opened, it may also close, so it is advisable to use a flexible stopping, not a rigid one.

Knots in hardwoods are usually unlikely to give trouble. But in softwoods a knot may dry out and shrink away from the surrounding wood, or it may even fall out. Be suspicious of a knot in softwood that has a black ring around it. The knot will almost certainly weaken and fall out. Avoid using such wood in a repair. However, if a knot has fallen out of existing work, the hole can be drilled to a true circle so a plug can be inserted. A small knot can be plugged with stopping. A softwood knot on a surface which is to be painted should be expected to exude resin after the paint has been applied. Shellac should be applied to the knot to prevent resin from breaking through the skin of the paint.

Rebuilding

18

Many pieces of furniture can be restored and given a new lease on life by minor repairs, touching up of veneers, or treatment of rot or borers. Much furniture that has been discarded by someone can be made presentable and attractive again with the exercise of a little skill and a lot of patience. But sometimes furniture needs, and deserves, more challenging repairs—repairs that involve rebuilding.

Such a project should not be rushed into. The amount of work involved has to be assessed, then the way it is to be accomplished judged. There may be joints that have to be discarded; new parts may have to be incorporated; woods may have to be matched. Damage must be assessed.

Rebuilding from a very badly damaged piece of furniture is a challenge, and only you can decide if it is worthwhile. It could mean a lot of work for a rather indifferent result. It could also be a very satisfying achievement. Although there is a lot of satisfaction in making a completely new piece of furniture, there are occasions when the charm of an old piece is such that time spent restoring it is justified.

PLANNING RESTORATION

The way to start is not to rush into the removal of damaged parts. Instead, check sizes and shapes. Compare opposing parts. In most pieces of furniture there are parts that are paired. If one is badly damaged, the other may provide a guide to the shape of the replacement part. If not, it may be necessary to make a drawing of what is left of a broken part before dismantling it. This can be on paper, but quite often it can be on a piece of scrap hardboard or plywood held against the part which is drawn around. Make sure you have all the facts you need before cutting out damage or removing joined parts.

Check for symmetry. If a framed structure has loosened joints, it could have moved out of true. If there is any doubt, get the whole thing pulled together with bar clamps or ropes and check corners with a try square. Measure diagonals too. This will have to be done at the final assembly, but testing now may show up distortion caused by a warped or broken part.

Whenever possible try to fit replacement parts in exactly the same way as the originals were fixed. This is not always possible because sometimes joints cannot be opened without damage to a part which is not to be replaced. If there have been mortise and tenon joints, they should be used if possible in the new work.

Usually even a simple restoration job involves several steps. It's always a good idea to think the steps through before starting. Let's run through the replacement of a chair arm. This should give you some idea of the kinds of things that must be anticipated. First, cuts are made on each side of the old joint at the front; a cut is made close to the joint at the back too (Fig. 18-1). Then cuts are made around the front joint to expose the edges of the tenon. This will give you an idea of the size of the mortise and tenon. When the dimensions of the joint have been defined (Fig. 18-2), the rest of the arm wood is cut

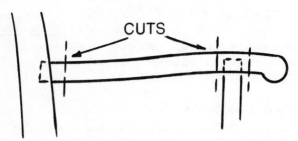

Fig. 18-1. To replace the arm of a chair, first cut off the old arm.

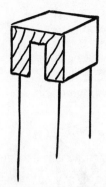

Fig. 18-2. Cutting around the joint helps to define its dimensions.

away (Fig. 18-3). Look for any nails or other metal fastenings. If necessary cut through these with a hacksaw. Quite often it is possible to cut away wood around them so they can be withdrawn.

At the back, the outline of the mortise will be exposed (Fig. 18-4), with the wood on the tenon still inside. Remove some of this by drilling, but keep the diameter of the drill less than the width of the mortise (Fig. 18-5). Avoid going too deep. If there is a nail or other metal fastening through the mortise, cut this with a metalworking drill. It is then usually possible to lever or punch the ends out. Cut out the rest of the tenon wood, trying not to enlarge the mortise.

The new arm is made to match the opposite one. If the arm is shaped, use a piece of wood large enough to allow for the curves. Outline the shape of the arm on the wood. Outline in

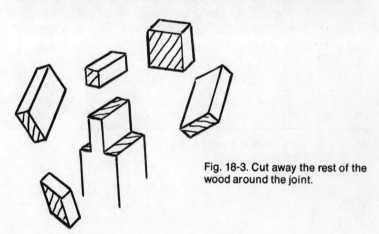

Fig. 18-3. Cut away the rest of the wood around the joint.

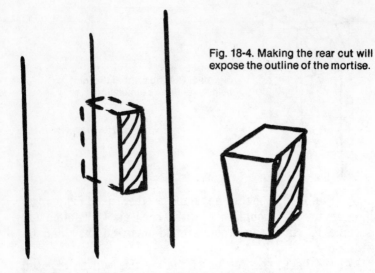

Fig. 18-4. Making the rear cut will expose the outline of the mortise.

one plane at a time (Fig. 18-6). Cut along the outline in the first plane, then mark the shape in the second plane. Usually, the tenon can be cut as the larger outline is cut—one plane at a time.

Aim to make the joints tight. Duplicate the *actual* dimensions of the old parts, not the theoretical dimensions. If the upright tenon obviously started 1/2 in. thick but is now mostly thinner and rounded on the end, try to make the mortise match that shape.

Get the arm to shape and do whatever rounding is necessary, but leave final sanding (maybe even final shaping at clamp points) until after assembly. This circumvents any marking as the parts are forced together.

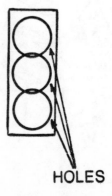

Fig. 18-5. Drill away the old tenon from the mortise.

HOLES

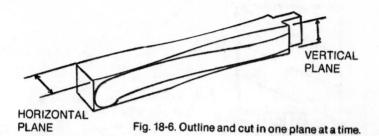

VERTICAL
PLANE

HORIZONTAL
PLANE

Fig. 18-6. Outline and cut in one plane at a time.

PANELS

If a panel has to be replaced, the problem is to get it out with minimum damage to surrounding woodwork. It will either be grooved into the framework (Fig. 18-7) or held into a rabbet with molding (Fig. 18-8). If it is a glass panel or a wooden one covered with tapestry or other nonwood decoration, it will almost certainly be in a rabbet, although this may not be immediately obvious. The molding is unlikely to be glued but will be held with a number of fine nails. They may not be easily seen, particularly if they have been punched and covered with stopping, which has been obscured by the subsequent finish. The loose side in the open rabbet is usually the side which has the least elaborate molding.

Sometimes a wide chisel or a knife can be eased under the center of the molding to lift it. It should be possible to spring the molding sufficiently to release the nails (Fig. 18-9) and

Fig. 18-7. Panels can be grooved into the framework.

199

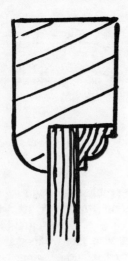

Fig. 18-8. Panels can be set into a rabbet joint braced by molding.

allow the miters to come away at the corners. When one length of molding has been removed, the others should come away with little trouble.

If possible, knock back and straighten the existing nails for use again. This will probably result in less damage and evidence of the repair than if new fastenings have to be used. The old panel should come out without difficulty. It can be used as a pattern for the new one. Be careful that the new panel does not distort the final assembly. Any errors in the old panel may have to be duplicated. The original may not have corners at exact right angles, particularly if it is a very old piece of furniture. Forcing the framework to right angles might affect some other part of the total assembly. Carefully scrape out the rabbet to remove blobs of varnish or other finish, particularly

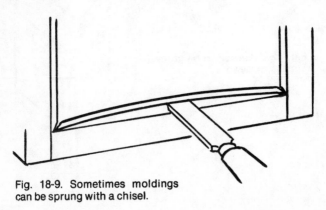

Fig. 18-9. Sometimes moldings can be sprung with a chisel.

at the corners, so the new panel will bed closely. Examine the treatment of the old panel. It may have been stained and polished before fitting.

Plywood and other plain wood panels, particularly in more recent furniture, are more likely to be in grooves. If a panel has to be removed and a new one fitted, one of the surrounding pieces may have to be cut away. But one way of dealing with a damaged panel is to leave it in place and cover one or both sides with plywood or hardboard (Fig. 18-10).

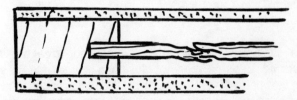

Fig. 18-10. Damaged panels don't always have to be replaced. They can be covered over.

If the surrounding framework must be removed, look for fastenings that might be withdrawn at a joint. These are unlikely, but if a joint is held by a screw, it may be possible to open it. It is more likely that the corners will be solidly glued and have either mortise and tenon or dowel joints. If the piece is old enough to have been made with animal or fish glue, it may be possible to soften the glue enough to open the joints without cutting (Fig. 18-11). This can be done with heat. A

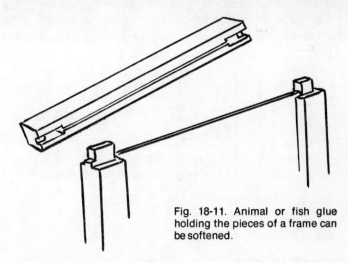

Fig. 18-11. Animal or fish glue holding the pieces of a frame can be softened.

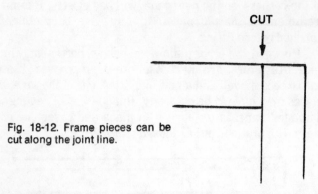

CUT

Fig. 18-12. Frame pieces can be cut along the joint line.

gradual soaking in heat is better than applying great heat for a brief period. Leaving the joint close to a heat source for some time may be effective. Hot water bottles tied over the joints for an hour or so may produce enough heat to weaken the glue.

An alternative to heat is moisture. Soaking the joint in water should cause old glues to weaken to the point of allowing release. Of course, a problem with the use of heat or moisture is that surface finishes may be damaged. If the piece is to be stripped for refinishing, this may not matter. But if the existing finish is to remain, heat and moisture should be avoided.

Sometimes the joints of a frame surrounding a panel can be cut. At a corner, one piece piece usually butts against the other on the surface, and the workings of the joint may not be apparent. But an inconspicuous cut can be made with a fine saw along the joint line (Fig. 18-12). If two joints along the same line are cut in this way, the long piece can be removed and the panel can be drawn out (Fig. 18-13).

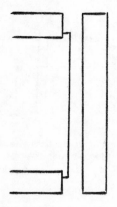

Fig. 18-13. If two opposing joints are cut, the panel can be slid out of the frame.

202

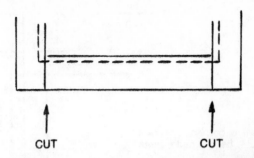

Fig. 18-14. The bottom piece of a frame can be cut out to remove a panel.

In a door it may be easier to make an inconspicuous repair by cutting out the bottom piece (Fig. 18-14), but this will involve springing the frame a little to to get the old panel around the ungrooved joint (Fig. 18-15).

If the side of a frame is removed and the new panel made and fitted, the corner joints can be remade with dowels, preferably two in each (Fig. 18-16). A jig can be made to insure matching holes (Fig. 18-17), or an adjustable dowelling guide can be used. If the bottom of a frame has been removed, it would not be possible to use dowels of adequate length, even if the framework could be sprung enough. Instead you can use open mortise and tenon joints because they will not show at the bottom edge of the door.

DRAWERS

If a drawer has been moved in and out for a very long time, there can be considerable wear on the meeting surfaces.

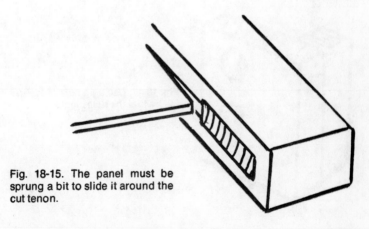

Fig. 18-15. The panel must be sprung a bit to slide it around the cut tenon.

203

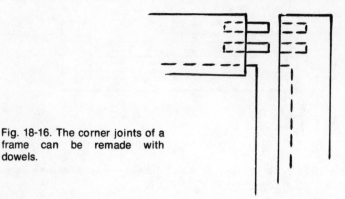

Fig. 18-16. The corner joints of a frame can be remade with dowels.

In modern pieces of furniture, there are metal drawer slides or the drawers may be hung with strips of wood sliding in grooves. But traditional drawers, as found in old furniture, usually have the bottom of the drawer itself sliding on guides. Some old drawers have kickers above (Fig. 18-18).

Wear occurs on the bottom edges of the drawer sides and on the runners (Fig. 18-19). It is not usually difficult to remove the runners and replace them if worn, because they are often screwed in or are ready to break away.

If examination of the drawer sides shows that building up the worn part would be difficult, it may be preferable to increase the width of the worn runner and add a mating piece below the drawer (Fig. 18-20).

If there is enough depth below the drawer bottom, it is possible to skim off the worn surface that rides on the runner. Then a new surface can be added to mate with a new runner (Fig. 18-21).

Fig. 18-17. Use a jig as a guide to insure that the holes match.

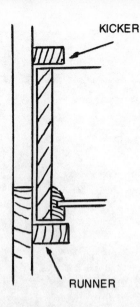

KICKER

RUNNER

Fig. 18-18. Kickers and runners act as guides for the movement of the drawers.

Examine the top edges of the sides at the back of the drawer. If a heavily loaded drawer has been pulled in and out over many years, a surprising amount may be worn off the top of the sides because of the weight of the contents tilting the drawer as it is pulled out (Fig. 18-22). Pieces can be inlaid to make up for this wear (Fig. 18-23), or in a bad case a full-length strip may be glued on.

There may be a temptation to use a harder wood when repairing a badly worn part of a drawer or its runners and kickers, but a hardwood rubbing on a softwood will cause rapid wear on the softer surface. It is better to use the same kind of wood as previously used, especially if an antique is being repaired. Wear can be reduced and movement of the drawer eased if the bearing surfaces are lubricated. Mineral oil is unsuitable, but the surfaces could be rubbed with wax polish or even candle wax.

LEGS AND FEET

Wear on old furniture often occurs at the points of support. Casters may wobble and wear away the wood, or the wood may suffer from direct contact with the floor. Legs, particularly at the rear of furniture, can suffer the attacks of borers without being noticed, and the wood can be so weakened that it will no longer support the furniture.

205

Fig. 18-19. Wear on the bottom edge of a drawer.

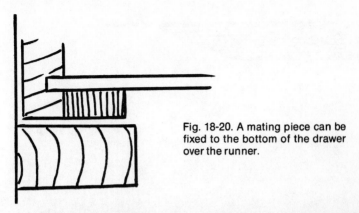

Fig. 18-20. A mating piece can be fixed to the bottom of the drawer over the runner.

It may be sufficient to reseat casters by plugging the worn screw holes in the legs and rescrewing the casters in place, possibly with longer screws. Screw-on casters are common on

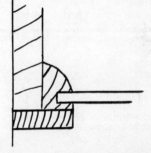

Fig. 18-21. A piece can be added to match the runner size.

older furniture, but modern pieces may have a type that has a stem in a hole in the leg. With an old piece of furniture it may be better to replace the screw-on type with the stem type, if

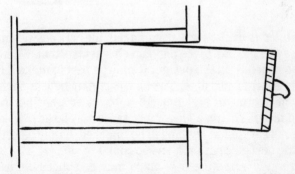

Fig. 18-22. Wear on a drawer can occur on upper surfaces as well as on lower ones.

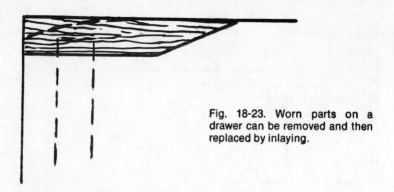

Fig. 18-23. Worn parts on a drawer can be removed and then replaced by inlaying.

there is enough sound wood into which to drill a hole. Of course, the new type of caster must match the piece of furniture.

Another way of dealing with worn leg ends is to add a foot that will plug into a hole (Fig. 18-24). The foot can be turned from wood, or it can be bought in plastic or metal. Even on an old piece of furniture such a new foot will be inconspicuous at floor level.

Fig. 18-24. If a hole is drilled in a leg end, a wooden foot can be plugged into the hole.

If a leg is badly worn or damaged, the only answer may be to cut away the bad piece and join on a new section. Where this is done depends on the design. It may be best to make the new part as short as possible. The new part may be less obvious if the joint is brought high enough to be under a shelf or rail. If the old piece is plain, a longer new piece may be advisable. But if there is carving or shaping to be matched, it may be better to keep the new piece as small as possible.

In many cases the new piece may be spliced on, using a long diagonal cut. The new piece should be slightly oversize so it can be trimmed to an exact match after the glue has set.

However, there is an alternative that may be considered better for the downward load of a leg (Fig. 18-25). The V may point upwards or downwards, depending on how this fits in with the design of the leg. This joint needs more care to make accurately. A simple splice is generally easier to make, so it does not show much when finished.

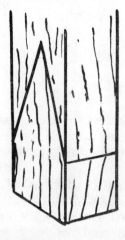

Fig. 18-25. New leg ends can be triangular.

RAIL JOINTS

Rails on tables and chairs can work themselves loose. Whether the rails are round, as in the underframing of chairs, or rectangular, there is likely to be wear both in the leg hole and the rail end. If rails are otherwise sound it may be advisable to keep them. Sometimes it is sufficient to reglue the joint using a synthetic resin glue filled with plenty of sawdust.

In a bad case there are several options. A false tenon can be fitted to the end of a rail, but it may be better to leave the rail end as it is and inlay a piece of wood in the leg. The piece of wood need not be much wider than the hole, but it should extend an inch or so along the grain in each direction. If possible it should be cut with bevelled ends (Fig. 18-26). The position of the hole should be marked carefully—preferably before the piece is glued in.

HANDLES AND KNOBS

Handles, catches, knobs and other such fittings may loosen with age and frequent use. Quite often they play an important part in the design of the piece. Then it would be unwise to replace them with something very different.

209

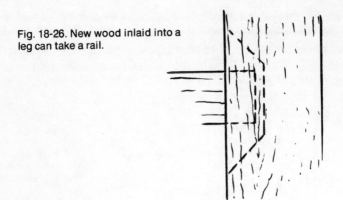

Fig. 18-26. New wood inlaid into a leg can take a rail.

Besides wear and damage to handles and knobs, years of handling may mar the surface behind them. So if a piece is being restored, it is usually best to do something about the area behind a handle or knob also.

A thin piece of matching wood may be put behind a fixture and finished to match the surrounding work. If the matching wood's edges are bevelled or rounded, a harsh shadow line will be avoided. The matching wood need not be a simple rectangle, but it can be shaped to match the handle or other features in the design (Fig. 18-27). The shape can also help disguise any repair if the door or drawer front has been badly worn.

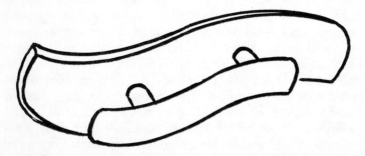

Fig. 18-27. A fixture's shape can be complemented by the shape of its base.

Sometimes screws in fixtures can work themselves loose, wearing away the screw holes in the process. No amount of tightening will correct this. It may be better to drill out the hole, insert a piece of dowel rod, and drill a new screw hole.

It's best to use a washer under the screw head. The washer should be large enough to spread the pressure to wood that has not been pulled in (Fig. 18-28). It may be possible to substitute a piece of metal or plastic tube for the drilled dowel. Another way of tightening the grip of the screw is to thread a piece of rubber tubing on it. The rubber tubing should be longer than the thickness it is to pass through. Then when the screw is tightened the rubber expands and fills the hole.

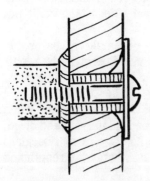

Fig. 18-28. A washer serves to spread the pressure exerted by the screw.

Wooden handles are not such a problem. It is usually possible to make new ones of similar pattern if the old ones are damaged. Or if the old fixing wood screws have worn their holes to a loose fit, new holes can be made and the screws can be driven in slightly different positions. If a backing piece is needed to cover a shabby surface, it can be made to match the wooden handle.

Plastic and modern metal handles can be very attractive. It is often possible to use a replacement handle to cover a surface damaged by an old handle. Obviously most plastics would not be appropriate for a piece of furniture that dates before the coming of modern plastics.

There were, however, plastics used on furniture in the last century. Celluloid is an example. So at least some plastics can be appropriate for older furniture. Black plastic, used with restraint, would be acceptable for a complete handle or part of one, used with wood or metal. Clear or semiclear plastic, particularly with a tortoise shell effect, might also be correct.

Some of the methods of plating metals are comparatively modern and it is safer to choose plain brass, which can be lacquered. Chromium plate and several other bright finishes would not be suitable handles on old furniture.

FIBERGLASS

An oldtime cabinetmaker or a modern perfectionist might regard the use of fiberglass and its synthetic resin as inappropriate for furniture, but this and some moldable plastic substances may provide the only sensible way of restoring a piece of furniture. There are modern pieces of furniture made completely from fiberglass. Some furniture has fiberglass shaped parts that are combined with wood or metal and may be covered with upholstery so the actual construction is not apparent.

The resins used with fiberglass will make a reasonable bond to wood, so it is possible to use fiberglass to repair wooden furniture. Fiberglass can also be bonded to fiberglass, providing the surface is sanded to expose new mat areas.

Fiberglass can be thought of as spun glass. When fiberglass (in a matlike form) is embedded in resin and dried, a remarkably strong material results. Layers of fiberglass may be built up in the resin to provide whatever strength and bulk is required.

Fiberglass is supplied in many forms. There may be a chopped strand mat, in which random short pieces of fiber are loosely bonded with an adhesive which dissolves in the resin. This is the cheapest form and the type most suitable for many small repairs to wooden furniture. Fiberglass may also be woven in several ways into cloth or tapes.

The resin used remains liquid for at least several months after it is obtained, but it has to be activated by the addition of one (sometimes two) chemicals. Once activated, it begins to set, and there is a limited time in which it can be used after hardening begins. For small repair work, a good way to buy fiberglass, resin, chemicals and mixing containers is as a kit sold for repairs to car bodywork.

The instructions provided with the kit should be carefully followed. Usually the resin is applied with a brush, using an up and down action after the first spreading. Fiberglass is cut to shape with scissors and laid in the resin while more resin is introduced with the brush. Permeation is indicated by the whiteness of the fiberglass changing to a clear appearance. If more fiberglass is needed, it can be put on top and covered with more resin. The first step in setting comes when the resin gels. If this happens in the mixing pot, it is too late to use it, and no attempt should be made to spread it.

212

If fiberglass is to be bonded to wood, the wood must be absolutely bare. This means it should be cleaned of every scrap of paint, varnish, or other finish; the surface should be scraped and sanded so the fibers of the wood are exposed uncontaminated. The resin needs to soak into the pores of the wood, so paint or varnish in the wood might interfere with this. But breaking up the surface by scratching or drawing a saw across sideways should provide a sufficient grip.

A fiberglass repair may be difficult to disguise, but such repairs can be done on the *inside* of furniture. Suppose a rail across the inside of a panel has broken under impact. It may very difficult to replace. The broken ends are brought together as well as possible (maybe with glue against the panel) and the worst of the frayed ends are cut off or fixed down (Fig. 18-29). All traces of finish are removed from the broken part and the immediate area of the panel. Resin is mixed and painted thickly over and around the damage. It is a help if the work can be turned so gravity helps the resin flow where it is wanted and not away from it. If the work has to be done in a near vertical position, there are thixotropic resins that resist any tendency to run. Pieces of fiberglass mat or cloth are put over the break and allowed to overlap on to the panel. Then more resin is quickly brushed on to penetrate the fiberglass. This is followed by more fiberglass, either the same size or slightly smaller, and enough resin to penetrate and cover it (Fig. 18-30).

The actual thickness of a fiberglass repair is usually not very much, and it is possible to sand the result and paint over

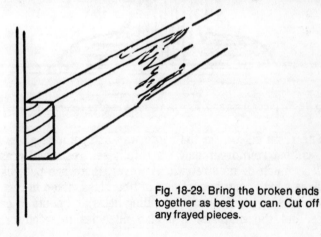

Fig. 18-29. Bring the broken ends together as best you can. Cut off any frayed pieces.

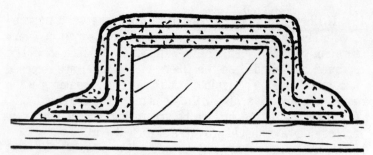

Fig. 18-30. Layers of resin and fiberglass are laid over the wood.

so it is not very obvious. This means fiberglass can be used on a visible surface of some painted furniture, like lawn chairs or workshop furnishings.

This method can also be used on internal parts that have come away from the main structure or on loose dividers. The surfaces must be cleaned off bare, and the fiberglass must be worked into the angles with plenty of resin (Fig. 18-31). This may be done on both sides or only one. There may be more than one layer of fiberglass. Woven fiberglass tape is convenient for this kind of repair.

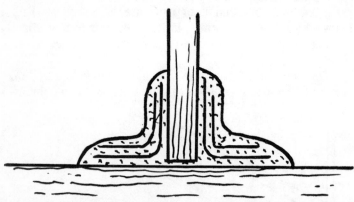

Fig. 18-31. Fiberglass and resin can also be used to secure a divider.

The resin suffers in the same way as synthetic glues if used without reinforcement. When fully set, resin will craze and lose much of its strength. However, there are puttylike mixtures which contain particles of fiberglass mixed in resin. These are sold particularly for filling holes and dents in car bodies, but the material will also fill holes in woodwork.

However, in making a fiberglass repair to a piece of furniture, any place that appears to encourage a buildup of resin without the mat or cloth reinforcement can have small pieces of fiberglass worked in to have the same effect as sawdust used with glue.

Fiberglass tape can be used like a bandage to strengthen a cracked or broken piece. It might be too obvious in a prominent position, but a rear leg or a floor lamp could be repaired in this way. With this method, the split or broken parts are brought together, possibly with resin in the joint, then resin is put on the outside, and the fiberglass tape is wrapped around as more resin is brushed on (Fig. 18-32). This is suitable for square legs as well as round parts. One overlapping wrap may be enough, but another layer can be added, either at the same time or after the first layer has set.

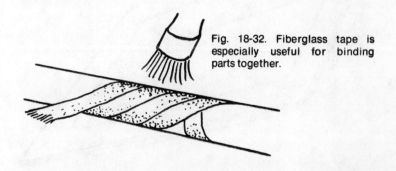

Fig. 18-32. Fiberglass tape is especially useful for binding parts together.

It is possible to build up a broken part with fiberglass and resin. This can be done a little at a time, using resin and pieces of fiberglass. Early layers can be allowed to gel or harden, then more can be added. This must harden. Under normal conditions and temperatures the result should harden overnight, but strength and hardness builds up even more over several days.

If there is any surplus fiberglass and resin, it can be trimmed with a knife after the mass has gelled, but after the result has hardened it can be sawn and filed to shape. If a broken part has been built up, filing and sanding will work the repair to shape and leave a mat surface ready for paint. Not all paints are suitable for fiberglass, and the instructions with the paint should be checked to see that the chosen finish is suitable.

There are other compounds available that will build up wooden parts and can be finished by filing and sanding. Although these come in colors to match certain woods, they are unlikely to become indistinguishable under a clear finish, so the best result will be by painting.

Fiberglass can be used in molding shapes too. This may sometimes be useful in producing replacement parts. A simple example is a tray for the bottom of an umbrella stand (Fig. 18-33).

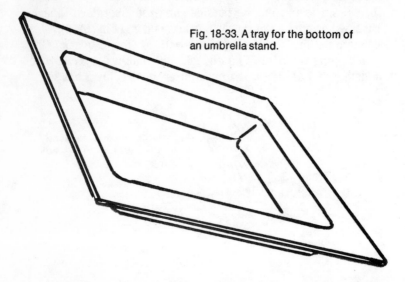

Fig. 18-33. A tray for the bottom of an umbrella stand.

First a mold has to be made. For an elaborate thing, there may first be a "plug" in the shape of the finished object. In industry, the making of the plug may be a long and expensive procedure. From the plug a fiberglass mold is made, and the production articles are molded in this. For a simple object, such as the tray, the plug stage can be omitted. A mold can be made straight away from convenient materials.

In the case of the tray, a block is built up in the shape of the recess. This can be several layers of wood or particle board, which are then fixed down to smooth-faced hardboard (Fig. 18-34). The better the surface of the mold, the better the surface of the fiberglass.

The next step is the coating of the mold with a parting, or release, agent. This is a wax compound that prevents the resin from adhering to the mold. Although wax polish can be used, it

Fig. 18-34. A mold can be made from pieces of wood.

is probably wiser to buy a special preparation. Over this goes the first coat or resin. There are special "gel coat" resins for this purpose, but the resin supplied with a repair kit should be satisfactory.

The gel coat is left to set. Then more resin is added and layers of fiberglass mat are laid in. Pieces of mat may be cut to follow the shape, but adjoining pieces should overlap. A second layer of resin follows, and this should be sufficient for our umbrella tray (Fig. 18-35).

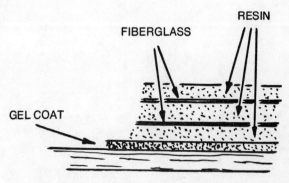

Fig. 18-35. A cross section of the fiberglass and resin layers.

Nothing has been done to restrict the outline, which will be ragged and uneven. When the whole thing has gelled, but has not become hard, the outline can be trimmed with a knife and straightedge. Alternatively, the edge can be trimmed later with saw and file. Leave the tray to harden on its mold for a day, then pry it off. Except for cleaning up the edges, it is finished.

Turning and Carving

19

Many pieces of furniture have turned parts. Carving is less common on modern furniture, but much old furniture was carved, some of it quite elaborately. Both of these skills have been regarded as specialist trades, but anyone repairing furniture should not be afraid of turning or carving. These skills can be learned with practice.

Of course, a complete replacement of an intricately carved panel may be more than a beginner can hope to tackle, but straightforward turning and carving, particularly if it is only a part of an original that has to be replaced, can be very rewarding.

TURNING

A lathe is a machine tool. The machine rotates the wood, but the operator shapes it by hand. There are large lathes and there are much more basic ones that occupy little room. There are others that are just an electric drill that serves as a lathe. The method of use is the same; the main differences are the scope and the size of work that can be undertaken. The simplest lathes are suitable only for spindle work—anything round which is greater in length than its diameter.

A lathe has a headstock, which usually takes its power from a motor via a belt and pulleys (Fig. 19-1). But an electric drill on a stand can power the lathe directly. Earlier lathes were operated by a treadle, or, as they still are in India, by

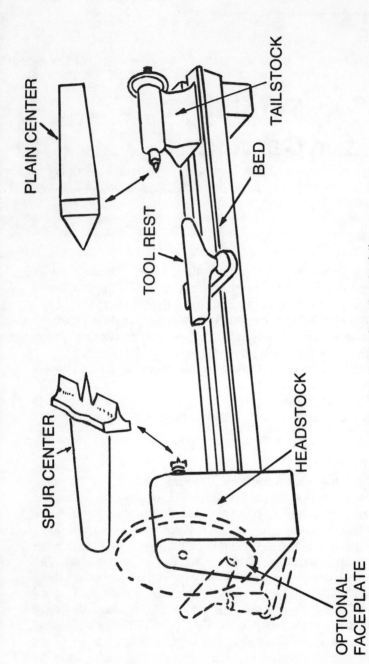

PLAIN CENTER

TAILSTOCK

BED

TOOL REST

SPUR CENTER

HEADSTOCK

OPTIONAL FACEPLATE

Fig. 19-1. A typical woodturning lathe.

220

hand via a reciprocating action with a bow. The headstock has a means of holding the wood. This can be done in several ways, but a simple device is a spur center. The parts of the lathe are normally on a bed, which may be two parallel metal or wood strips, a casting, or a large tube or rod. Sliding on the bed is a tailstock which carries a plain center that supports the other end of the wood. The tailstock can be locked in any position on the bed, and there may be a screw adjustment for accurately positioning the center.

Tools are held in the hand, but they rest on a toolrest, which is usually T-shaped. Normally the top of the toolrest is at about the same height as the center of the wood being turned. The simplest rest is fixed at this height, but a better one is adjustable and may have interchangable rests. In any case, the rest has to be movable so it can be kept close to the work.

A standard woodturning lathe has no more parts than these. There is equipment for special purposes, but for ordinary turning it is better for the lathe to be unobstructed. It is possible to do woodturning on a metalturning lathe, but the slide rest and other complications interfere with the free use of hand tools. In any case, woodturning throws wood chips in all directions, and there is soon a buildup of wood dust that will get into parts of a metalturning lathe and interfere with its operation.

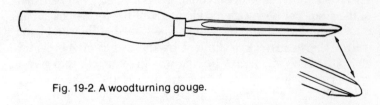

Fig. 19-2. A woodturning gouge.

Most woodturning is done with gouges and chisels. Regular chisels could be sharpened to suit, but standard woodturning tools are longer because there is sometimes an advantage in the use of length for leverage. A woodturning gouge is ground outside (Fig. 19-2). Some turners favor having it sharpened square across the end, but most gouges have their ends rounded. For small work, a 1/2 in. turning gouge will serve for general work, and a 1/4 in. one can be used for smaller curves. Larger gouges are only used for large work, and even then their only advantage is in speed of working.

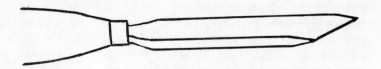

Fig. 19-3. A woodturning chisel.

A woodturning chisel is bevelled on both sides and is normally given a skew end (Fig. 19-3). Some turners prefer the end square across. A parting tool is a type of chisel sharpened across the end and narrowed behind the point (Fig. 19-4).

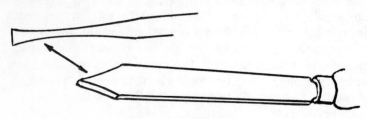

Fig. 19-4. A parting tool.

For large diameter work the lathe may have a faceplate (Fig. 19-5) to which the wood being turned can be screwed. There are other chucks and holding devices that can be fitted to the mandrel nose (the driving part of the headstock). The maximum wood diameter that can be turned at the right-hand end of the headstock is limited by the height of the center above the bed, which may be cut away in some lathes to give a greater clearance. Some lathes are arranged to take another faceplate at the other side of the headstock (Fig. 19-6). With

Fig. 19-5. A lathe faceplate.

the toolrest kept out of the way, almost any diameter is possible, and the limitation then is more likely to be the ability of the motor to turn the wood.

For turning between the centers, the grain of the wood is usually lengthwise. But for turning disks, the grain must be crosswise. For bowls and similar things, the tools used have more of a scraping action. They are thick and have flat section obtuse scraping ends. The blades may be straight or curved (Fig. 19-6). These scraping tools may be bought but are often made by grinding old files.

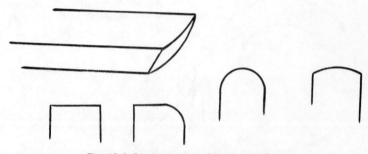

Fig. 19-6. Blade shapes of turning tools.

Wood to be turned between centers can be square, although some workers prefer to plane off the corners (Fig. 19-7). The centers of the ends can be marked with a center punch, and the driving end for spur center may be given a saw cut. The wood is pressed or lightly hammered onto the driving center. Then the tailstock is brought up and the center at that end is entered. It may be lightly lubricated. The toolrest is brought close and its clearance is checked by pulling the wood around by hand before switching on the motor.

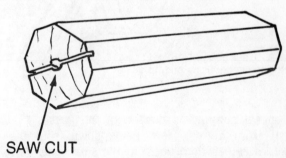

SAW CUT

Fig. 19-7. Turning can be easier if the corners of the wood are planed off.

A gouge should be brought squarely to the rotating work. One hand holds it down on the toolrest; the other hand stays near the end of the handle. There will have to be some experimenting with the angle the tool approaches the wood because this is affected by the height of the rest. If the handle is held too high, the edge only scrapes, but if the handle is lowered, a point will be reached where the edge slices off shavings (Fig. 19-8). Move the toolrest in as the diameter is reduced.

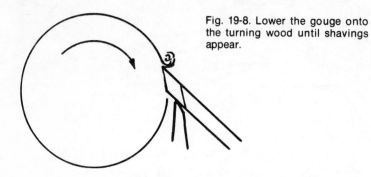

Fig. 19-8. Lower the gouge onto the turning wood until shavings appear.

First, round the wood over its whole length with a gouge. There may be a succession of cuts inwards, but once the more angular parts have been removed, the gouge can be drawn along the rest to make more of a slicing cut (Fig. 19-9).

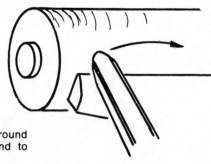

Fig. 19-9. Use a gouge to round the turning wood from end to end.

General shaping is done with the gouge. Hollows are worked from high to low, going down from the greater diameters rather than up from the small ones (Fig. 19-10). Although the wood looks good while rotating, stopping the lathe will show that quite a rough surface is left from the gouge. This is purely an exercise for removing the bulk of the surplus wood and no part is taken right down to size.

If a gouge is tilted towards the direction of cut, it will slice along the wood so the quality of the surface is improved. In some work, sanding after this may be all that is needed, but a good surface is normally the result of work with a chisel.

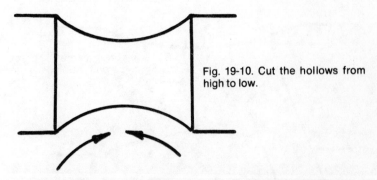

Fig. 19-10. Cut the hollows from high to low.

There is not much risk of damage to the wood when using a gouge. At worst there may be a rough surface, due to scraping instead of cutting, but more care is needed with a chisel. Its misuse can cause it to dig in and spoil the wood. A chisel is used with a slicing action. The chisel is held so the lower corner of the blade is presented to the work, allowing the point to slice (Fig. 19-11), moving along the wood lengthwise. To

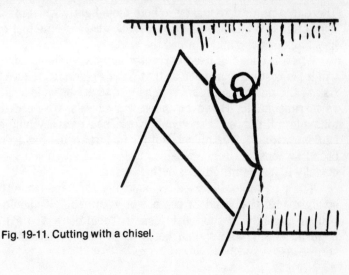

Fig. 19-11. Cutting with a chisel.

avoid digging in, the far side of the cutting edge should be kept well clear of the surface of the wood. In following a curve in profile, cuts are always made from large to small diameters, with cuts meeting at the center of a hollow (Fig. 19-12). For heavy work, the hand on the toolrest may have the fist upwards, but for more delicate work, progress is more easily seen if only the thumb is on top.

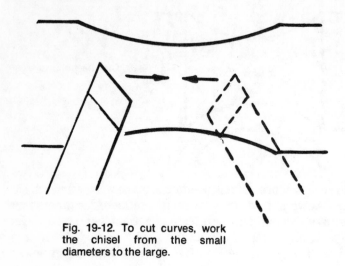

Fig. 19-12. To cut curves, work the chisel from the small diameters to the large.

With all turning tools it is necessary to hold on very tightly. There is a natural tendency to hold tools lightly when making light cuts, but this should be resisted, otherwise the tool may kick back or twist and damage the wood.

When a chisel is used correctly and has a sharp edge, it will leave a surface as good as that from a plane. To reduce the risk of the point digging in, it is helpful to use as wide a chisel as is reasonable. However, narrower chisels are needed to follow small curves. For repair work, nearly everything can be done with a 1/2 in. chisel. But for large parallel surfaces or broad sweeps, a 1 in. or wider chisel is better, while a 1/4 in. chisel will have limited uses in finer work.

The parting tool is used for squaring ends and for cutting straight into the wood to remove a waste end. It should be pointed straight at the work, usually level at first; then the hand on the handle should be lowered so the tool cuts, not scrapes (Fig. 19-13).

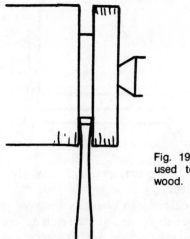

Fig. 19-13. The parting tool is used to cut straight into the wood.

The sequence of tool operations is very important. Let's take a small replacement spindle as an example. If the spindle has to match other spindles, a marked piece of wood or card can be used as a guide (Fig. 19-14). These and other diameters are checked by using calipers.

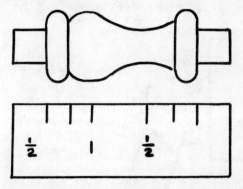

Fig. 19-14. Mark the dimensions of the spindle on a piece of wood or card. Use the markings as a guide.

Have a piece of suitable wood an inch or so too long. Round it on the lathe. Use a gouge to reduce it to close to the maximum finished diameter. The end next to the tailstock center can be squared by using the parting tool or by cutting in with the long point of a chisel (Fig. 19-15). With this cut as a

227

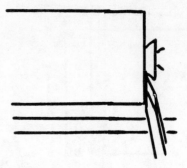

Fig. 19-15. Squaring can be done with a parting tool or the point of a chisel.

guide, a pencil can be used on the rest to mark main cuts. They can be cut in with the long point of a chisel.

The dowel at the tailstock end can be made now, but it would be inadvisable to reduce diameters at both ends before working on other cuts: the wood could spring under the pressure, producing a distorted or rough shape. Cut in with the parting tool or by successive cuts with a chisel as the wood is reduced. Remove the waste wood with a gouge. Then cut the dowel size with a chisel (Fig. 19-16). Since the dowel will have to fit a hole, check it carefully with calipers or use a hole in a piece of scrap wood to try over the end of the dowel after withdrawing it from the tailstock. For ease of entry into the final position, taper the end of the dowel slightly.

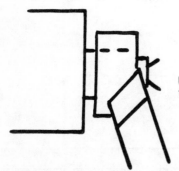

Fig. 19-16. The dowel can be cut to size with a chisel.

Narrow rounded parts, called beads, are found in much turned work. To make a bead on a chisel with its bevel against the wood, its lower corner towards the direction it is to cut. Then roll the chisel so this corner cuts in, towards where the line marking the limit has already been cut in with the long point (Fig. 19-17). Turn the chisel over and do the same to the

228

Fig. 19-17. Roll the chisel to round the wood.

other side of the bead (Fig. 19-18). After practice, many small beads can be cut in one smooth sweep, but a more cautious approach with many light cuts is better at first. On a spindle, it is probably best to make the beads first, then do the other shaping, mostly by slicing cuts with a chisel.

Fig. 19-18. Roll the chisel over the other side of the bead.

The other dowel is reduced to size in the same way as the first one, except its end is cut in. But do not make the parting tool cuts much ahead of gouge cuts. If parting tool cuts are made much below the dowel size before any of the waste has been removed, the whole piece could snap during turning. However, it may be necessary to remove some of the waste part of the wood to allow easy use of the tools (Fig. 19-19).

An expert turner is proud of being able to produce a tool finish that requires little or no sanding, but the revolving wood in the lathe lends itself to easy sanding. Poor tool work may be made good by using a fairly coarse abrasive. But a coarse abrasive can also make prominent scratches around the work,

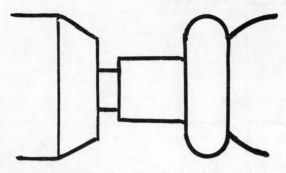

Fig. 19-19. If necessary, remove some of the waste wood so you can get at the dowel.

and therefore across the grain. It is better to use abrasive paper no coarser than needed, and follow with even finer grades so abrasive marks around the wood are too fine to be seen. The spindle may be cut off with the parting tool, although there is always a risk of the final small part snapping and leaving a ragged mark. For a dowel going in a hole, a broken end may not matter, but elsewhere it might be better to remove the work from the lathe and saw off the last small diameter piece.

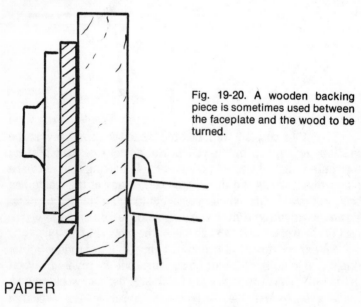

Fig. 19-20. A wooden backing piece is sometimes used between the faceplate and the wood to be turned.

PAPER

For turning a disk-shaped piece on a faceplate, the wood is first cut round with a bandsaw. The wood could be screwed directly to the faceplate with wood screws through the slots. But is is more usual to use a backing piece between the wood and the faceplate (Fig. 19-20). The backing piece can be sandwiched between the wood and faceplate with screws. Or once the backing piece is screwed to the faceplate, the wood can be glued to the backing piece (with paper in between). After turning, the wood can be broken away with a chisel.

Although some disk turning can be done with a gouge, it is more usual to do it all with scrapers, which are either used level or tilted slightly downwards to the position that gives the best cut (Fig. 19-21).

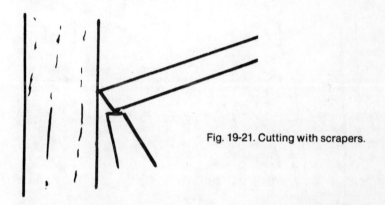

Fig. 19-21. Cutting with scrapers.

It is usual to turn the outside of a disk to a true circle and then skim across the face to get a good surface. After this, whether to work on the rim or on the surface depends on what is being made. A bowl may be brought approximately to shape outside, then the bulk of the hollowing can be done. After that the outside can be finished before getting the inside to the desired shape. For a thing like a lamp base (Fig. 19-22), the general profile is roughed out, the outside is shaped, and key points are pencilled on the revolving wood.

Any angles in the disk will have to be cut with the square corner of a scraper tool or the long point of a chisel. Most other turning, whether roughing to shape or finally turning, is best done with a scraper tool having a moderate curve on the end. This is put on the rest, which is kept close, and swung in a series of small arcs (Fig. 19-23).

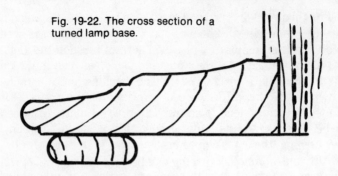

Fig. 19-22. The cross section of a turned lamp base.

If a hole is needed at the center of the disk, it can be made in the lathe. A hollow can be started with the corner of a tool (Fig. 19-24). If the wood is being turned over the bed and if the

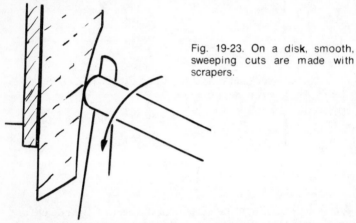

Fig. 19-23. On a disk, smooth, sweeping cuts are made with scrapers.

tailstock will take a chuck, a drill may be used. This is impossible in many simple lathes and would be impractical if turning at the other end of the headstock. It is possible though

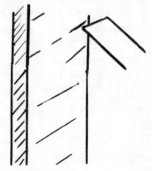

Fig. 19-24. A hole can be started in a disk with the corner of a chisel.

232

to turn the hole with a chisel. Use a chisel no wider than about three-quarters of the size of the hole and feed it straight in (Fig. 19-25).

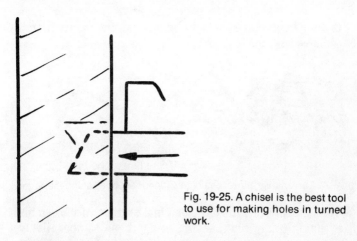

Fig. 19-25. A chisel is the best tool to use for making holes in turned work.

CARVING

If carved work has been damaged, the state of the work will have to be examined to determine the best way of carrying out a repair. In many cases it may be better to cut away much of the old carving so the joint between old and new will be less obvious. If the glue line can come along an existing line in the design, it may be so inconspicuous as to be visible only after a careful search. A joint that is in a recess will be less obvious than one that is on high surfaces.

It is easier to get a close fit with a straight joint, but sometimes there may be an advantage in following the moderate curve of some part of the carving (Fig. 19-26).

Fig. 19-26. Sometimes repairs to carved wood must follow curved lines.

Attempting to follow an intricate cut is inadvisable unless you are prepared to spend a lot of time exercising considerable patience and skill. With most carving on furniture, breaks or damage are most likely to occur at edges, so repairing is usually done by gluing on new wood and carving that to match after the glue has set (Fig. 19-27).

Fig. 19-27. Fortunately, most repairs to carvings are done along the edges.

With some old furniture the original craftsman showed his skill by doing fairly fine carving in depth, so comparatively fragile pieces projected high above the base surface. These projections might break off. A repair then has to be done by inlaying a piece of sufficient thickness and carving it to match (Fig. 19-28).

Fig. 19-28. Sometimes pieces must be inlaid before carving can begin.

A difficulty with repairs to carving may be in matching wood and grain. Check the direction of grain on the damaged part before cutting it away and replacing it. Grain will usually be lengthwise in the direction needing greatest strength. The wood may have been selected with a curved or wandering grain to follow the lines of the carving, so the greatest success in a repair would be in using wood with similar grain pattern. This is not always easy and you may have to compromise.

Wood for carving should be without flaws. Any sign of a crack should cause the piece of wood to be discarded. Unless the original had knots or other flaws that have to be matched, it is better to use wood with a mild grain, this means wood with an even grain pattern with no radical twists in the grain lines. Unless it is necessary for matching purposes, it is likely to be easier to carve wood with little contrast in the grain colors than to use wood with prominent grain markings. Carving cuts have to be made in many directions, and there is less risk of tearing out in wood in which the grain lines have little prominence.

The traditional wood carver used a very large range of tools, most of them gouges. This means that antique carved furniture was worked with the facility of this great range. Fortunately, most repairs to carvings can be done with a few woodworking chisels, some woodworking gouges, a router, a power saw, and two or three Surform tools.

Obviously, no repair should be left with evidence of power tools. But in some work, power tools can lessen the labor by taking the wood almost to size, leaving only light finishing cuts for hand tools. For instance, a router can take a background down to a uniform depth, then work with gouges can remove a further 1/16 in. to leave the hand-tool-carved look.

Of course, much carving can be done with general woodworking chisels and gouges. This is particularly so with the bolder type of carving done in more recent years. Earlier carving was more intricate; finer carving tools are more appropriate for imitation of this kind of work.

Fig. 19-29. Some gouge blade shapes.

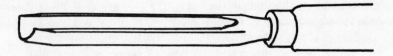

Fig. 19-30. A common carving gouge.

The larger number of tools in the original carver's tool chest was due mainly to the great range of sweeps or curves in each width of carving gouge, going from near flat to deeper than semicircular (Fig. 19-29), with probably eight intermediate sweeps. Common carving gouges are straight (Fig. 19-30), but they may be curved (Fig. 19-31) to get into hollows, or spooned to get into smaller hollows (Fig. 19-32). A carving tool maker may still produce most of these tools, possibly only to special order, but there are smaller sets available. For repairs it is probably advisable to accept one of these sets as an expert's selection of what is most likely to be required.

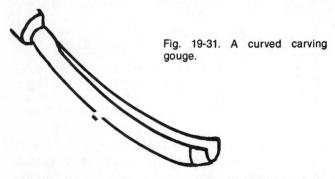

Fig. 19-31. A curved carving gouge.

Other tools with gouge ends have been made, with the body of the tool curved in different ways or reduced in size to get into hard-to-reach places. If there is an opportunity to obtain

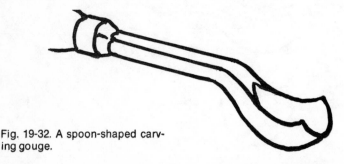

Fig. 19-32. A spoon-shaped carving gouge.

old tools of this type, they are worth having, but they are not the sort to buy just for repairs.

Carving chisels are thinner than regular chisels and may be sharpened on both sides, with the greater bevel to one side. The end may be square across or slanted. Traditional carving involves fine grooves and lines. A narrow gouge, called a veiner, cuts lines like the veins of leaves, hence its name. It is possible to cut a V-shaped groove with a chisel, but there are parting tools available in several angles and sizes which can also make a V cut too (Fig. 19-33).

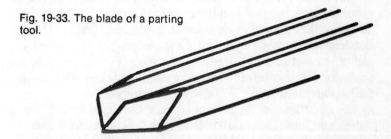

Fig. 19-33. The blade of a parting tool.

It is important that carving tools are kept sharp. While *outside* honing can be done on an ordinary oilstone, sharpening *inside* calls for slip stones that are used like a file on inside surfaces. A slip stone with a round edge and a chisel-shaped edge (Fig. 19-34) can get inside gouges and V-shaped tools. But if there are many different gouge sweeps, it may be better to have two or more stones that approximate the curvature of the sweeps. For the best sharpening it is worth having two grades of stone; a coarse one will quickly remove metal, and a fine one will produce a good edge. For ordinary chisels and gouges it is

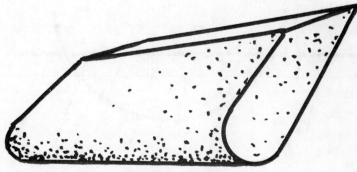

Fig. 19-34. A slip stone.

usual to sharpen tools with a flat surface opposite the bevelled one, but a carver likes to have a slight bevel on the second side.

Anything being carved should be securely held. Both hands should control the tool, so the wood should be fixed to a bench, unless it is so massive that it will not move. Clamps, bench holdfasts, and vises can be used. For most carving work, it is necessary to arrange the surface being carved so that the tool can be brought to it from any angle without obstruction. It is usually best to have the surface slanting upwards, but this is not always possible.

Much carving can be done with hand pressure. One hand should ride on the tool handle to provide pressure and control. The other hand should ride over the blade, assisting in control but ready to provide restraint if the tool tries to go ahead too far or too fast due to softness of the grain. For fine work and the greatest control, hand pressure should be used, particularly where new work adjoins existing carving.

For harder woods or deeper cuts, the carving tool may have to be hit with a mallet. There are special round carver's mallets, but any available type is suitable. The carving tool should be held in one hand with the fingers around the handle and the thumb towards the end being hit by the mallet. The wrist or arm should rest on the wood or somewhere else solid so the carving tool direction can be controlled. Mallet blows should be frequent and light, rather than heavy; progress can then be controlled.

For most cuts the corners of the tool should be above the surface (Fig. 19-35). If the final shape is deeper than the tool, it should be worked down with several cuts. Avoiding burying the corner of a tool reduces the risk of splitting. Sometimes

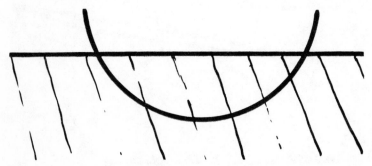

Fig. 19-35. In carving, the upper edges of a gouge must ride above the wood surface.

Fig. 19-36. If you want to break away waste wood, dig into the surface with the corner of a gouge.

breaking away waste wood is intentional, then a tool may have a corner entering below the surface (Fig. 19-36).

Carving often has to be done in all directions, but if the grain is understood and cut accordingly, a smoother finish will result and there will be less risk of the wood breaking out. The lines of grain can be thought of as pieces of straw. An upward sloping cut will shave the ends off (Fig. 19-37), while trying to cut the other way might bend their end over (Fig. 19-38) and either cause splits or a ragged end. Therefore an upward sloping cut should be used even when cutting across the grain, going diagonally up the slopes of grain rather than down. A sharp tool is much less likely to case the grain to break out

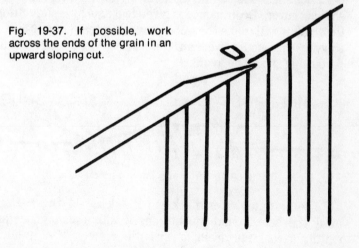

Fig. 19-37. If possible, work across the ends of the grain in an upward sloping cut.

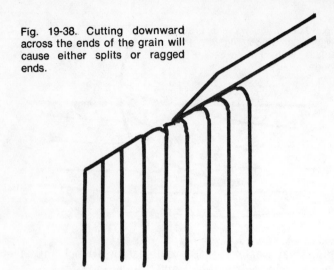

Fig. 19-38. Cutting downward across the ends of the grain will cause either splits or ragged ends.

than a blunt one, and slices can be made across the grain with a sharp gouge with confidence so long as the tool corners are kept above the surface.

An attraction of carving is the way it gives a three-dimensional look. If a piece of good carving on furniture is examined, it will often appear to be much deeper than it really is. The sense of depth is due to the way the carving was done. Nowhere on the carved part is there any flatness. When carving such a panel, none of the original surface should remain as it was before carving started, even if all that has been done has been some light cutting with a gouge having a shallow curve. Prominence is given to a part by undercutting; the shadow will make the wood above stand out (Fig. 19-39). Of course, this could weaken the carving, so excessive undercutting should be avoided.

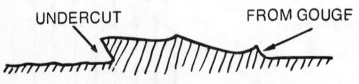

Fig. 19-39. Undercutting emphasizes raised area.

The first step after marking out a design is usually to cut away the background by outlining it with a deep gouge and cutting across the grain towards the outline (Fig. 19-40). If

240

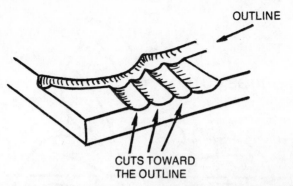

OUTLINE

CUTS TOWARD
THE OUTLINE

Fig. 19-40. Outline the background first. Then cut towards it across the grain.

there is no need for undercutting, the edge of the raised part is stronger with the curved edge left from a gouge.

With the background lowered, the remaining raised part is where most of the carving usually occurs. If the repair is part of a repetitive design, there will be guidance elsewhere on the furniture. Laying a straightedge across parts of equal depth will show you how deeply certain parts should be cut. Even if there is not an identical pattern elsewhere, the general arrangement of the design will show you how deeply to cut. Cut in broad sweeps, not in hesitant, light jabs.

If there are leaves or foliage to be cut, there is no need for machine-like duplication of each part. Nature did not make the originals all alike. A leaf has curves all over, some upwards and some downwards. Sweep your gouge around to get the general effect (Fig. 19-41) before cutting in veins and other details. A leaf or any other object can be made to look deeper if its surface is not level with the general plane of the wood. Instead, the high part may be undercut, and this part of the carving will stand out more than if left near flat.

Some early furniture was decorated by chip carving. The only tool used was a knife. In most repair work, chip carving will consist mostly of a series of triangles cut in patterns (Fig. 19-42).

In the basic triangle, lines from the center to the corners are cut with a knife (Fig. 19-43). Then slices are made towards the center from the outline with a knife or chisel (Fig. 19-44). Sometimes there are curved lines, but the multiplicity of patterns that may be found can usually be broken down into a large number of these triangles.

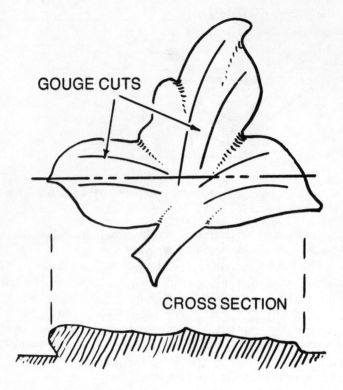

GOUGE CUTS

CROSS SECTION

Fig. 19-41. Preliminary cuts are made with a gouge.

The oldtime carver did all of the work with his gouges and chisels. If repaired work has to adjoin such carving, the new work should have a good tool finish. Sanding a carving alongside an unsanded part will usually make the repair look shabby. If the quality of tool work is not as good as was hoped, it is better to scrape a poor surface than to sand it.

A cabinet, or hook, scraper may be used, but to get into shaped and narrow parts a special scraper may have to be made. This is a piece of tool steel, of the type used in saw blades, and might be from a discarded hacksaw blade. The end is curved and sharpened like a chisel, including honing (Fig. 19-45). A burnisher (any hard steel) is rubbed over the edge to put a burr on it. This scraper is used so the burr does the cutting (Fig. 19-46).

Where the carved repair includes broad curves at an edge or other part accessible to large tools, it may be possible to use a plane or a Surform tool. The Surform tool may have flat or

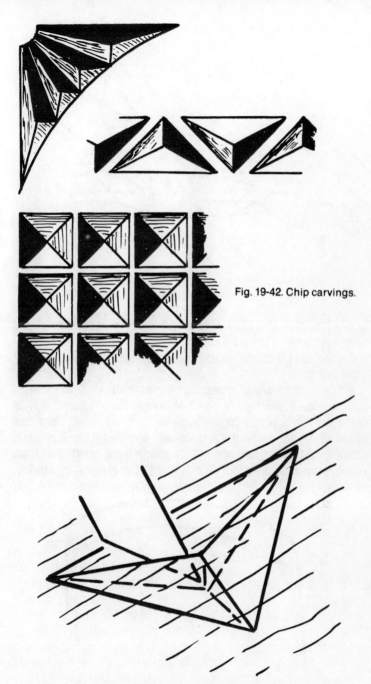

Fig. 19-42. Chip carvings.

Fig. 19-43. First cut from the center of the triangle to the corners.

Fig. 19-44. Most of the cutting is done with a chisel.

curved disposable blades and will quickly reduce to shape flowing curves. The surface may need further treatment by scraping or sanding, but the general shape can be obtained quickly.

The intricacies of most carving make it very difficult to get an even finish by sanding because of the inaccessibility of some parts. This may not matter if the wood is left bare, but staining or lacquering may result in different coloring on sanded and unsanded wood. Check adjoining wood. The final finish may match better if none of the new work is sanded.

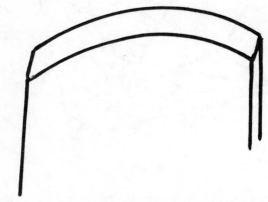

Fig. 19-45. The end of a cabinet scraper is sharpened like a chisel.

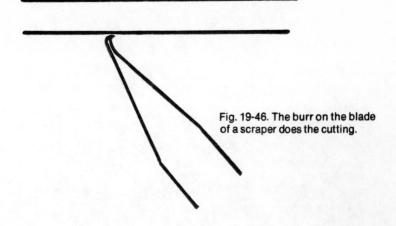

Fig. 19-46. The burr on the blade of a scraper does the cutting.

Scraping is not so likely to affect absorption of the stain or finish. In any case, only hand sanding is advisable. Any sort of power sanding is likely to lower high spots or cause flats where they are not wanted.

Upholstery and Seating

20

Seating furniture may have plain wood seats, which can be reasonably comfortable if shaped, but for prolonged sitting and the greatest comfort there has to be some softening of the surface. This may be minimal and restricted to the part actually taking the weight. Part of the wooden structure may be visible, or the whole thing may be completely upholstered, with no wood showing except a few inches along the legs.

UPHOLSTERY

There have been many changes in upholstery materials and methods. How a repair is to be made depends on whether there is a need to maintain a semblance of the original work. Early covering materials were derived from wool or cotton, with a few other cloths of natural materials. Leather was also used. Modern upholstery materials, which are often more durable, are usually either woven from man-made fibers or are plastics. Fortunately, many of the modern alternative materials look so much like earlier materials that it may be possible to substitute them without spoiling the effect of an old piece of furniture.

New furniture usually has cushioning that is very different from that of old furniture. If an old upholstered seat is dismantled, it may be found to have many layers of different materials. Canvas and muslin were used as well as the surface material. Softness was provided by a variety of fillings. Feathers and down gave a flexible and soft seat or back, but horsehair, coir fiber, and many other things found their way into upholstery. Some of the materials used were not hygienic, and even if a traditional finish is expected of the repair, it might be better to change to modern, cleaner materials for the inside.

Fig. 20-1. Some latex or polyester foam cushions have holes on one side.

Nearly all new furniture has latex or polyester foam interiors. These are provided as cushions of various thicknesses, usually with hollows underneath (Fig. 20-1) or inside (Fig. 20-2). These cushions may be already shaped with rounded edges. It is possible to fix tape to them with adhesive, so a square edge can be pulled to a curve. If there are hollows on one side, the square edge will form a good curve (Fig. 20-3). The more solid cellular foam will pull to a curve better if cut at an angle (Fig. 20-4). Where cutting an edge exposes hollows that might show through the covering or affect comfort, there is an edging strip to stick on (Fig. 20-5).

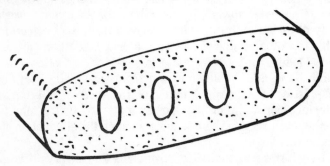

Fig. 20-2. Some foam cushions have holes on the inside.

Chair and stool seats with only nominal softening often have a liftout panel fitting in a recess. The covering material is stretched over the top and tacked underneath (Fig. 20-6). For

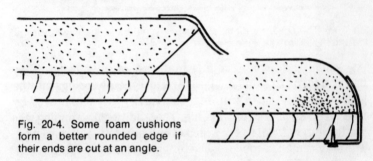

Fig. 20-3. The end of a foam cushion can be taped down to form a rounded edge.

neatness there may be a piece of plain cloth stretched over the underside with its edges turned under.

What goes between the covering and the panel depends on the design. An old seat may have a few layers of cloth or

Fig. 20-4. Some foam cushions form a better rounded edge if their ends are cut at an angle.

something similar that has flattened almost hard with age. This can be replaced with thin foam, if no more softening is required, or there can be a thicker pad of foam, with its edges curved, as already described.

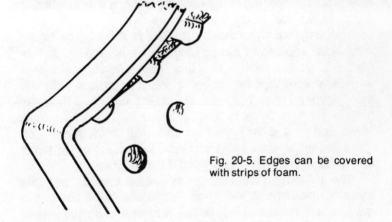

Fig. 20-5. Edges can be covered with strips of foam.

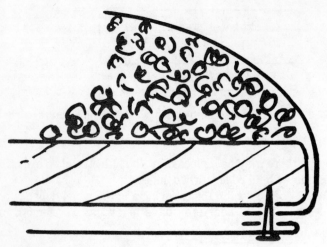

Fig. 20-6. The covering material on some furniture is stretched over the top and tacked on the underside.

Much traditional furniture made use of coil springs. They are also found in some modern furniture. Some springs may be supported on wooden framing, but usually they are braced by interlaced strapping or webbing. The traditional strapping was made from natural fiber, which eventually rotted or gave way. The only repair needed may be to replace this strapping.

If a chair of this type is turned over, it will usually be found to have a coil spring at each crossing of the webbing, with a few stitches made with string to prevent the spring slipping out of place. These stitches can be cut away so the old webbing can be removed. The springs should remain attached at their other ends. Note the spacing of the webbing and mark its location, if this is not obvious, on the wooden frame.

Webbing, which is usually canvas, is fixed to the frame with tacks. If a repair has to be made to the woodwork, it is advisable to use beech or other close-grained wood that provides a good grip for the tacks. When fixing new webbing, avoid driving tacks into old holes. At one end the webbing is tacked down, with some surplus extending. This surplus is folded and tacked over the first part (Fig. 20-7). A common arrangement is three tacks arranged in a triangle; the top is held down with three tacks arranged the other way.

The webbing should be given a good tension, and this means using some sort of lever. A tool can be bought, or one can be made (shown in Fig. 20-7). This has a round end to bear against the framing and a hand grip at the other end. There is a slot wider than the webbing and a peg to push through a loop of webbing. The tool is levered to get a tension, with the surplus webbing held by one hand, while the other hand uses a hammer to drive the three tacks. Sufficient surplus is then cut off and folded over the first tacks; three more are then driven as described before.

Although it is usual for the webbing in the two different directions to be woven over and under alternatively, this probably does not matter. What is more important is securing the springs in place. This is done with string and a large needle. There are special upholsterer's needles, but any needle with an eye that will take the string can be used. Use enough stitches to hold the spring. Knot the string securely, but do not make an unnecessary number of stitches; too many might weaken the webbing.

In some upholstery, the seating is suspended on a system of coils or other springs stretched across the frame. With foam cushioning above it, this dispenses with the perpendicular coil springs and makes a thinner total section. Repairs may be necessary when springs break or come away from their fastenings. Since the springs are likely to be on the cushion side of the framing, it will usually be necessary to lift the covering to get at the springs. If the covering is examined, it will usually be found that there are tacks or nails which can be pried away so the covering can be turned back to expose the foam, which will have to be removed to get at the springs.

There are several types of these springs, but failure may be due to ends becoming unhooked. Simple hand tension may not be enough to get a spring back into place. If a cord loop is attached, a lever can be used to stretch the spring into position

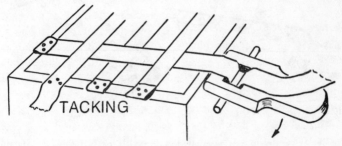

TACKING

Fig. 20-7. A tool for putting tension on webbing.

(Fig. 20-8). If springs have broken, not much can be done except replace them, which may mean a whole section if they are bonded together.

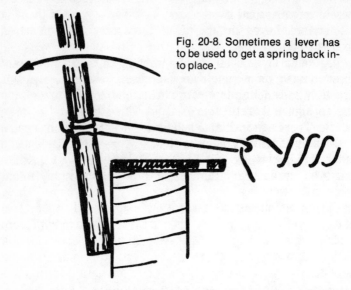

Fig. 20-8. Sometimes a lever has to be used to get a spring back into place.

Another method of support is the use of rubber strapping. This looks like webbing but is actually reinforced natural or synthetic rubber. This is used on the surface next to the cushioning, which may lift out so that servicing the strapping is simple. The strapping may be fixed at the ends just as ordinary webbing is. But there are other techniques used, including the use of a groove in the woodwork. A metal clip is squeezed onto the end of the strapping to provide a rigid end to press into the angled groove (Fig. 20-9). If new rubber

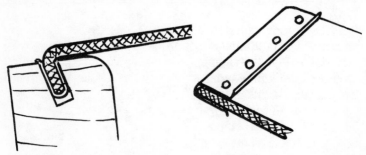

Fig. 20-9. Strapping can be easily fixed into a groove if it has a metal clip on its end.

strapping is to be fitted, new end clips should be used, although it may be possible to remove an old end carefully, cut off the stretched strapping, and fit and end clip again.

With the older cushionings, there was a risk that they would move around if nothing was done to restrict them. This movement might have been prevented by the use of compartments, but buttoning was commonly used. It prevented a large area of padding from ballooning instead of remaining in shape, and it did something to stop movement of the filling. Although foam cushioning is in a form that cannot move around, it is still common to find buttoning, partly for the sake of appearance.

There is usually a top and a bottom button, joined with stout thread or sting (Fig. 20-10). The top button has a loop at its back, while the bottom one can have two or four holes. Special buttons suitable for covering with chair material can be bought for use on the surface.

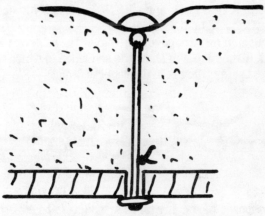

Fig. 20-10. Buttoning usually consists of top and bottom buttons.

There are long double-ended upholsterer's needles intended for buttoning work. The thread tension has to be adjusted to give the right appearance on the surface. The first experimental knot can be made with the cushion compressed (Fig. 20-11). If this is satisfactory when released, the knot can be tied and the thread can be worked around so the knot is hidden within the cushioning. In some upholstery there may be a peg instead of a button on the underside.

For the most durable repair, use a synthetic thread, so there will be no rot. The majority of synthetic threads are

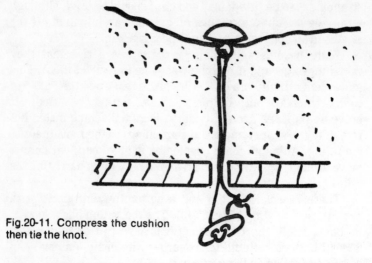

Fig.20-11. Compress the cushion then tie the knot.

more slippery than natural fiber ones, so make sure the knot cannot slip. A reef knot, one with the ends half-hitched before cutting off, should hold (Fig. 20-12).

If cushioning or covering have to be removed and replaced, inspection will show the sequence in which the work was done. Dismantling is in the reverse order.

Fig. 20-12. A reef knot.

On exposed parts, any tacks are likely to be covered with a tape, sometimes called gimp, which may be anything from a simple strip to a decorative piece with tassels. There are tack lifters with forked ends, but a thin screwdriver pushed under the head and twisted 90° usually lifts the head enough to allow the use of pincers (Fig. 20-13).

Modern furniture makes more use of adhesives. This means that it may be necessary to break away old material that has been glued on. This does not matter if it is to be replaced, but make sure you understand the function of the particular piece and how it will have to be cut and affixed.

Covering material has to be arranged so its main surface is evenly tensioned and any pattern is symmetrical. All other

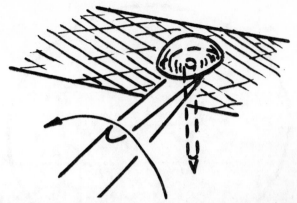

Fig. 20-13. Usually a thin screwdriver is all that's needed to lift upholstery tacks.

work on it is dependent on this. It is unwise to cut any exposed surface. Corners are dealt with by careful folding. If a curve has to be followed or there is some other shaping, it is often possible to avoid one large fold or crease by using a series of narrower tucks along an edge, each being controlled by a tack. This can be decorative. Do not try to trim the cloth to size in advance. Allow some excess around the edges. This gives you something to hold and pull while adjusting tension and fixing. Final trimming can be done with a sharp knife.

There are now adhesives for just about every material. If you can find the right adhesive, it is possible to put on a patch. It is difficult to make it inconspicuous, but if a hole has been made in an otherwise good covering, a patch may be preferable to an expensive, complete recover, at least for a short time. Any tear or cut (under the patch) more than 1/2 in. long should have a few threads sewn across it. This is to relieve the patch of tension. How the stitches are arranged depends on the damage. A few large zigzag stitches should be made on a straight cut; a coarse darn should be used on a more open hole. The patch will stay down better if its corners are rounded. Sharp corners are the first parts that will lift away. Cut the patch so it matches any pattern there may be. A circle or ellipse may be less apparent than any patch with straight lines (Fig. 20-14).

If the patch is a plastic imitation leather or other fairly thick substance, it can be sanded down on the underside to thin the edges (Fig. 20-15). Some material can be pared with a razor blade or knife.

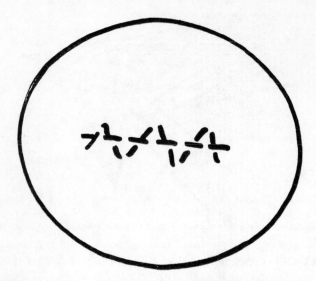

Fig. 20-14. Circular or elliptical patches are less noticeable than straight-line patches.

Follow the manufacturer's instructions for the adhesive used on the patch. Avoid getting adhesive around the repair: Pencil in the shape of the patch and carefully spread the adhesive within the outline. It is usually helpful on plastic surfaces to scrape the old surface with a knife just before spreading adhesive. This gets rid of dirt and grease on the surface and removes the oiliness present on the surface of some plastics.

RUSH SEATING

The alternative to a plain wooden seat or an upholstered one is a seat made of flexible material that provides its own cushioning. The country craftsmen in Europe and the pioneer settlers employed any material at hand. One result was the use of rushes in a configuration that has become known as a "rush pattern" (Fig. 20-16).

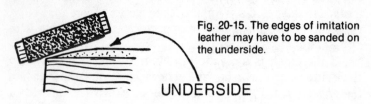

Fig. 20-15. The edges of imitation leather may have to be sanded on the underside.

UNDERSIDE

Fig. 20-16. A rush pattern.

Sedges and rushes grow in marshes and along river banks. There are several types, some of which are suitable for seating. But at one time locally available rushes were twisted and plaited so they could be used for baskets, mats, and other things, as well as chair seats. Probably the best type for seating grows in deep water and may reach 8 ft in length. This type is called the golden rush or bulrush. This is dried, and it is this stringy, dried rush that is bought for chair seating.

For use, rush has to be twisted into a kind of rope. Most rush has to be wetted as it is used. As a chair seat is built up, the rush is twisted in as needed. And having the damp rushes scattered around means it is not work to be done in a living room. Because of this problem there are several rush substitutes, which may have to be used anyway when rush is unavailable. These are long ropelike materials, so wetting and twisting as you progress is unnecessary. Consequently, the work is less messy.

The material nearest to rush in appearance is seagrass, which is rush colored. It is supplied in hanks as a two or three strand rope. Several thicknesses are available and the coarser type is most rushlike in the finished seat. This may be important when reseating old furniture, but the finer grades may make a more interesting seat for modern furniture. Rushes should never be colored; they do not take dye well. Seagrass may be bought colored, which may suit the furniture color scheme, but would be inappropriate if you were trying to simulate rush.

Any type of rope can be worked into a rush pattern. Dacron or other synthetic rope could be worked into the pattern to make an interesting seat on modern furniture. Natural fiber rope, with its more hairy appearance, gives a finish between seagrass and the synthetic rope.

Usually the fault that develops in an old rush seat is sagging, which develops into breaking of the rushes and a hole at the center. Rushes and seagrass are natural materials which will rot as they get old, but they have a long life if kept in a dry atmosphere. There is no satisfactory way of patching these materials, so when they wear out they should be cut away and burned.

There may be a few nails or tacks in the rails to remove. It is interesting to see how the rails of an old chair will show the

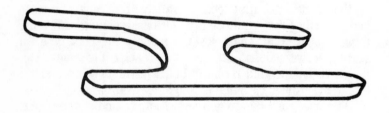

Fig. 20-17. A wooden shuttle.

marks of shaping with a draw knife. More recent furniture will have machined wood or be hand planed. In any case this is an opportunity to sand the wood and reglue weak joints, as well as attend to the finish of the chair in general before reseating.

Fig. 20-18. A wooden needle.

It is helpful to make a few wooden shuttles, on which to wind the seagrass or rope (Fig. 20-17). For the last part of the seating process it is useful, although not absolutely essential, to have a wooden needle (Fig. 20-18). A piece of wood that can be used edgewise to push the material along a rail or to open a hole is another tool with occasional uses (Fig. 20-19). A hammer, pincers, knife, and scissors are the only other tools needed.

Fig. 20-19. A piece of wood with a point can be used to force the line into crevices or along rails.

The first step in creating the rush pattern on a chair frame is to nail the knotted end of the line (of rush, rope, or similar material) to a rail (Fig. 20-20). The line is then taken over a rail near a leg, under it, and up through the center of the frame

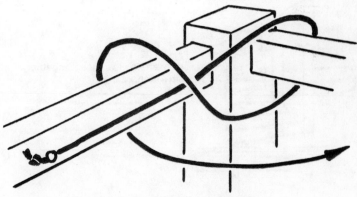

Fig. 20-20. Starting a rush pattern.

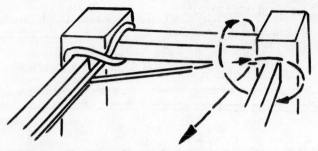

Fig. 20-21. The wrapping is repeated at the other three corners.

to the other rail. From this corner, take the line to the next corner, where the process is repeated (Fig. 20-21). This is all that has to be learned. A repetition of this action completes a seat. One trade secret is exposed.

> A good tension should be kept on the line at all times. This means holding the line against the wood whenever it crosses, until the next turns have been made. It is helpful it two people can position themselves at opposite sides so one can maintain tension while the other puts on the next turns.

As the work progresses it will be seen that the pattern builds up from the corners, and the lengths of line between the corners disappears inside. The pattern on the underside will be the same as that on the top. After a few times around the seat, the squareness of the corner patterns should be checked. The pattern should be close knit, with no bare wood showing between. It should be square to the corner. In a rectangular

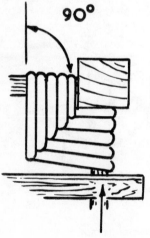

Fig. 20-22. Keep the angles true by pushing the lines together with a straightedge.

stool, a straightedge can be tried across. But any discrepancies are likely to be obvious to the eye without testing, and the line wrapped around the rails should be pushed along with the edge of a piece of wood to keep the angles true (Fig. 20-22). Check for squareness after every two or three rounds.

Rushes have to be twisted in as needed, but stagger the lengths of the separate strands so joints come at different places along the line. With seagrass or rope, connecting knots are made between corners so the knot will be hidden (Fig. 20-23). If knots are needed in rushes, put them in the same place.

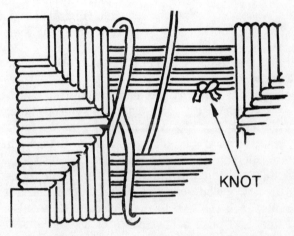

Fig. 20-23. Connecting knots should be concealed.

With a rectangular stool, a point will be reached where no more turns can be put on the short sides. Force in as many as you can by squeezing strands along the rails. If this is not done, there is a tendency for gaps to show after some use. Continue working across the other way by an over and under figure-eight action (as in Fig. 20-23).

Another problem comes with a chair that is wider at the front than the back. If turns of line are continued in the ordinary way, the back would fill before the front. To correct this, occasional early turns are made twice around each of the front legs (Fig. 20-24). It is better to do this after every two or three complete rounds in the early stages than to wait until the bulk of the seat has been done before bringing in these double turns. Use enough of these occasional twice-round turns at the

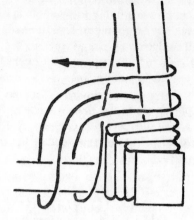

Fig. 20-24. Double turns should be taken around the front legs to keep the pattern square.

front until the remaining gap at the front is about the same as that at the back rail.

Making rush patterns gets harder toward the end of the process. You must use a pointed stick to force open the center to pass more line. Use a wooden needle for the last few passes. Get as many turns around the rails as they will take. The edge of a steel rule can be used to push the line along and get in another turn. Using the maximum number of turns helps reduce the risk of a hole showing at the center of the pattern.

Finally, tack the line to the underside of a rail, cut off excess line, and push a few inches of it into the seat from below. The finished seat will be quite taut and may not seem very comfortable at first, but as the material settles down and the slight natural stretch takes place, there will be sufficient flexibility for comfort.

As the pattern is worked, the hollow interior between top and bottom will become obvious. With manufactured seagrass or rope, there is no need to do anything about this space. With some types of rush it may be advisable to fill the interior. When the rush pattern has been half done and the spaces are very apparent, waste rush can be pushed in, followed by more as the pattern progresses. This padding gives body to the seat and prevents the rushes from loosening excessively under pressure.

CHAIR CANING

Cane-seated chairs were in use in France and were introduced to England during the reign of Charles I, but they did not become popular until Charles II came to the throne. They have retained their popularity until the present day. The method of caning has changed little in this time, and the seats of much modern and antique furniture will be found to have been worked in the same way (Fig. 20-25). Similar caning may be found on bedsteads and the sides of antique tables.

Several methods of weaving cane have been used, including a very close weave that was taken over the sides of the chair to give a covering almost like upholstery. Attempting to repeat this sort of covering is not advised. More common is an open pattern that makes use of holes drilled in the framework. There have been other methods devised that reduced some of the tedium of threading through holes, and it is possible to buy woven cane, already arranged as a patterned sheet, to fix as a panel.

Most chair cane grows in hot swampy places, and may be imported from Java and Sarawak. It trails and may grow to hundreds of feet in length. It has hooked thorns which grip other vegetation. It is harvested into quite long pieces, which are then split and prepared for use. There are plastic substitutes that can be used, but obviously these would be inappropriate on a period piece of furniture.

Interweaving cane to make a seat can be done in many ways, and even in the more common patterns there are minor variations. If a damaged cane seat has to be stripped, or the repair is to a chair or stool that forms part of a set, detail work should be examined and noted before and old cane is removed. Old cane may be cut away and discarded. All holes in the framework should be cleaned out. At this stage the woodwork will almost certainly benefit from cleaning and probably repolishing.

Chair cane is supplied in bundles. Width may be indicated by numbers. Pieces of the old cane may be used as patterns when buying new cane. As supplied, the cane may be rather hard and brittle, but it can be made supple by soaking in cold water for a few minutes. It should be used damp, but not soaking wet. Plastic cane does not require soaking. The natural cane has to be accepted in whatever lengths it comes, but since 8 ft or so is about as much as can conveniently be worked at one time, this does not matter. Plastic cane may be supplied in a continuous length.

Fig. 20-25. A cane chair.

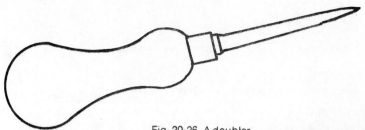

Fig. 20-26. A doubler.

Essential tools are few. A good knife is used, and there have to be pegs. A pointed awl, called a doubler, can be used (Fig. 20-26). A similar tool with a long shaft and flat end is useful for cleaning holes (Fig. 20-27). Instead of the doubler, a piece of waste wood pointed with a chisel or knife can be used. Pointed pieces of wood can also be used for temporary or permanent pegging. For permanent pegging, the pointed end is pushed in and snapped off, then a new point is cut for the next time. A larger wood or steel spike can be used for opening spaces between canes. A bodkin, or spike, with a hole in its end (Fig. 20-28) is used to pull strands through close weaving. A longer weaver (Fig. 20-29) performs a similar function across a seat.

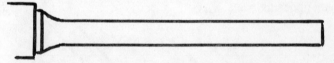

Fig. 20-27. A flat-ended tool is used to clean holes.

The holes in the chair frame need to be without obstruction. They should be bigger than the size of the cane. Cane makes a pattern in a single thickness. It is threaded down through one hole, underneath, and up the next hole (Fig.

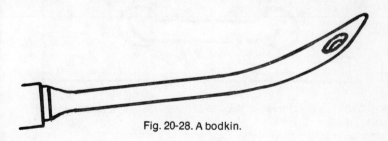

Fig. 20-28. A bodkin.

265

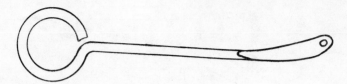

Fig. 20-29. A long weaving tool.

20-30). Avoid twisting the cane and keep the glossy side uppermost all the time on the exposed parts.

It is possible to start a new length of cane by pegging old and new ends in holes, but it is safer to knot. The end of the old piece goes up through a hole, making a loop underneath. The new end goes down through this hole and is half-hitched around the loop (Fig. 20-31). The knot is pulled tight and work is continued with the new piece. Waste ends can be trimmed later.

Most cane patterns used have strands directly across the top at right angles to each other with more strands woven diagonally. Variations come in the number of strands and how the overlaps are arranged. There are two basic patterns: "single-setting," with only one strand between opposing holes in the first weaving, and "double-setting," with two strands between opposing holes.

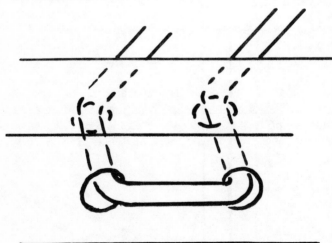

Fig. 20-30. Cane is threaded through one hole then through an adjacent hole.

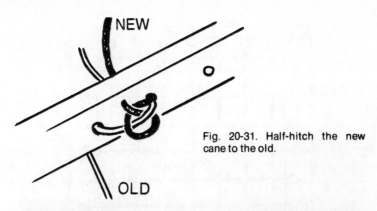

Fig. 20-31. Half-hitch the new cane to the old.

NEW

OLD

Double-setting, of course, is a little harder to do than single-setting. Use a single strand. Thread it through a hole near a corner with about 3 in. sticking out below and secure it with a peg. Pull the strand across the frame to the opposite hole; thread it down this hole and up the next. Repeat the process. But do not thread through the corner holes. Put on a good tension each time and use a temporary peg to hold the tension at each hole while the cane is being worked to the next stage. This process puts strands of cane across one way (Fig. 20-32). Do the same in the other direction, with the strands on

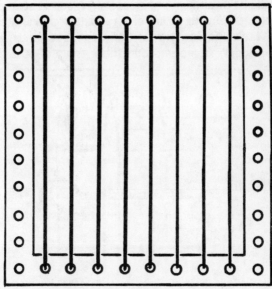

Fig. 20-32. The first step in double-setting.

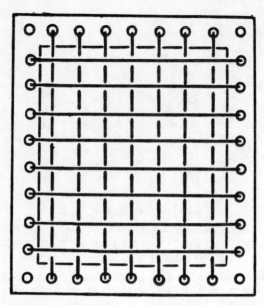

Fig. 20-33. The second group of strands are threaded perpendicular to the first.

top of the first (Fig. 20-33). Now thread strands in the opposite direction, using the same holes as were used initially. But this time, pull the strands *over* the second group of strands (Fig. 20-34). Next, a fourth group of strands are pulled across the frame in the same direction as the very first strands, weaving over and under the second and third group of strands (Fig.

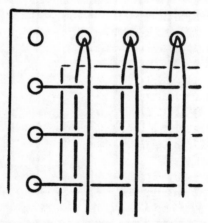

Fig. 20-34. The third group of strands are threaded over the second. The second and third groups are parallel to each other.

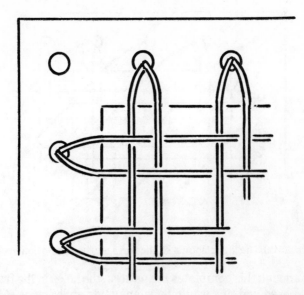

Fig. 20-35. Weave the fourth group of strands over and under the second and third.

20-35). This can be done by hand, but it is quicker to use a bodkin.

For a single-setting pattern, only one strand of stouter cane is used instead of the pairs of strands each way. From this point onwards weaving is very similar. In both methods, tension should be maintained on the strands by pegs as the work progresses.

In the double-setting method, push the crossing patterns close together so there is no doubt which are the spaces to be used for diagonal weaving. Pairs of strands in double-setting are treated as single strands when doing diagonal weaves.

To weave diagonally on a double-setting pattern, start at a corner hole and go across to the opposite corner, over and under all the way (Fig. 20-36). Do this again between the same holes, but start under if the previous tucking started over, or vice versa. Do this between the other holes, paralleling the first diagonal weave.

Weave the other opposing diagonals in the same way, starting with two strands corner to corner and continuing until all holes are linked (Fig. 20-37). The pattern will get very tight and a bodkin will be needed near the corner, if not also in the body of the seat.

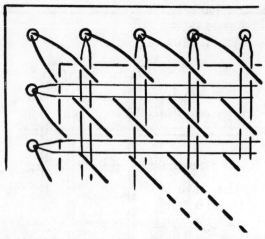

Fig. 20-36. The first diagonal strands on a double-setting pattern.

Although this completes the pattern, the holes in the frame are exposed and this would have an untidy appearance if left. The final step is covering the holes with a strand of cane (called beading cane), which may be wider than that used for weaving the pattern. It is held in place by thinner cane through the holes. The beading cane is in a single length along one side, then another piece is used on the next side. It is not bent around a corner.

First, point the end of the beading cane and push this end down a corner hole. Bend it and lay it over the holes along one side. Bring the thin cane up a hole, over the beading, and down the same hole to go underneath to the next hole, where the

Fig. 20-37. After the diagonal strands are woven in, the pattern looks like this.

action is repeated (Fig. 20-38). Do this all the way along the side, with a good tension. Then point the end of the beading cane and thrust it down the next corner hole. Repeat on the other sides.

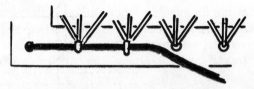

Fig.20-38. Starting the beading cane.

If any ends have to be secured, pegs can be used and concealed by the beading. Ends of diagonals may be secured by twisting around any convenient loops underneath. Stray ends should be cut off flush.

Complications come when seats are not square or true rectangles. It is usual to make the woven pattern squared, rather than trying to conform to the frame shape. Traditional chairs are often wider at the front than the back. The original arrangement will almost certainly have allowed for a square pattern. Start by caning between holes at back and front. Work outwards. When all the rear holes, except the corners, have been used up, keep the canes parallel, but go to the side holes (Fig. 20-39).

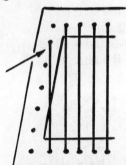

Fig. 20-39. Threading cane strands between side holes.

Covering a round seat with cane is similar to covering a square seat. But holes around the curved perimeter have to be taken up where they are convenient to make the pattern. This means not every hole is used every time, but tucking through holes is arranged as needed to keep pattern lines parallel.

With a circular or elliptical seat, count the holes and divide by four so as to obtain four points which can be regarded as centers of four sides of the pattern. Work from the center outwards and keep the canes parallel. Farther around the curve it may be necessary to miss some holes to retain parallel lines.

Arrange the diagonals so they will cross the first strands at 45°. With a circular seat this means starting at the holes halfway between those used to start the setting canes, but with any other sort of curve, positions will have to be judged that will give the correct angles.

The foregoing instructions cover what is probably the best known pattern, but if existing seats are examined, many variations can be seen. The seat may have had the diagonals put on first and the parallel canes put on singly or in pairs in a variety of patterns through them. Different sizes of cane may be mixed to give a different appearance. In all cases the basic technique and tool work is the same as described, but the different patterns have to be followed.

Section 3
Refinishing Old Furniture

Planning Refinishing

21

Do-it-yourselfers should use a certain amount of caution before starting on the restoration of furniture. Planning is essential. This is important with modern furniture as well as antique furniture. But with antique furniture, a mistake in refinishing could mean disaster. The more valuable the piece, the more important it is to get an expert opinion.

Older furniture is classified according to its period or according to who designed or made it (see Table 12-1). Genuine examples from earliest days are unlikely to come the way of an amateur refinisher. There are many reproductions around, and there are a great many later examples of antique furniture around that may require attention.

Until about two hundred years ago the design and quality of British and American furniture lagged behind that of some European countries, particularly the Netherlands. Most items surviving from those days, on both sides of the Atlantic, are chests. Oak was by far the most used wood. During the Cromwellian period the manufacture of fine furniture was discouraged. After that, cabinetmaking began to make progress. There was an upsurge in the use of walnut and imported woods that allowed the making of more delicate furniture with designs inappropriate to oak.

This continued with increasing refinement into the Queen Anne period. During the reigns of the Georges there was a great upsurge in the quality and design of British furniture, which found its way into the American colonies.

Table 21-1. Antique Dates, Periods, and Styles

Tudor period	Henry VIII	1509 to 1547	
	Edward VI	1547 to 1553	
	Mary	1553 to 1558	
Elizabethan period	Elizabeth	1558 to 1603	
Jacobean period	James I	1603 to 1623	
	Charles I	1625 to 1649	
Cromwellian period	Cromwell	1649 to 1660	
Carolean period	Charles II	1660 to 1685	
	James II	1685 to 1688	
Queen Anne period	William and Mary	1689 to 1702	
	Queen Anne	1702 to 1714	
	George I	1714 to 1724	
Georgian period	George II	1724 to 1760	
	George III	1760 to 1820	
	George IV	1820 to 1830	
Victorian period	William IV	1830 to 1837	
	Queen Victoria	1837 to 1901	
Names given to styles:			
Chippendale I	1720 to 1779	Production from about 1750.	
Chippendale II			
Chippendale III	1779 to 1805	Very little furniture output.	
Brothers Adam	1728 to 1792	Designers of furniture made by others.	
Hepplewhite	1760 to 1800	Firm carried on after death of Hepplewhite in 1786.	
Sheraton	1751 to 1806	Designer, but some furniture made by him.	
English Empire	1802 to 1840	Often copies of French pieces: in vogue until Victorian period.	

This was the time of the great furniture designers and makers. All of the great designers and makers put their designs into books, and these pattern books were used by other craftsmen besides those employed by the famous-named cabinetmakers. At their peak, the Chippendales employed 20 to 30 cabinetmakers. But the large amount of Chippendale furniture about could only have been produced by the efforts of many other craftsmen as well.

Of course many colonists brought furniture from England and other countries, so many original pieces from these days are in existence. However, it was not long before American craftsmen were using the pattern books of Chippendale, Hepplewhite, and Sheraton as guides for making furniture with local woods. This applies to furniture of modest homes as well as pieces appropriate only to large houses.

An example is the Windsor chair. It is said that George I, when hunting near Windsor, England, went into a farmhouse for a rest and liked his chair so much he had some made for use in Windsor Castle. By 1725 the design had reached America and was being made here. The English Windsor chair is made of beech, elm, and yew. It is still being made. American Windsor chairs had pine seats, local hardwood legs and bent parts. Before long the Windsor chair from Massachusetts had developed distinct differences from that of Virginia and other states.

By the end of the 18th century, furniture of a high standard was being made in America. Most pieces made before that are probably imported.

Of course, not all colonists were from England, and immigrants from elsewhere brought furniture or ideas from their own countries. So American furniture of a century or more ago had characteristics derived from this mixed background. The expert may be able to recognize these influences of what was becoming a distinctive American style.

This is not a book on antique furniture, but the foregoing paragraphs should warn the refinisher against rushing into working on a piece of furniture without finding out more about it.

Some idea of the history and age of a piece of furniture will provide a guide to its construction and the methods and materials to be used in preparing and refinishing it.

Any furniture made before World War II was almost certainly built with animal glue or fish glue, which have very little resistance to moisture. Even casein glue soon breaks down in damp conditions. This means that too much water should not be used when cleaning this furniture. Do not soak the furniture. Water can be applied with a cloth or brush and removed before it has a chance to soak into joints and weaken them. This also applies to any plywood of that age. If water soaks in, the glue will part and the veneers will pucker. If hosing down of any furniture is necessary to remove a violent chemical used in stripping or another process, the job should be done quickly. Doing this outside on a hot day, so moisture soon evaporates, is a good plan.

If contact cement has been used on modern veneers or for fixing Formica tops, be careful with lacquer thinners because they will dissolve this cement.

The oldest furniture will almost certainly have an oil or wax finish. Some old furniture, particularly Victorian, may be French polished. But after World War I, sprayed lacquer came in. This is now the most common finish. The approximate age of a piece of furniture tells you what finish to expect. This is important if you want to touch up, or have to finish a new part to match old parts. It is also important if you want to strip the finish and start again. Solvents differ in their effects. Alcohol which softens French polish may have little effect on oil.

With an opaque finish, brush marks will indicate paint rather than lacquer, which is usually sprayed. The constitution of paint has changed over the years. The natural oils, resins, and other ingredients usual up to the 1950s have given way to very different things. The solvents for old paint may have little effect on modern paints. The solvents needed for lacquer may be different again.

Clear brushed finishes are likely to be shellac or varnish. Even when a brushed finish has been there a long time and repeatedly polished, it is usually possible to look across the surface towards a light and distinguish brush marks. Spraying has a different appearance.

Shellac and varnish are very different things. Don't assume that you can always treat them alike. And although modern and traditional varnish may look alike on the wood, their chemical constitutions are very different.

If the old furniture being examined is dirty and thick with polish, and you are unable to identify the finish through it, a part of the surface may be cleaned with domestic detergent and water. Another mixture that will remove dirt and old polishing wax without much risk to the original finish is a mixture of denatured alcohol, vinegar, and kerosene in equal proportions. This will soften and remove most dirt, grease, and stain.

Assessing the surface to be refinished is largely a matter of collecting evidence and weighing it. After a little experience most people are able to distinguish one existing finish from another. The age of the piece will show what original finish was probably applied. But remember, that is not necessarily the one on the wood now.

Refinishing seldom means stripping away the original finish and replacing if with a better one. The original finish may have been removed and replaced years ago. Refinishing usually entails stripping away the existing finishing and applying one that resembles the original.

An antique will have acquired a patina of age. There is no instant finish that will reproduce this if it is stripped off. It would probably be better to keep as much of that existing finish as possible and concentrate on repairing and touching up where necessary.

If the finish has to come off, there are two principal ways of doing this: mechanically and chemically. Chemical stripping is probably the only method for a large or intricate piece of furniture where there is no doubt that the only way to make a good job of it is to work up from the bare wood. Mechanical stripping is done by scraping and sanding. This is usually more laborious, but if it be possible to revive the appearance without completely getting down to completely bare wood, this method may mean less total work in finally reaching the desired finish. Chemical stripping is messy, but effective. If your only work place is unsuitable for this, you may have to settle for mechanical stripping.

It is sometimes possible to refinish only part of the furniture. You need to be certain of the previous finish so you can use the same type again. The difficulty is in matching exactly. Even when you have the same materials, the new ones may not be able to duplicate the look of an aged finish. It is never advisable to join new and old finishes along a surface. Even if there has been new wood spliced on, it is better to clean off the old part down to bare wood. If the new finish goes up to the angle of a joint, a slight difference in appearance will usually be less obvious than if an attempt is made to blend new and old finishes along a rail or arm.

Minor Repairs to a Surface

22

Minor surface repairs sometimes must precede a refinishing damaged surfaces, and these techniques can mean the difference between a complete restoration and a discarded piece of furniture. Sometimes it's even possible to avoid refinishing altogether: a few repairs to an old finish can bring it back to life.

CLEANING: THE FIRST STEP

Dirt is not to be regarded as essential to antique furniture, as some people assume. It is merely a sign of neglect and ought to be removed. It may be difficult to identify the finish through layers of dirty polish. So the first step in doing minor repairs is to clean the surface to reach the finish.

Any household detergent may be tried, but use it with cold or lukewarm water—never hot water. Remove surplus detergent with clean water, otherwise it may affect finishing materials that follow. The surface must be really dry before anything else is applied. Nearly all finishing materials are based on oil of some sort, and oil does not mix with water, so the application of oil-base finishes over a damp base will result in poor adhesion and a surface that may blister or crack and come away.

Besides detergent, you can use a mixture of equal parts of denatured alcohol, vinegar, and kerosene. Vinegar and water may also work. Kerosene or alcohol may be added to soap and water. A warm mixture of water, turpentine, and linseed oil (in the proportions of 1 tablespoon of turpentine, 3 tablespoons of oil, and 1 quart of water) can be used too. Any of these mixtures has the capacity to get through dirt, dissolve wax, and loosen other things that are marring the surface without much risk of damaging the applied finish beneath. More powerful solvents and cleaners might dissolve or soften the finish as well as remove what has accumulated above it.

If the dirt resists all these mixtures, then you may need to introduce friction. If the dirt or other foreign material is only on the surface, you can use steel wool, but use this with an oil or one of the cleaning mixtures. Thin machine oil is suitable. Pumice powder on a cloth moistened with oil can be used instead of steel wool. In any case, wipe off frequently and inspect progress so you do not go too far.

To get at dirt in carvings, the recesses of moldings or other intricate parts, use a brush such as an old tooth or shaving brush to apply the cleaner. Something with stiffer bristles, such as a nairl brush, may be needed for stubborn dirt.

WHITE RINGS AND SPOTS

Hot or wet beverage containers stood on a surface may cause rings which dry out as white marks. If the marks are not very bad or deep they many disappear if one of the modern furniture polishes containing a cleaner is used. If a polish is not effective, it must be removed before trying another treatment.

Metal polish is effective on some marks. Use liquid metal polish and rub it over the surface gently. Cold cigarette ashes, dry or with a little water, rubbed over the marks may be effective. With both methods, follow with wax polishing.

Flicking a cloth containing ammonia over the mark may work, particularly on lacquer. Do not rub with the cloth. It is the fumes that do the work. On some finishes it may help to lightly wipe over with a cloth soaked in alcohol. If it is a brushed shellac or French polished surface, the use of alcohol may cause some of the existing finish to flow over the damage to hide it. On mahogany, wiping with linseed oil followed by rubbing with half a Brazil nut may hide the blemish.

BURNS

Hot liquids cause white rings, but flames or cigarettes may actually burn the finish and go through it to char the wood below. Of course, charred wood has completely lost its characteristics and there is no way to revive it. Another piece of wood may have to be inlaid, or the surface may have to be stripped and levelled. If the burn is only in the finish or isn't too deep, it may be possible to deal with it as a local minor repair.

Scrape out the charred dust with a curved knife blade. Wetting the hollow with paint thinner will show up any burned dust remaining. Remove all the dust to expose sound wood or finish.

There are several ways of filling the hollow. Artist's oil paints can be used, mixed to match the surrounding wood. Do not dilute. Smudge it into the hollow a little at a time. Wipe away surplus and leave to harden. Spray it with lacquer or brush on another clear finish. Sand or use fine steel wool and apply more finish. Sight across the surface to see that it is level. When the repair has been levelled to your satisfaction, go over the whole surface with wax or other furniture polish.

There are other ways of filling the hollow. Beeswax may be colored and pressed in while warm.

Colored shellac sticks may be used too. Melt the appropriate color, press it in the hollow, level it, then polish. Wax crayons also have possibilities. They can be melted in a spoon over a flame and mixed to get the right color. If a stove is used, there is less risk of soot getting into the wax. This wax is not as hard as wood, so after levelling, it should be protected with shellac, varnish, or lacquer.

SCRATCHES

Minor scratches can be dealt with by regular polishing. Most furniture polishes will clean out dirt from little scratches, and they have enough body to fill the scratches and make them less apparent.

Dirt trapped in a larger scratch may look even darker if polished over, so the dirt should be removed with one of the cleaning mixtures or even by poking it out with a pointed tool.

Shallow scratches can sometimes have their edges run together without introducing any new material. But this depends on the finish. If a shellac finish is moistened with alcohol along the scratch and this is left for some time—say two days—the softened edges may close. Rub over the surface with a cloth containing fine pumice and oil. When this is polished, the scratch should be gone. A minor scratch on a varnished surface can sometimes be closed up with turpentine. Thinners may work on lacquer, but if the equipment is available, a respray is the best coverup.

Plastic Wood can be used in very large scratches. It is unsuitable for fine cracks. Its color should match the surrounding finish, but if this cannot be arranged, it is possible to stain it. Plastic Wood will take the same finish as the surrounding wood.

Shellac sticks can be melted into large recesses of all kinds. These colored sticks are used like sealing wax with a hot knife blade. A shellac stick may be described as a beaumontage, although this is the name of a traditional mixture used for filling holes. One version of the mixture consists of equal parts of beeswax and resin melted together. This may be done with the can directly on a stove. But since the materials are combustible, an open flame should be avoided. Using an outer container of water removes the risk of overheating. When the wax and resin are liquid, add a small quantity of shellac and some coloring matter to suit the repair. This mixture is pressed into the damage and levelled.

BLACK RINGS AND SPOTS

Black spots are not as easy to remove as white spots. The black is due to long wetting, so the black tint has to be bleached out. Domestic bleach may do it, or a concentrated solution of oxalic acid can be brushed on. This solution works almost instantaneously, so be ready to wipe it off with a damp cloth. A concentrated solution can be made with about 3 tablespoons of oxalic acid crystals and a cup of hot water. Pour the crystals in the hot water while stirring. Stir until all the crystals are dissolved.

WARNING

Oxalic acid is very poisonous so take care in its use, storage, and disposal.

This bleaching is unlikely to have much effect on the existing finish, so after the black mark has been dealt with, a polish should be all that is needed. Ink or other dark liquids that have penetrated the finish may be bleached in the same way.

HAZE

After a long time the atmosphere will affect most finishes. There may be a greyish or whitish haze to the finish, sometimes only apparent when viewed from particular angles. This effect is only on the thinnest surface layer of the finish.

To get rid of this effect, the outer film of the finish has to be removed. Clean off dirt and polish to completely expose the finish. Go over the surface with the finest steel wool, working with the grain as much as possible. The dulling effect of this will obscure the haze. To check if you have rubbed far enough, moisten the surface with turpentine. If the haze can still be seen, rub more but do not wear the finish away unnecessarily. Wipe the dust away, preferably with a tack rag. Go over the surface with wax or liquid furniture polish.

CRACKED FINISH

An old finish may become covered with a mass of small cracks. This may be due to expansion and contraction of the wood underneath or it may be due to age. It does not happen with wax or oil finishes, which remain sufficiently elastic, but some lacquer and shellac finishes may eventually become hard and brittle so any movement of the base will crack them. It may be necessary to strip them and start again, but there are ways of running the cracks together again.

If it is a lacquer surface, go over it with lacquer thinner. Work in a ventilated but dry and warm place. Any humidity may cause clouding of the finish. Work quickly all over the surface. The whole surface should become a paintlike consistency and can be lightly brushed smooth. Let this dry completely. Then go over it with steel wool and finish with a furniture polish.

Shellac surfaces are dealt with in the same way lacquer surfaces are, except alcohol diluted with about 10% lacquer thinner is used.

Furniture Stripping

23

If the finish on a piece of furniture is in such a state that it is not worthwhile attempting to revive it, the only hope for the furniture, if it is structurally sound, is to strip the finish and start again from the bare wood. This can be a very satisfying activity and may result in a wreck being brought back into use. Something that was properly designed and constructed may justify a considerable amount of work in removing the old finish and applying a new one. There could be a surprising increase in value, possibly from negligible or no value to something that commands the price of an antique.

The early stages may be very messy, and most people would not regard the work as pleasant. The chemicals needed to remove some finishes have to be handled carefully because they can be dangerous, both to the user and to things in the vicinity. Something that will dissolve a finish may also ruin clothing, eat into upholstery, and do other damage if allowed to go where it should not. If chemical strippers are used they should be applied outdoors in a place where plenty of water can be used.

The first thing to do with an article that is to be stripped is to clean it. Although chemical strippers will often attack a finish rapidly, they may not attack the dirt on top of it. Dirt should be removed with water and detergent, which will not affect any wax on the surface. Wiping with a cloth soaked in turpentine should remove wax. If the surface still seems dirty after this treatment, use detergent and water again. Much old furniture was joined with glues that are not waterproof, so use a minimum amount of water and wipe it off after cleaning each part. Do not soak the furniture when washing it.

You need to know what the existing finish is. Paint is fairly obvious, but there may be doubt about a clear finish. Even an opaque finish that looks like paint may be lacquer. Use an inconspicuous part for testing. Rub with turpentine. If the surface softens and begins to dissolve, it is paint or varnish. Try using alcohol. If the surface is shellac it will soon soften. If it is a lacquer finish, only lacquer thinner will have any effect on it.

If the furniture has knobs, hinges, handles, or other metal or plastic parts that can be removed, take them off. If the furniture will come apart in any way, separate all you can and deal with parts individually. Drawers should come out; taking off hinges may release doors and allow shelves to be withdrawn. Some tables have tops made up of moving leaves that can be released. Even some tables with apparently fixed tops have screws below that will allow the top to come off.

DRY STRIPPING

Although most stripping is done with liquids and pastes, it is sometimes possible to get down to the bare wood by mechanical means. This is called dry stripping. If the piece of furniture was discarded by someone and left outside, it is likely that much of the finish has peeled away. Mechanical methods may then remove what is left and, at the same time, do something to improve the surface in readiness for the new finish.

Usually, mechanical stripping is more appropriate to small items. The mess associated with liquids and pastes may not be justified then, but for large items with the finish still firmly attached, they would be more efficient and less trouble.

Stripping can be done with a hand scraper, either the cabinet type or the hook type that can be pulled (Fig. 23-1). The edge of a piece of broken glass will also make an effective scraper. Use enough pressure to get the cutting edge of the scraper through most of the finish. Experiment with the angle that gets the best cut. Holding the scraper so it travels with a slicing action may be more effective than a straight pull or push.

Hand sanding is possible but can be rather slow. Use a coarse abrasive paper at first. Many finishes produce a dust

Fig. 23-1. A hook type scraper.

that quickly clogs fine paper. Use the paper wrapped around a block and work with the grain in case any grit scratches right through to the wood. The marks would show if made across the grain. When bare wood is within sight, change to a finer abrasive.

A belt or orbital sander will be quicker than hand sanding. Start with a coarse grit, say No. 80, because of the risk of clogging, and change to a finer grade as bare wood is reached.

Sanding and scraping may become tedious and unsatisfactory on intricate moldings and other places where there is not much flat or broadly curved areas. Even on small work it is then probably wiser to use a chemical stripper.

WET STRIPPING

There are a great many chemical strippers. Some are simple solvents, but those needed for paint and varnish are chemical mixtures. They can be obtained in prepared form, and for occasional use this is the best way of getting them. If much stripping is to be done, the trouble of mixing your own stripper may be justified. The various constituents bought in bulk should be cheaper, but some of them need careful handling and storage.

Certain precautions should be taken when using chemical strippers. It is usually best to work outdoors. If you do work in an enclosed place, see that there is adequate ventilation so any fumes given off are dispersed rapidly. Otherwise, some of them may harm your eyes, throat, or skin. Ventilation is also important because many of the fumes are combustible: they might ignite spontaneously if allowed to concentrate. Obviously, you should not smoke or have an open flame anywhere near the work area.

Old clothes and a rubber apron are advisable. Have your arms covered and wear stout rubber gloves. You may also wish to use a barrier cream on your skin. Wear goggles.

If possible, work on a concrete surface and have a hose available that can wash the surplus stripper and its resultant gunk away. Even if you have these facilities, a few buckets to collect the mess that is scraped off are advisable. If you have to work inside, the floor may be covered with paper, plastic, cloth, and other things. But many chemical strippers will attack these, so be prepared to gather them up and dispose of them. If a hose isn't handy to wash away residue, there will have to be plenty of water to apply with brush and sponge.

Don't work around children and livestock. Store the strippers in a secure place. Do not leave any of the liquids in open containers; they can evaporate quickly.

Chemical strippers are rather harsh on anything they touch, so you have to be prepared to discard things. Old brushes can be used and will have a reasonable life. Cloth pads can be used and it is possible to use fine steel wool, which will function something like a sponge as well as provide some abrasive qualitites. Stiff-bristled brushes are needed to get into crevices. Old tooth and nail brushes can be used on carvings and moldings. For the grooves between parts of turned work, string soaked in chemical stripper can be pulled around. Burlap or other coarse material can be broken into pieces to get chemical stripper into awkward places.

Remove the softened finish with a scraper. The best type has a broad blunt end (Fig. 23-2). It is not intended to cut but merely lifts the gunk as it is pushed along. A sharper end might dig into the wood. A putty knife, the type cut square across the end, can be used in the same way. Wooden scrapers can also be used (Fig. 23-3). Scrapers can be quite crude, as long as they have thin edges to get under the paint or varnish that has softened.

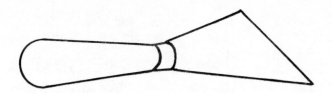

Fig. 23-2. A blunt-ended scraper.

CHEMICAL STRIPPERS

Lacquer can be removed with lacquer thinners or shellac mixed with alcohol. Both solvents evaporate quickly, so they have to be applied fairly lavishly, and the softened finish must be removed before the solvent in it has evaporated. This usually means working on only part of an area at a time, scraping almost immediately after putting on the solvent. If spray equipment is available, the solvent can be sprayed with one hand while the other hand follows with a scraper.

It may be necessary to work on a part several times if there is much lacquer or shellac to be removed. Paint stripper can also be used on shellac and may work with some lacquers. If a surface has been stripped with alcohol or lacquer thinners, a new finish can follow without neutralizing the surface.

Chemical strippers for paint and varnish are broadly divided into solvents and caustics. The solvent types are less harmful, but the recommended precautions should still be observed. Paint and varnish removers bought in a can are likely to be of the solvent type. Liquid removers are suitable for flat surfaces, but there are paste removers that contain starch or other stiffeners that helps them to resist sliding away on vertical or sloping surfaces.

A solvent paint remover contains wax. The wax forms a thin skin as the remover is applied and prevents the volatile liquids in the remover from evaporating too quickly. Because of this, the remover should not be brushed or rubbed over after

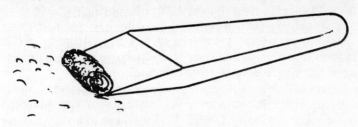

Fig. 23-3. A wooden scraper.

it is applied. Flow it on generously and leave it. Working the brush or cloth backwards and forwards breaks the wax skin and makes it ineffective.

Ater using a stripper containing wax, go over the surface with a cloth soaked in alcohol. Rub hard with this and change the cloth surface frequently so any residue of wax is pulled out of the pores of the wood. Also go over carvings and moldings with a brush and alcohol. This is important. Although wax is a good thing to put on top of a finish, if it is allowed to remain under a new finish it will affect its adhesion.

Solvent paint and varnish removers contain a mixture of individual solvents. One remover that can be made consists of one part denatured alcohol, one part acetone, and one part benzol, to which has been added a small amount of paraffin wax shavings.

Of the caustic removers or strippers a common one is lye (caustic soda). This is used with water and a little cornstarch. First, dissolve the cornstarch in cold water—one cup of cornstarch to two cups of water is about right—and heat until the mixture thickens. Set this mixture aside. In a plastic bucket dissolve 12 oz (3 or 4 tablespoons) of lye in 1 quart of cold water.

WARNING

Add the lye crystals to the water, not the water to the lye. Adding water to lye can cause boiling and spattering with danger to eyes, skin, and clothing. Remember to protect your eyes and wear rubber gloves. Have the cornstarch mixture in another plastic bucket and slowly mix in the lye solution. This mixture can be used warm or cold.

Apply the solution to the finish and let it work for about 10 minutes. Watch the reaction and add more if necessary. The paint or varnish should completely loosen so it can be pushed off with a scraper. A scrubbing brush may help on stubborn parts, or steel wool can be used.

Next, use water to wash the surface after stripping. If this is done thoroughly, there may need to be no other treatment, except drying, before starting to refinish.

Another caustic stripper is trisodium phosphate. A fairly concentrated solution is made in hot water (2 or 3 pounds of the powder in a gallon of water). It is used hot in a very similar way to lye, with several applications if necessary.

Caustic strippers are cheap to make up and they use household chemicals, but they must be used with great care. If the furniture is suspected of being vulnerable to water, there is a risk of damage to glued joints.

It is inadvisable to mix different strippers. But sometimes you may not get much success with the first stripper you try. Do not go straight into using another stripper, but carry the first treatment through to its end, particularly washing off or neutralizing. However, it is safe to follow a commercial solvent paint remover with trisodium phosphate, using it to remove the remains of the first paint remover as well as the reluctant paint.

After working with chemical strippers, dispose of cloths and other things that have been used with the solutions. Do not pack cloths soaked in solvent or chemical stripper into a bucket and leave them. Spontaneous combustion may result. In any case there may be unpleasant or harmful fumes. Put the cloths in water and dispose of them away from the work area. Similarly remove paper, plastic and other materials that have become soiled.

Take the stripped furniture away from the place where it was stripped. Put it where it can dry in a well ventilated place. Although it is possible to go ahead with the new finish soon after using some strippers, it is better to let the wood dry, particularly if sanding and scraping are expected to be needed to get a good surface for refinishing.

Clean the work area and put away any remaining chemicals. You have not finished stripping until all risk of danger has been removed.

Refinishing Preparations

24

When all of the old finish has been stripped, the furniture is ready to receive its new finish. If the new finish is to be paint or opaque lacquer, any discoloration will not matter because it will be hidden. If the new finish is to be clear, even if there will be stain underneath, there will probably have to be some evening of the color in the wood before new treatment is commenced.

Stain and some of the previous finish will almost certainly be trapped in the pores of the wood. This may not matter, if the color is even. In fact some collectors of restored antique furniture regard this as evidence of age and something that improves rather than detracts from the quality and value of the furniture. What has to be guarded against is uneven color and texture that will show through the new finish.

Some stains may be difficult to remove from the pores of the wood. Whether much stain comes away with stripping of the finish depends on the type of stain. A water stain may need a wipe with water to remove more stain or to even streakiness. Spirit stain may have responded to a solvent type chemical stripper, but any local clearing after stripping can be done by wiping with alcohol. If the stain had an oil base, wiping is better done with benzene or naphtha. The type of stain may have become apparent during earlier treatment, as one of the chemical strippers used may have dissolved it. Otherwise, it may be necessary to experiment to discover what to use for removing or evening the stain.

The aim, at this stage, is to get an even color. It may not be the natural color of the wood, but the general appearance should be uniform.

Getting an even color means either darkening light parts or lightening dark parts or both. Wiping with solvents may be all that is needed. Using a cloth pad soaked in solvent in all directions on a surface may break down the streakiness left from stripping. The solvent can be used to lift some stain from dark parts and to blend parts that show sudden changes from dark to light. Change the surface of the cloth pad frequently.

If a dark part has to be lightened, use one of the bleaching techniques described in Section 1. Oxalic acid will probably be the most convenient. The bleach can be applied with a cloth over a broad area or with a small brush for local reduction. Besides uneven stain, there may be marks in old furniture due to rusting screws or prolonged contact with metal parts. There may be marks from spilled ink or other liquid. Now is the time to attack these marks by careful application of bleach. Oak is particularly prone to staining due to contact with steel. Brass is much less troublesome.

If you have to darken a light part, use thin stain. Apply the stain and wipe off most of it. Continue to do this until you have the color you want. Using a thick or dark stain the first time is risky. You could overdo it and find yourself with a bleaching problem before making another attempt.

Pine and other softwoods can suffer from uneven coloring as they age. Some old softwood furniture was made from several woods. They could have aged to different colors. Even two parts of the same wood may be different. Sapwoods and heartwood are no different in appearance in most softwoods when newly worked, but sometimes the sapwood ages to a grey color alongside the unchanged heartwood. Fortunately, this greyness usually responds to bleach.

Much pioneer and colonial furniture was made of softwoods, and the treatment given varied according to available materials. Some stains and finishes were made from pigments and liquids available locally, but most should respond to strippers and further treatment as already described. Knotty pine was not always regarded as attractive, and finishes were used to disguise the knots without completely hiding the grain. One of these finishes used a red pigment dissolved in skim milk. The color was like cherry or mahogany, although the pine grain was visible.

This is a stubborn finish to remove, and there has to be a combination of mechanical and chemical stripping. Alcohol will soften the finish, but while the surface is kept moistened with alcohol, it should be rubbed with steel wool or coarse abrasive paper, by hand or with an electric sander. The red pigment has a considerable penetration into softwood, so even when the surface has been brought down to bare wood there will be redness in the grain. This is attractive and may be preserved as evidence of age showing through the new finish.

Staining and bleaching usually must be used in conjunction with sanding and scraping. It is unlikely that a stripped surface will be left in a fit state for the immediate application of paint, varnish, lacquer, or other finish. The grain may have been raised due to the use of liquids. This may respond to scraping or sanding. Detailed instructions for obtaining a good wood surface are given in Section 1. These should be followed, but remember that sanding and scraping may affect coloring. Scraping takes away some of the surface—not as much as planing, but more than sanding. This reduction of surface can affect appearance, which may not matter if the whole thing is scraped; but if only part is scraped and it adjoins a sanded part, there may be a slight difference in appearance after finishing, although the untreated wood looks the same.

If you are dealing with an antique, too drastic a treatment of the surface should be avoided. Do all the sanding necessary, but avoid having to work down to a new surface, unless the old surface is so badly damaged that planing, scraping, or heavy sanding is needed. The old surface will have acquired a patina of age and this should be preserved if possible.

Don't get carried away when using a power sander on an open surface. In the more inaccessible parts, you will have to use a considerable amount of hand sanding. Moldings and carvings can be particularly troublesome, but if an even result is to be achieved, these need just as much cleaning and sanding. Be particularly careful of deep grooves and recesses. Get the residue of stripping and sanding out with a spike or pointed scraper. It is useful to have a vacuum cleaner and a tack rag to go over the furniture before starting on the new finish.

If any repairs have to be made, work them in with the surface preparatory work. If a joint is loose, it may be more convenient to sand while the pieces can be pulled apart. In general, repairs should be done before sanding. This also applies to any dents or holes that have to be filled. Some stoppings tend to change color slightly after sanding. Coloring, bleaching, and sanding have to be coordinated, and there may have to be some trial and error to get a coloring result that is reasonably uniform in the finished piece of furniture.

As a final step before refinishing, look over the work towards a light. There should be a uniform flat mat appearance. If there is a hint of a sheen anywhere, that could indicate a little of the old finish still remaining. It may not matter for an opaque finish, but with a clear finish it could affect the color or texture, showing a difference at that spot. A little more sanding over the particular area is probably all that is needed.

If there has been any new gluing, see that there is no surplus on the surface. Use the minimum necessary in a joint. But if there is an excess it is not usually sufficient to just wipe it away. With most modern glues this leaves glue blocking the wood pores around the joint and this prevents an even penetration of stain or finish. It is better to let the glue almost harden and cut it away with a chisel, followed by light sanding.

Refinishing  25

Before starting to build up a finish again after stripping and preparing the wood, spend some time deciding on what you are aiming at. If it is a genuine antique that you are working on, it should be given a finish that is appropriate. When you have finished your work, the result should look as it might have a century ago. It may not, in fact, be finished in exactly the same way, but it will look like it. There is no reason why you should not take advantage of improvements in methods and materials, providing they achieve similar results to those originally employed. But it would be inappropriate to spray a high-gloss lacquer on something that would only look right with a more mellow and subtle sheen of wax. However, there would be nothing wrong with using spray in the early stages of shellac finishing, if this would speed the eventual buildup of a suitable hand-polished surface.

Of course, if the furniture is not an antique and is a comparatively modern piece thrown out or discarded by someone else, you can do almost anything you like to it. Whatever you do should improve it. If it is made of softwood and plywood and has been neglected, it may only be suitable for an opaque finish, applied by brush or spray. If it is hardwood but has been left in the open, the many parts may have weathered or absorbed dirt. So despite your efforts at bleaching and cleaning, a natural finish would look uneven and unattractive. This may be better covered with paint or opaque lacquer. If you still want the grain to show through, a fairly dark stain may be the only way to disguise the differences in wood color.

Many furniture restorers try to keep the wood grain showing if possible. They prefer wood in its natural color. If that is impossible, they stain it and use a transparent finish, so all of the beauty of the texture and grain of the wood shows through. Only as a last resort would they cover the wood with an opaque finish. When you cannot see through the finish, the base material might be metal, plastic, or other material, instead of wood. Though those materials have their places in modern furniture, there is nothing like wood for the best furniture. So why destroy the evidence?

Of course, all these considerations have to be tempered with a knowledge of where and how the restored piece is to be used. If it will be in a kitchen or laundry, a tough opaque finish is more appropriate than a natural one. If it is to go in a room where everything else is stained a dark color, a very light or natural finish might be inappropriate. If the only hope of getting an acceptable finish on a restored piece is to apply dark stain, and the place where it is to be used is stocked with light furniture, think about it. The furniture in a room does not have to be uniform in finish; something which contrasts with the other things can look right. Much depends on your sense of interior design.

If the furniture being restored can be regarded as an individual piece, without consideration of where it is to go, your choices are multiplied. If it is a rescued piece of no particular value and it is to be a present or for sale, it can be finished in any way you wish and may provide an opportunity for experiment. However, do not be too daring. Multicolored surfaces or a covering with fairy tale decals may be objectionable—to friends and customers. Those sorts of things are better done to order. If the eventual recipient does not know about the work, it is better to be more conservative in the finish you use.

The actual methods of refinishing are similar to those described for finishing new wood. There may also be need of some of the repairs described in Section 2. Only methods of dealing with wood that has already had one finish applied and removed are given here.

The difference between stripped wood and new wood is mainly that stripped wood will almost certainly have remnants of the earlier finish trapped in the pores of the grain. How much depends on what the original finish was and how thoroughly the stripping was done. It is almost impossible to completely remove particles of an earlier finish that have entered the pores. The solvents may get some out, but they also wash some farther in. This does not matter, but should be allowed for, particularly when staining.

Another difference may be in the quality of the wood. Seasoning is a long process. Despite the efficiency of modern methods of seasoning, wood needs time to achieve the stable condition that results from thorough seasoning. New wood may be in acceptable condition, with the correct degree of moisture content arrived at by modern scientific control. But as it ages, cracks may develop or open, knots may loosen, or other flaws may slowly become apparent. The wood in an old piece of furniture should have passed this stage. The condition in which you find it after stripping is unlikely to change, and you can go ahead on the assumption that no problems due to the wood should arise after you have finished work on it. This is also one reason for keeping old wood in sound condition. If a piece of furniture has to be broken up, wood rescued from it may be better for repairing another piece than new wood from the mill or wood yard.

Make sure the wood is absolutely dry. If you have had to moisten to raise grain before sanding, let all of the moisture evaporate. Wiping with a cloth soaked in alcohol will pull out water. If the chemical stripper has required neutralizing, make sure the neutralizer has evaporated. If there is no rush to refinish, the wood may benefit from drying for several days.

Use the vacuum cleaner and a tack rag on the wood immediately before starting refinishing. Going slowly over the surface with the end of the hose of the vacuum cleaner pointing straight at the wood will pull out any dust in the pores that is free enough to come away. Follow immediately with the first finishing stage so as to seal the wood before it can take up any more dust.

If the first treatment is stain, apply it thinly, preferably with a cloth. Use a water or oil stain. Spirit stain might dry too quickly. Spread the stain and wipe off surplus. In this way, variations in absorption can be watched. There will almost certainly be some variations due to varying amounts of residue in the pores of the wood. Continue to appy thin coats, allowing more stain on parts that need darkening. Building up to the required color in this way is more likely to result in an even appearance than if a liberal coat of dark stain is applied in one application.

Variations in absorption may be a problem with whatever is applied next. What is applied next depends on the chosen finish, but several layers may be needed to obtain an even finish. Shellac can be used where it suits what is to follow. Rub down between coats as necessary to fill the grain and provide a smooth base for further finishing. Lacquer may be sprayed on and rubbed down in the same way.

Since the wood should have been filled under the old finish, it is unlikely that any very lavish treatment will be needed with paste or other filler. If there is doubt, test an inconspicuous part of the furniture with and without filler. If there are obviously open parts of the grain, filler may be advisable all over, if an even finish is wanted. On antique oak there may never have been any filler, so the hollows over the wider gaps in the grain may be accepted in the new finish as being appropriate to the particular furniture, even when the application of filler would have given a smooth, even sheen.

Varnish will make its own filler, unless the stripped wood is very absorbent. If too many coats have to be applied merely to fill the grain, another filler would be quicker and more economical.

Consider the final effect wanted. A hard gloss is protective and easily cleaned, but too brilliant a sheen may not be appropriate to the piece of furniture. An antique may have its sprayed or brushed finish rubbed down and waxed, or it may be finished by French polishing.

For a painted finish, pay attention to the quality of the prepared surface, but do not worry if the wood color is uneven. Shellac makes a good quick base for painting. Watch absorption and look across the dried surface to see where dullness indicates soaking in. Apply more where necessary and sand level. Once the surface has been sealed in this way, painting is no different from dealing with new work, as described earlier.

Special Techniques

26

Special restoration methods demand imagination. You can make furniture look old or individual or elegant or anything you wish. All you need is a knowledge of a few techniques and some good ideas.

AGE SIMULATION

New work and old furniture which are being restored can be made to look old. This is sometimes called furniture faking, but that implies deception, which it would be if an attempt was being made to pass off the furniture as a genuine antique. But the look of antiquity is attractive, and there is certainly nothing wrong with trying to achieve such a look.

There are certain processes which are described as antiquing, which would certainly not deceive anyone. There are antiquing kits available that will give a finish that has some semblance of antiquity. Other treatments can be applied to old furniture to make it look older. If you like an antique appearance, there is no reason why you should not set out to make an apparent antique from new wood.

A knowledge of furniture faking is useful when old furniture has to be repaired. If a new part has to be made and built into a genuine antique piece of furniture, it is obvious that it must be made to match, by methods already described. Steps must be taken to give it the same appearance of wear and age as the adjoining wood.

Try visualizing how the parts of a piece of furniture might wear over a century or so of use. Unless it has been kept almost in museum conditions, fair wear and tear will have taken its toll. A rail on which feet may have rested will have the squareness worn away. If it is a turned rail, there may have been enough foot wear to have hollowed a side of the turning. Similarly, table legs may have been knocked by a chair or other seat. A table top used for meals may have had slight hollows worn by the regular use of dishes on one spot. The exposed edge of the top of a table or cabinet is likely to have been knocked and worn, so there are irregularities in the appearance. These are all wear marks that can be simulated.

Simulating wear and damage is aptly described as "distressing." With new wood, some of the distressing will have to be done before applying stain or finish, but it would be wrong to imitate all the damage and wear on the bare wood and then finish over it. Wear to the old work would have happened *after* the surfaces had been finished. Much of the finish would have been worn through. But almost certainly polish or other treatment to revive the finish would have been applied at intervals, and this would have gone over the bare, or near bare, wood as well as over the parts retaining their full finish. This has to be taken into account. If heavy wear is to be assumed, as when a rail was used as a footrest, some shaping may be done before applying a finish, but you can simulate durther wearing away followed by more wax or other polish.

Such shaping can be done with abrasive paper wrapped around a strip of wood and used like a file. If the wood is given a curved cross section (Fig. 26-1), the resulting shaping will be more realistic. Rock the tool both in the length and sideways. The shaping must not appear too regular or obviously made much quicker than normal wear would have achieved. Definite cuts, as might results from the use of a chisel or knife, are not wanted. If such tools are used to shape something near the required depth, make sure there is plenty of sanding afterwards that destroys tool marks and disguises any evenness of tool cuts.

Besides wear in appropriate places, very old furniture will have suffered from dents. A dent compresses the wood fibers instead of wearing them away. So dents have to be made by striking the wood, not by cutting or wearing away dents and hollows.

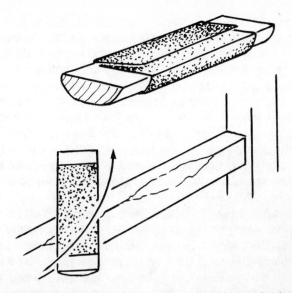

Fig. 26-1. Shape with abrasive paper wrapped around a wood strip curved on one side.

The effect of dents over the years can be obtained in several ways. A piece of chain may be gathered into a ball and pounded on the surface by hand (Fig. 26-2). Another way is to use a piece of rock in the hand. Various rocks can be tried, but coral rock is favored. There may be direct hits with an iron rod, either its side or end, depending on what sort of damage is to be simulated.

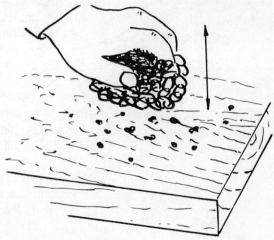

Fig. 26-2. "Distressing" with a piece of chain.

Whatever method is used, avoid uniformity. Damage due to dents over the years would not follow a regular pattern, so make sure your pounding of the surface is random. Do not be over enthusiastic with your denting. Most furniture owners would have used reasonable precautions over the years and it is unlikely they will have let the wood get excessively battered. Any marks will be due to accidents that escaped their care. Try to make your simulated damage give this impression.

Quite often dents cause a darkening of the wood, so your applied dents may have to be stained. This has to be kept local to the damage. Stain used should not soak along the grain and blend gradually into the wood.

Instead of one of the usual stains, use artist's oil color in turpentine. Vandyke brown, mixed fairly thickly, should give the right effect on most woods. A small artist's brush can be used to paint on the stain, but avoid uniformity. A better way of getting uneven stain marks is to cover the ball of chain with stain so it deposits stain at the same time it makes dents.

An old finish sometimes acquires small dark dots. This random arrangement of small dots can be simulated by splattering with a brush. Use a paint or varnish brush and a stick. Use the same thick stain as suggested for the dents. Experiment first on scrap wood or a piece of paper. Hold the

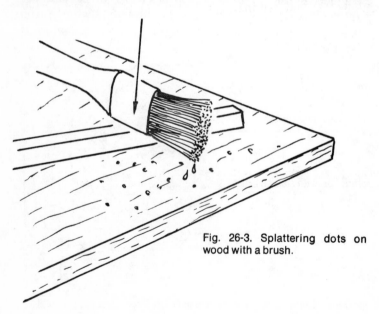

Fig. 26-3. Splattering dots on wood with a brush.

stick in one hand and knock the ferrule or handle of the brush against it so stain is thrown on the surface (Fig. 26-3). Varying the amount of stain and hardness of hitting will regulate the size and position of the dots. Only quite small dots are required. When practice splattering has produced a satisfactory result, work over the wood.

Distressing with dents and splatter dots may be done before final finishing but after some finish has been applied. For color treatment, shellac, lacquer, or varnish rubbed in makes a suitable base. If the surface of the wood is absorbent, there is a risk of the color spreading. When color has been applied, it should be left to dry completely then protected by further coats of finish.

Sometimes a very old finish acquires many fine dark lines, probably due to cracking of the finish and the entry of dirt. This may have been polished over, but the dark lines remain. The effect is not due to the grain of the wood, so the lines may be in any direction.

Wood can be distressed with these lines by painting them on. Use artist's brushes. A fine one will do all the lines, but having more than one brush allows an easier application of lines of different sizes, as they would be in genuinely aged furniture. Draw fine lines with the same stain as suggested for splattering and denting. Let the lines be random and mostly short (Fig. 26-4). Have very little stain in the brush at each application so the lines are irregular in outline.

Fig. 26-4. Age lines can be painted on with a small brush.

After distressing wood, it spoils the effect to give a finish that could not have been used a century ago. Oil and wax are safe choices, while French polishing would be acceptable. Shellac or lacquer may be a quicker way of filling the grain and building up something on which to base the final finish, but it is what goes on top that is most important.

Whatever the original finish on an old piece of furniture, it is likely that the patina of age is the result of polishing at intervals over a very long time, usually with wax. In making a simulated antique, particularly if it is to be a repaired part of a genuine antique, wax polish, furniture cream, and other things that are really finish revivers will have to be used. For the best results there will have to be intervals between applications. So a few weeks, at least, should be allowed for these stages before the work can be considered finished.

ANTIQUING

The surface of painted furniture can be mellowed by antiquing. This kind of antiquing involves the application of "antique glaze." The glaze is usually darker than the surface it is to be applied to. It is rubbed on, then most of it is rubbed off. Irregularities, such as carvings and moldings are emphasized, by the glaze. Angles and corners become more defined. Contrasts are emphasized. Light colors benefit from the treatment.

Suitable antique glazes can be bought, alone or in complete kits. Alternatively, the glazes can be made. This is done by using the appropriate oil color with an equal amount of linseed oil, which is then thinned with a little turpentine. A very small amount of dryer may be added. In another mixture the oil color is mixed with turpentine in about equal amounts; then about half as much varnish is mixed in. Do not mix more glaze than is needed for the work at hand, and try to get a creamlike consistency that can be brushed.

The choice of oil color has to be related to the base color and the desired effect. A yellowish-brown is obtained by the use of burnt umber or raw sienna. This mixture is used when the base paint is a pastel or light shade; it can be used with white or any pale color, but it is unsuitable for the more pronounced colors, such as red and green. Umber may also be used over gold paint. Lamp black is used in the glaze over red, green, or other strong background colors. It can also be used on silver paint.

If the background paint has been newly applied, make sure it has dried completely. Otherwise the glaze will mix with it, causing a muddy result.

Brush on the glaze so as to cover the surface being treated. Only a portion of the surface can be done at a time if it is a large object. The glaze will cover and obscure the original color. Work into any corners, grooves, and other irregularities. Wipe off unwanted glaze with a clean cloth. Normally this is done immediately. Remove most of the glaze from the center of the panel and from highlighted parts of the framing, but leave some in depressions. Work with the cloth to get the effect desired. If you overdo the wiping, apply more glaze and wipe again.

Wiping with the cloth should get the general effect wanted, but there will be marks from the cloth and a general roughness of definition of the glaze color edges. This can be evened out by using a large, dry brush. This is stroked over the work, always working from a lighter to a darder area. On a panel, this brushing is from the center to the sides. But on framing, the direction of movement will have to be regulated to suit the disposition of the light and dark parts. Clean the brush by wiping occasionally with cloth. The brushing action can be varied on some parts by working the brush up and down on the surface while it is held vertically.

Look at the work from all directions and see that the glaze color changes gradually and that emphasis is given where it is wanted. Be careful not to smudge the work by handling. There will probably be signs of the glaze in depressions of the main color, even in parts that have been wiped most. This is part of the antiquing and should be left. It all builds up the appearance of age in the furniture. Leave the glaze to dry completely, at least overnight, then apply a clear finish over it. The clear finish may be white shellac or clear lacquer. After it dries, rub it down lightly with fine abrasive or steel wool. Follow with wax polish.

A similar antiquing treatment can be used over a clear finish. The wood may be bare or stained. First, the surface is lacquered or French polished, over filler if necessary. But only one or two coats need be used before antiquing. The glaze can be one of those suggested for a painted finish. Apply the glaze as described above, wiping and brushing to get the effect desired. In carved or other shaped parts, remove glaze from the higher parts and leave it in the recesses, but do not leave an excess which will accumulate on the surface when dry.

Finish the antiqued surface after drying with coats of shellac or clear lacquer. Rub it down with an abrasive and polish with wax polish.

If the finish is to be antiqued gold or silver, follow the directions that come with the gold or silver mixture. It is possible to buy the powders to mix with a special bronzing liquid to make a pint. Normally, the wood is sealed, possibly with shellac, and one or two coats of undercoat paint appropriate to the finish are applied. Keep the gold or silver mixture stirred and have it thick enough to cover in one operation. Let it dry; then coat it with shellac. Use a burnt umber glaze over gold or a lamp black glaze over silver, applying and shading as already described.

It is possible to get gold and silver bronzes in aerosol containers. It is also possible to get lacquer shading stains which can be used for antiquing, but spraying has to be done exactly where wanted since the sprayed lacquer cannot be wiped or brushed.

USING PLASTER

There was a demand, particularly in Victorian days, for wood decorated with plaster, which was then given a gold or silver finish. Although paints were used, some of the coating was actually gold leaf. Picture frames were the most common things treated in this way, but the technique was also used on other woodwork.

Plaster of Paris does not have much resistance to damage, so old furniture treated in this way is likely to have damaged parts. If plaster of Paris cannot be bought at a hardware store, a more refined, expensive type may be found at a drugstore. Anyone inexperienced with plaster should experiment before doing an actual repair. Setting is very quick, so have all your preparations made before adding water to the plaster powder. Stir in water to a thick creamy consistency. Mix only a little at a time. Once it sets, whether on the wood or in the pit, nothing can be done to make it liquid again.

Mixing is best done in a throwaway container—old cans, plastic jars, etc. Mix with a piece of wood that can then be used to lift blobs of liquid plaster onto the repair.

Most repairs will have to be done by placing plaster in position and molding it into shape with a stick, knife blade, or other tool. But it may help, particularly along a straight edge, to use a piece of plywood or card to keep the plaster within bounds (Fig. 26-5). To prevent the plaster from sticking to this, coat it with wax or grease.

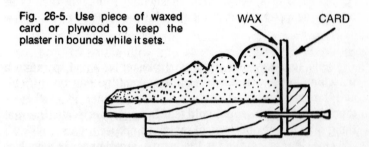

Fig. 26-5. Use piece of waxed card or plywood to keep the plaster in bounds while it sets.

WAX   CARD

Much of this plasterwork is in the form of molding, often with beads. When made originally, beads would have been cast in a mold, giving uniform patterns. Things like free flowing curves, stylized leaves, and even straight flutes, are not too difficult to shape with hand tools. But it is difficult to get a true spherical shape for the series of knobs forming beads. It may be easier to find round shot or other little spheres and press these into the plaster (Fig. 26-6).

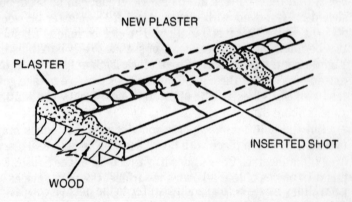

NEW PLASTER

PLASTER

INSERTED SHOT

WOOD

Fig. 26-6. Shot can be pressed into the plaster as a substitute for carved beads.

You can expect to have up to 5 minutes working time, so you have to work quickly and carefully. Leave the plaster a little too thick anywhere that you do not think you can get exact. The dried plaster can be shaped by sanding. With

311

abrasive paper wrapped around wood and used like a file, the surface can be worked to match adjoining areas.

Dry plaster is extremely absorbent. If a gold or silver mixture is to be brushed or sprayed on, the surface should first be sealed with several coats of shellac. Finishing then is as already described. Antiquing may follow.

USING GOLD LEAF

Gold leaf may be used over plaster or wood to make a matching repair. But successful application can be difficult and the use of a liquid mixture is much simpler. Nevertheless there is nothing to equal gold leaf in appearance, and the real thing may be the only way of making a proper repair.

Gold leaf is supplied in the form of small pages of a book of probably twenty sheets. The gold has been rolled or hammered extremely thin—0.001 in. is the thickness you will be handling. There are fine sharp gilder's knives, but the same work can be done with a razor blade, preferably in a handle. The gold is not picked up by the fingers, but is lifted by a gilder's tip, which is a thin flat brush with log hairs. Gold leaf is applied with an adhesive.

If the gold leaf is to go over parts adjoining the repair, check that the surfaces are clean. Detergent can be used, but should be removed with clean water. If the plaster or wood absorbs water, it must be allowed to dry completely before proceeding. Apply several coats of shellac to any bare plaster. Lightly sand this smooth. Clean off dust. Small lumps on the surface may show through. Coat surfaces that are to take gold leaf with the adhesive and allow this to get tacky. The waiting time is about 2 hours.

Cut the gold leaf to approximate shapes, but edges may overlap. Pick up a piece with the gilder's tip and put it in place over the adhesive. Coax it down with the tip of the brush. Do this with pieces of leaf all over the surface. Use small pieces of leaf to fill any gaps. Make sure all leaf is in close contact with the adhesive. Although the thin gold will adapt to shapes, smaller pieces are easier to fix over intricate designs. Use the gilder's tip to position the leaves—not your hand or any other tool.

The finished surface can be given a more even appearance and a semblance of age by using a little gold bronze powder on a cloth, which is lightly rubbed over the surface. Allow a day for everything to dry hard before any further treatment. The repair will probably benefit from a coat of shellac to protect it.

BAMBOO FURNITURE

The normal wood of a tree gains a layer on the *outside* each year; bamboo starts as an outside tube and grows *inside*. This means that the strong wood is on the outside. In most bamboo used for furniture, this hard outside skin is also smooth and glossy when new. In any bamboo repair, it is inadvisable to break through this skin since its destruction may mean weakening, possibly out of proportion to the actual amount removed.

Bamboo furniture may be stripped and cleaned in the same way as other wood furniture. If there are any hollow ends exposed, avoid letting stripper enter and become trapped: it may harm the core. Some sanding may be needed, but avoid sanding excessively. In any case, bamboo has a certain character and the aim of restoring is to renew or emphasize this character.

RESTORING METALS

Much metal furniture is made of iron or steel. Very old blacksmith-made furniture will almost certainly have been made of wrought iron, which has a good resistance to rust. Newer furniture is made of mild steel, which is much more prone to rust. Its first rusting tends to make a barrier to further attack, but neglected steel furniture may be riddled with rust and so eaten away that not enough sound steel is left to justify restoring. Painting over rust is only disguising the trouble temporarily. Rust will continue under the paint and soon show through as brown marks.

Painted iron or steel furniture can be stripped with the same strippers as wood. Since there is no grain for the paint to have entered, it may come away easier. A wire brush may also be used, either a hand type or a rotating one driven by a power drill. In both cases, spring steel "bristles" are needed. It is impossible to remove every bit of rust. Instead, work on the surface until it is generally bright; there may be some pitting still containing rust. Do not leave the surface at this stage. A bright smooth steel surface will acquire a new film of rust overnight, even in an apparently dry atmosphere.

Paint on a rust-inhibiting fluid, which prevents rust spreading and discourages further rusting. Follow the manufacturer's instructions, particularly about the time to be left before painting over. Painting iron or steel furniture is simple: there are undercoats to provide a base and a top coat. Since the metal is not absorbent, be careful not to leave excess paint anywhere. Excess will be likely to run and leave unsightly blobs.

Normally there is no need to start with any special paint for a first coat on wood furniture. But for iron or steel furniture that is to remain outdoors, some paint manufacturers (particularly those catering to the boating industry) have special primers which etch their way into the surface to get a grip on the metal and provide a longer lasting paint base.

If old metal fittings are to be restored, it will usually be found that they originally did not have an applied finish, but any quality of appearance was due to the smoothing of the metal itself. Iron hinges and fastenings on an antique chest may have had a coat of paint, but nonferrous metal fittings, usually loosely described as "brass," probably had polished surfaces. Brass is a copper/zinc alloy. Bronzes may be copper/tin, or they could be the same as brass with the addition of a small quantity of some other metal. Most old brasses have a more golden color than new brass, indicating a higher proportion of copper in the alloy. So it is not always satisfactory to replace an old fitting with the only equivalent obtainable today.

The first step in dealing with a dirty old fitting after it has been removed from the furniture is to look at its back, which will be cleaner and provide a clue to the alloy. Paint or polish which has gone over the edges may be scraped off, but be careful to avoid cutting into the metal. Some old alloys are quite soft. Scrub with water and detergent to remove dirt. If there is wax from wood polish, dissolve this with turpentine or thinners.

When all of the buildup on the surface has been removed, the surface will still be dull. This dullness will be corrosion—the equivalent of rust on iron. But it is not usually more than just an even coating on the surface. It is possible to clean off the corrosion with acid, but this can be dangerous because the metal has to be soaked in a fairly strong solution of acid. The result is rapid, but the risk to the article and worker is great. Another way is to use an ammonia solution. Avoid breathing the fumes while inserting or removing the article. Leave until you can see that the metal has been cleaned—probably about 20 minutes. Then wash off the ammonia in running water and dry the metal.

If a polish is to be built up and the surface is not evenly clean from the ammonia treatment, use fine steel wool followed by a damp cloth or a scrubbing brush with pumice powder or domestic cleaning powder. This should reduce the surface to an even appearance.

Polish on bare metal is the result of working on the surface with successively finer abrasives, with each completely removing traces of the work of the previous stage. Pumice powder is the first stage. There must be no traces of pumice left and the surface must be dry. Follow with a cloth or brush and a liquid polish of the type intended for brass. This may be sufficient to give a satisfactory finish. But for the highest polish on any metal, follow with a polish intended for silver.

Power polishing is much quicker than hand polishing, but there is a risk of rounding edges and taking off decorative ridges and beads. This might be considered one way of simulating the wear of age, but machine wear might not follow the same lines as natural wear and therefore not be regarded as authentic. Power polishing is best done with a mop consisting of a large number of cloth disks on a spindle rotating at a high speed. To create enough pressure, a 6 in. diameter mop needs to turn at about 3000 revolutions per minute. Use a polishing compound with a coarse cut for first polishing, but soon change to finer compounds. Have the mop turning *towards* you and hold the metal sloping downwards. Pause frequently to allow the mop to cool. Do not dip it in water.

Of course, polished metal will become dull again after exposure to the atmosphere. At one time the only action possible was repolishing at intervals. The alternative today is to spray with clear lacquer. This might be the same lacquer that is used for a clear finish on wood. But there are also special transparent lacquers intended for use on metal that dry to an almost invisible hard film to prevent the atmosphere from getting at the surface and causing dulling.

Index

Index